Many years ago, a secret government organization abducted the man called Logan, a mutant possessing razor-sharp bone claws and the ability to heal from any wound. In their attempt to create the perfect living weapon, the organization bonded the unbreakable metal Adamantium to his skeleton. The process was excruciating, and by the end there was little left of the man known as Logan. He had become…

SAVAGE WOLVERINE

SAVAGE WOLVERINE VOL. 1: KILL ISLAND. Contains material originally published in magazine form as SAVAGE WOLVERINE #1-5. First printing 2014. ISBN# 978-0-7851-6722-8. Published by MARVEL WORLDWIDE, INC., a subsidiary of MARVEL ENTERTAINMENT, LLC. OFFICE OF PUBLICATION: 135 West 50th Street, New York, NY 10020. Copyright © 2013 and 2014 Marvel Characters, Inc. All rights reserved. All characters featured in this issue and the distinctive names and likenesses thereof, and all related indicia are trademarks of Marvel Characters, Inc. No similarity between any of the names, characters, persons, and/or institutions in this magazine with those of any living or dead person or institution is intended, and any such similarity which may exist is purely coincidental. **Printed in the U.S.A.** ALAN FINE, EVP - Office of the President, Marvel Worldwide, Inc. and EVP & CMO Marvel Characters B.V.; DAN BUCKLEY, Publisher & President - Print, Animation & Digital Divisions; JOE QUESADA, Chief Creative Officer; TOM BREVOORT, SVP of Publishing; DAVID BOGART, SVP of Operations & Procurement, Publishing; C.B. CEBULSKI, SVP of Creator & Content Development; DAVID GABRIEL, SVP Print, Sales & Marketing; JIM O'KEEFE, VP of Operations & Logistics; DAN CARR, Executive Director of Publishing Technology; SUSAN CRESPI, Editorial Operations Manager; ALEX MORALES, Publishing Operations Manager; STAN LEE, Chairman Emeritus. For information regarding advertising in Marvel Comics or on Marvel.com, please contact Niza Disla, Director of Marvel Partnerships, at ndisla@marvel.com. For Marvel subscription inquiries, please call 800-217-9158. **Manufactured between 2/28/2014 and 4/7/2014 by R.R. DONNELLEY, INC., SALEM, VA, USA.**

10 9 8 7 6 5 4 3 2 1

1

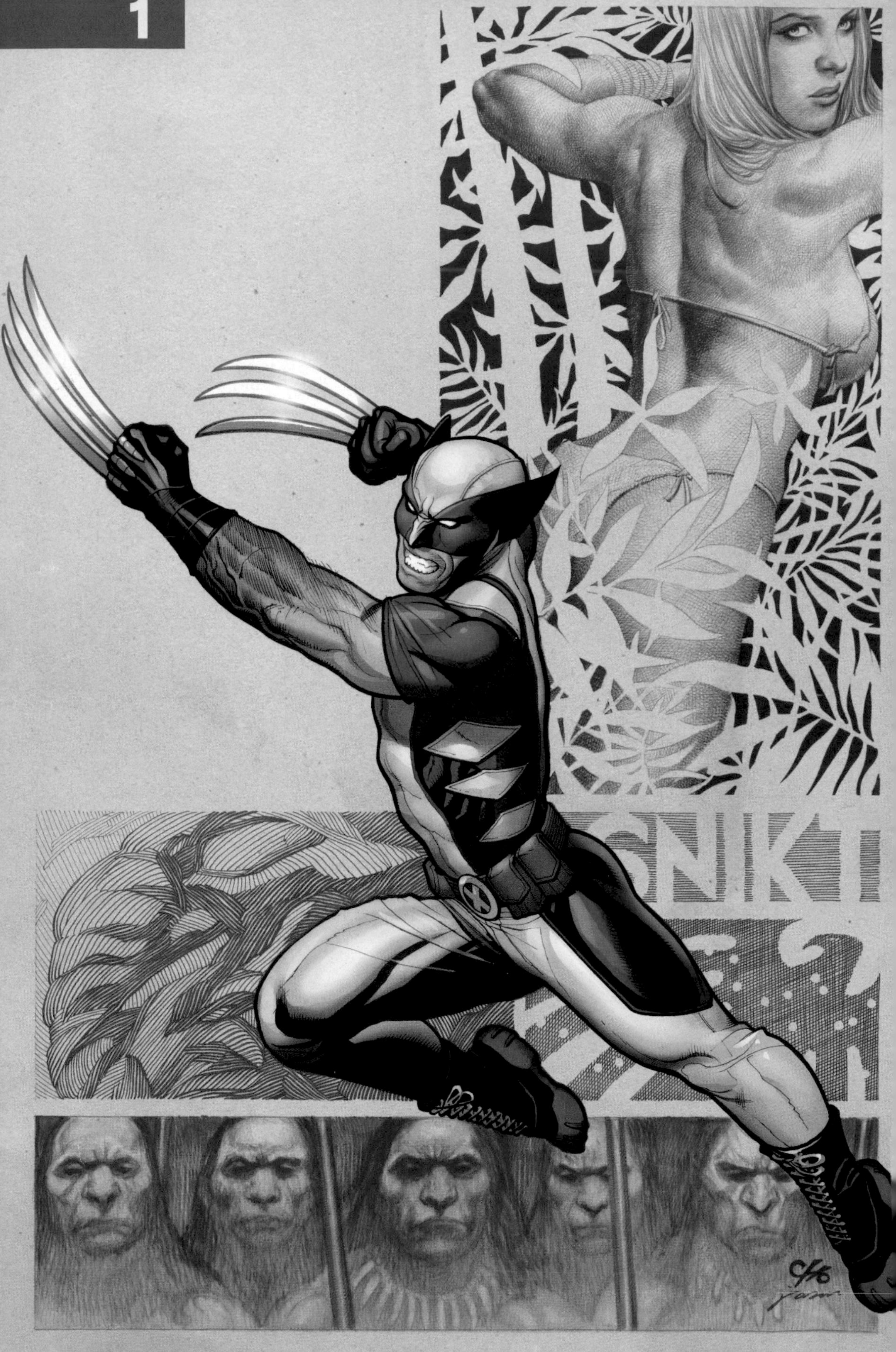

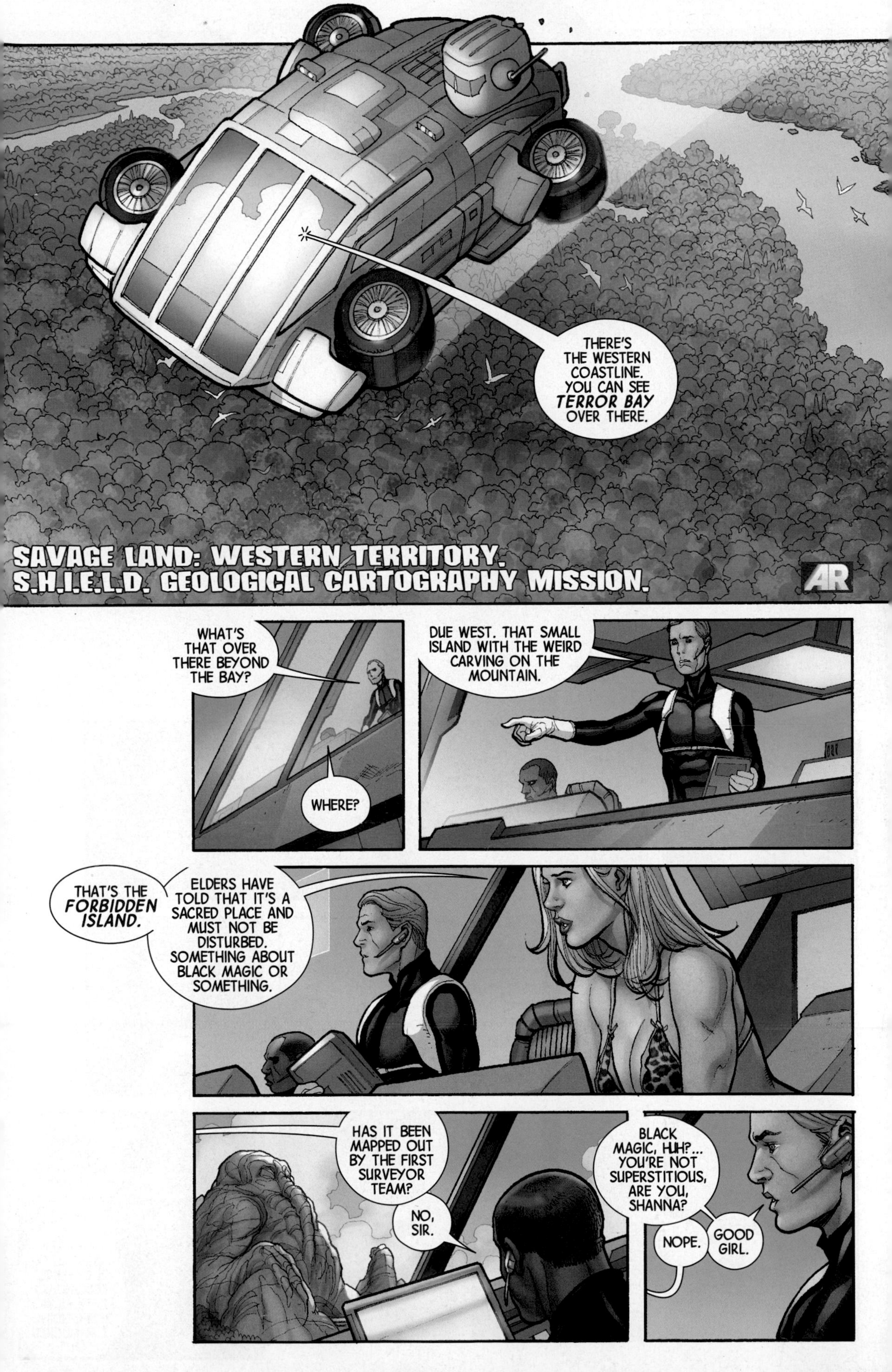
THERE'S THE WESTERN COASTLINE. YOU CAN SEE TERROR BAY OVER THERE.
SAVAGE LAND: WESTERN TERRITORY.
S.H.I.E.L.D. GEOLOGICAL CARTOGRAPHY MISSION.
WHAT'S THAT OVER THERE BEYOND THE BAY?
WHERE?
DUE WEST. THAT SMALL ISLAND WITH THE WEIRD CARVING ON THE MOUNTAIN.
THAT'S THE FORBIDDEN ISLAND.
ELDERS HAVE TOLD THAT IT'S A SACRED PLACE AND MUST NOT BE DISTURBED. SOMETHING ABOUT BLACK MAGIC OR SOMETHING.
HAS IT BEEN MAPPED OUT BY THE FIRST SURVEYOR TEAM?
NO, SIR.
BLACK MAGIC, HUH?... YOU'RE NOT SUPERSTITIOUS, ARE YOU, SHANNA?
NOPE.
GOOD GIRL.

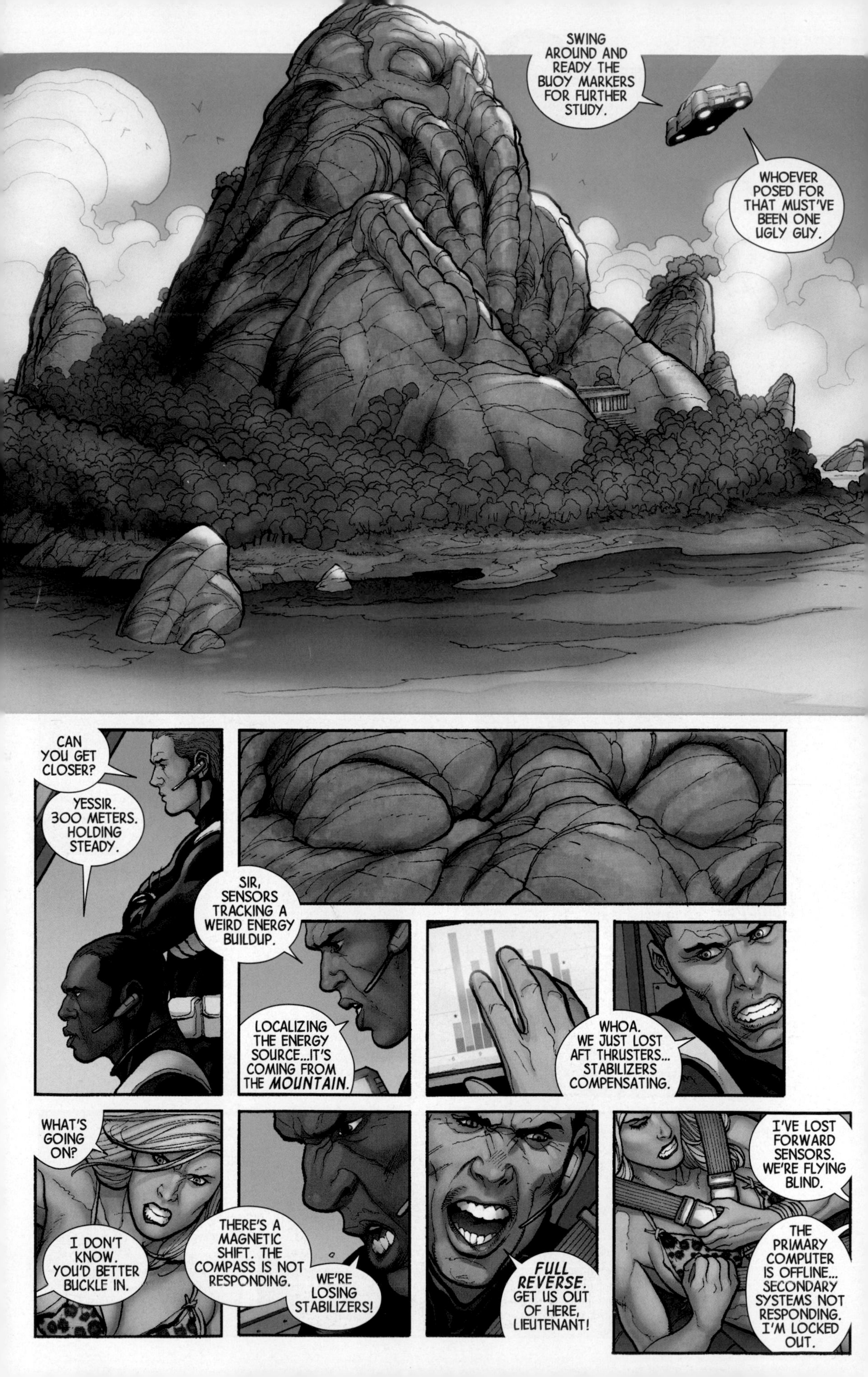
SWING AROUND AND READY THE BUOY MARKERS FOR FURTHER STUDY.
WHOEVER POSED FOR THAT MUST'VE BEEN ONE UGLY GUY.
CAN YOU GET CLOSER?
YESSIR. 300 METERS. HOLDING STEADY.
SIR, SENSORS TRACKING A WEIRD ENERGY BUILDUP.
LOCALIZING THE ENERGY SOURCE...IT'S COMING FROM THE MOUNTAIN.
WHOA. WE JUST LOST AFT THRUSTERS... STABILIZERS COMPENSATING.
WHAT'S GOING ON?
I DON'T KNOW. YOU'D BETTER BUCKLE IN.
THERE'S A MAGNETIC SHIFT. THE COMPASS IS NOT RESPONDING.
WE'RE LOSING STABILIZERS!
FULL REVERSE. GET US OUT OF HERE, LIEUTENANT!
I'VE LOST FORWARD SENSORS. WE'RE FLYING BLIND.
THE PRIMARY COMPUTER IS OFFLINE... SECONDARY SYSTEMS NOT RESPONDING. I'M LOCKED OUT.

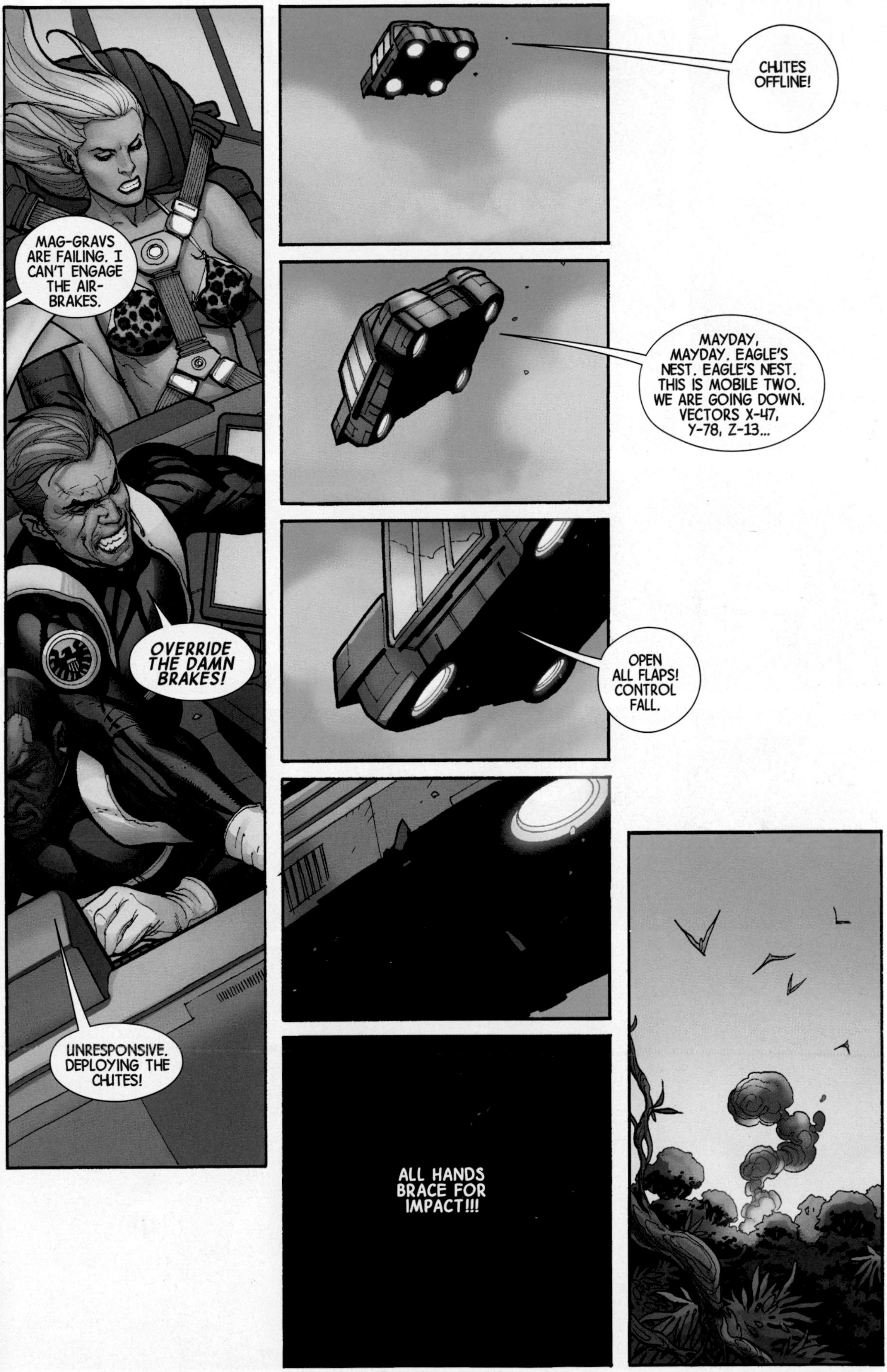
MAG-GRAVS ARE FAILING. I CAN'T ENGAGE THE AIR-BRAKES.
OVERRIDE THE DAMN BRAKES!
UNRESPONSIVE. DEPLOYING THE CHUTES!
CHUTES OFFLINE!
MAYDAY, MAYDAY. EAGLE'S NEST. EAGLE'S NEST. THIS IS MOBILE TWO. WE ARE GOING DOWN. VECTORS X-47, Y-78, Z-13...
OPEN ALL FLAPS! CONTROL FALL.
ALL HANDS BRACE FOR IMPACT!!!

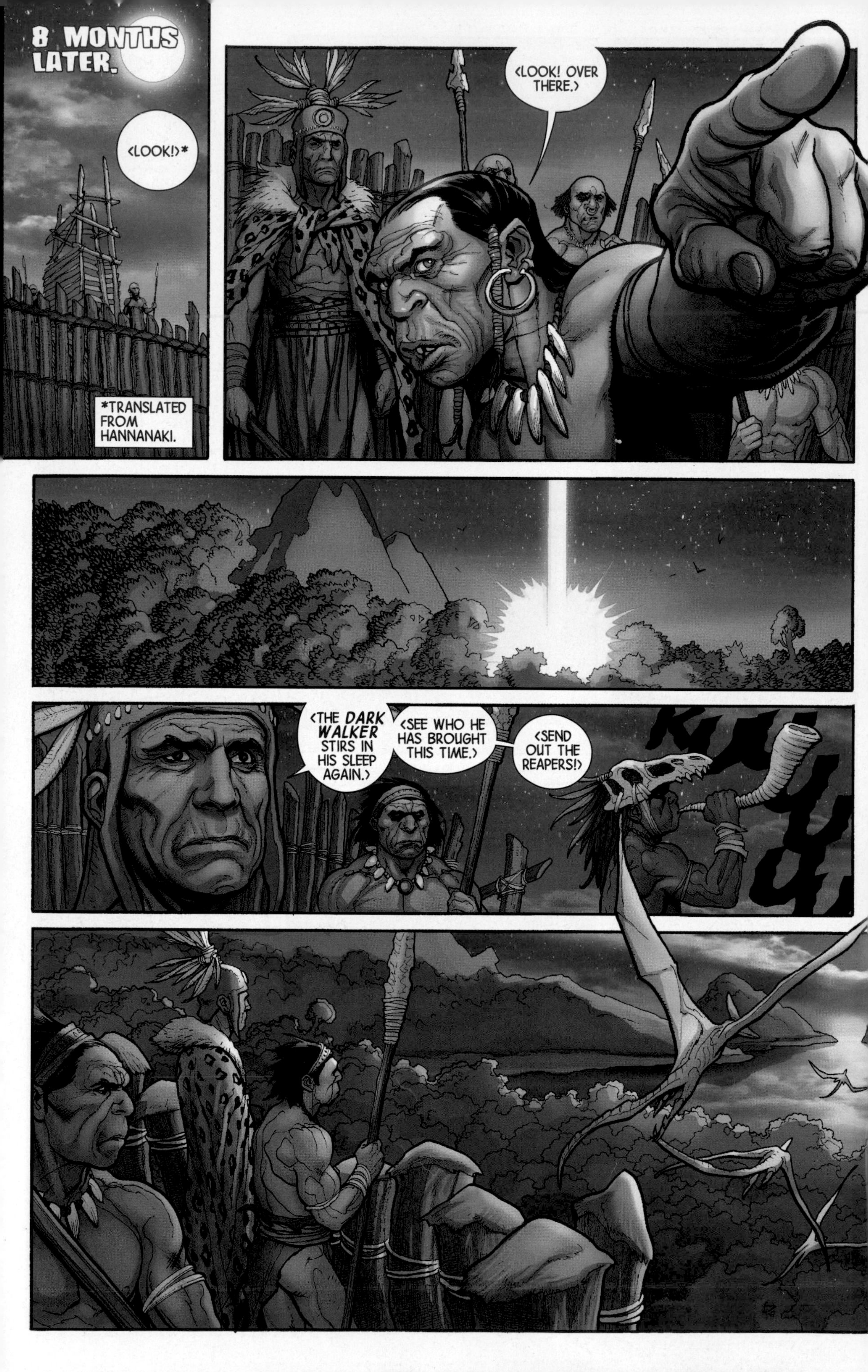
8 MONTHS LATER.
<LOOK!>*
*TRANSLATED FROM HANNANAKI.
<LOOK! OVER THERE.>
<THE DARK WALKER STIRS IN HIS SLEEP AGAIN.>
<SEE WHO HE HAS BROUGHT THIS TIME.>
<SEND OUT THE REAPERS!>

CRIPES.

WHERE AM I?

HUMID.
TROPICAL POLLEN.
VOLCANIC ASH.
POLAR BREEZE...

...SMELLS
LIKE THE
SAVAGE
LAND.

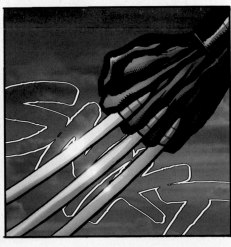

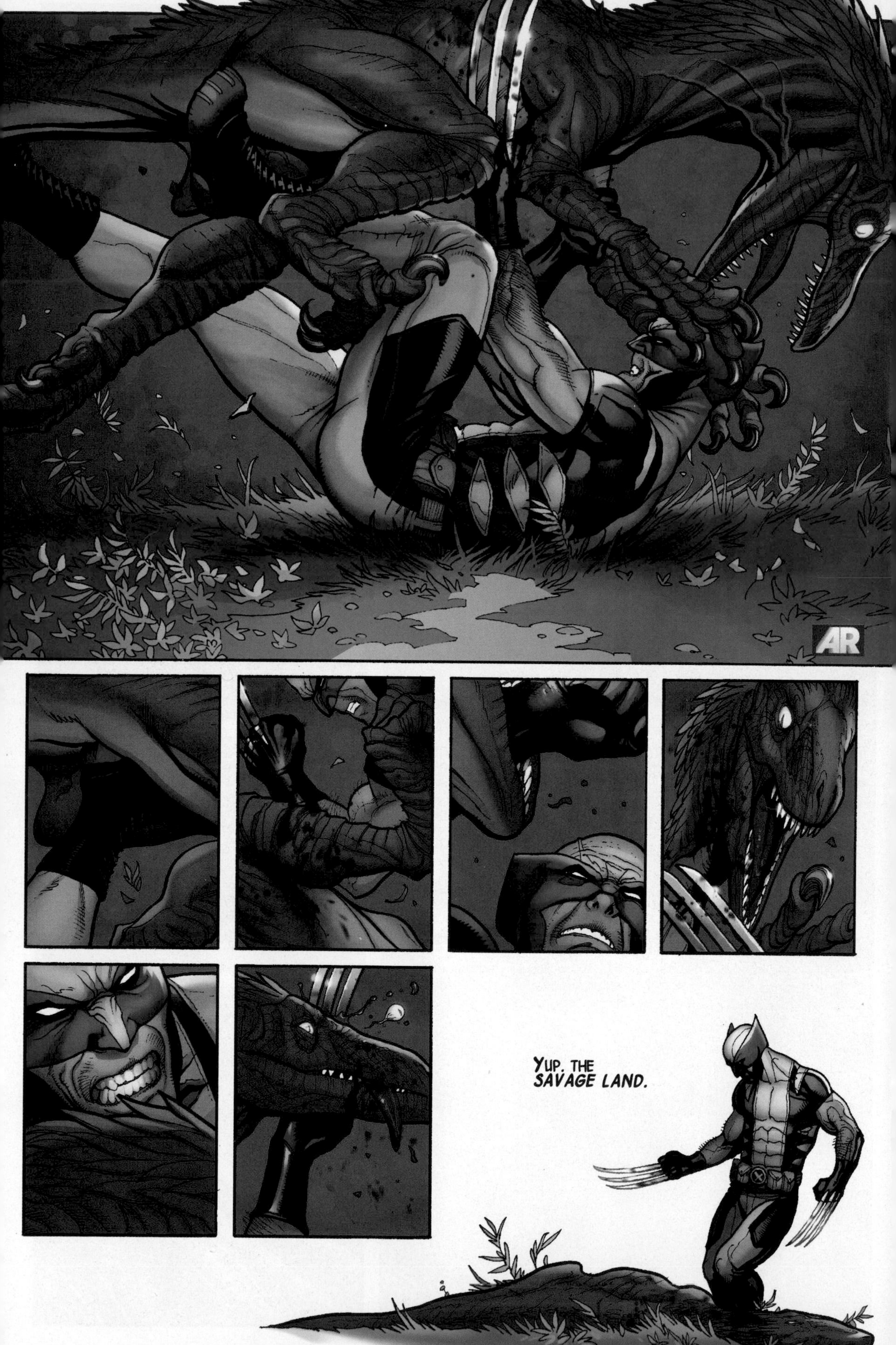
YUP. THE SAVAGE LAND.

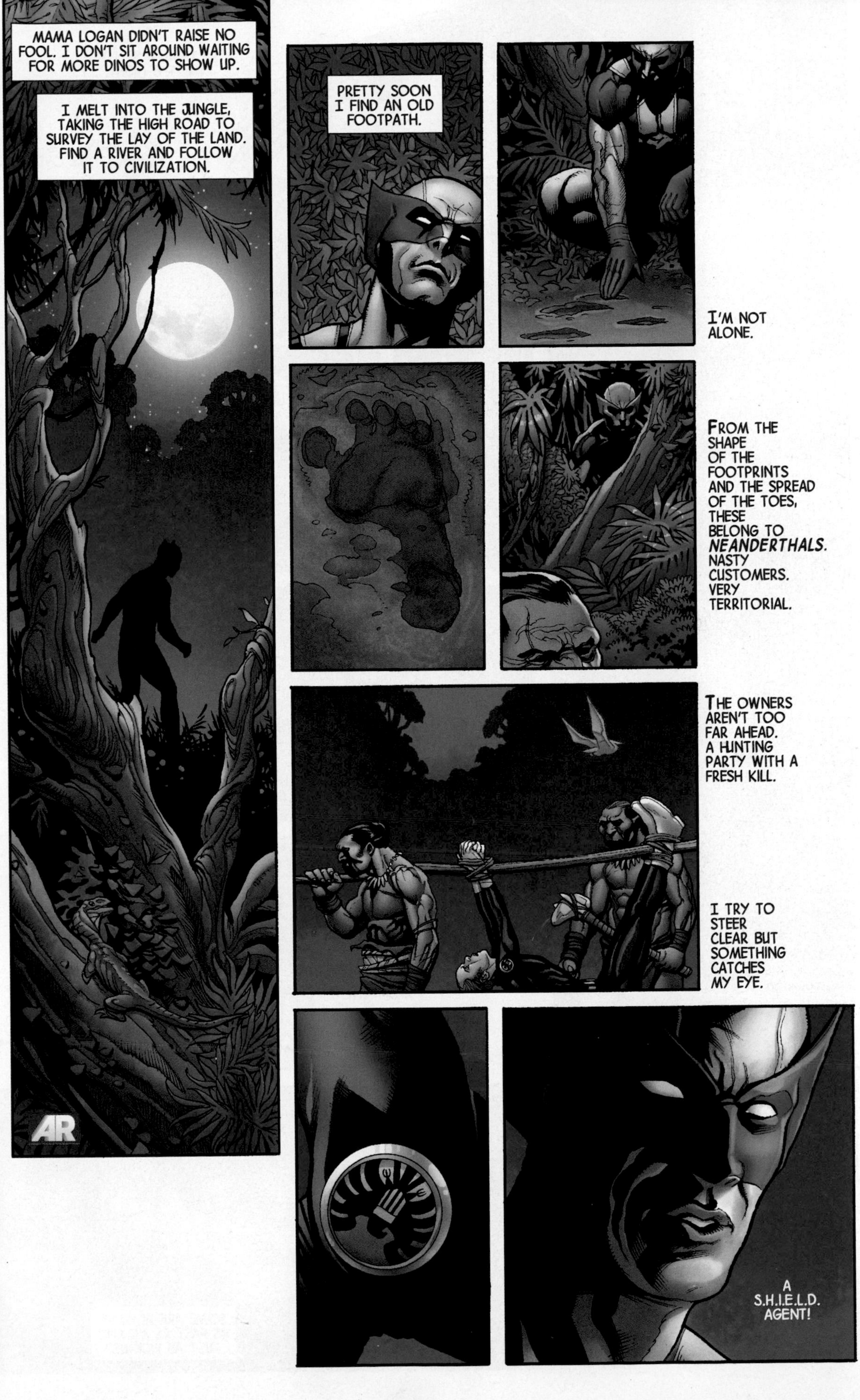
MAMA LOGAN DIDN'T RAISE NO FOOL. I DON'T SIT AROUND WAITING FOR MORE DINOS TO SHOW UP.
I MELT INTO THE JUNGLE, TAKING THE HIGH ROAD TO SURVEY THE LAY OF THE LAND. FIND A RIVER AND FOLLOW IT TO CIVILIZATION.
AR
PRETTY SOON I FIND AN OLD FOOTPATH.
I'M NOT ALONE.
FROM THE SHAPE OF THE FOOTPRINTS AND THE SPREAD OF THE TOES, THESE BELONG TO NEANDERTHALS. NASTY CUSTOMERS. VERY TERRITORIAL.
THE OWNERS AREN'T TOO FAR AHEAD. A HUNTING PARTY WITH A FRESH KILL.
I TRY TO STEER CLEAR BUT SOMETHING CATCHES MY EYE.
A S.H.I.E.L.D. AGENT!

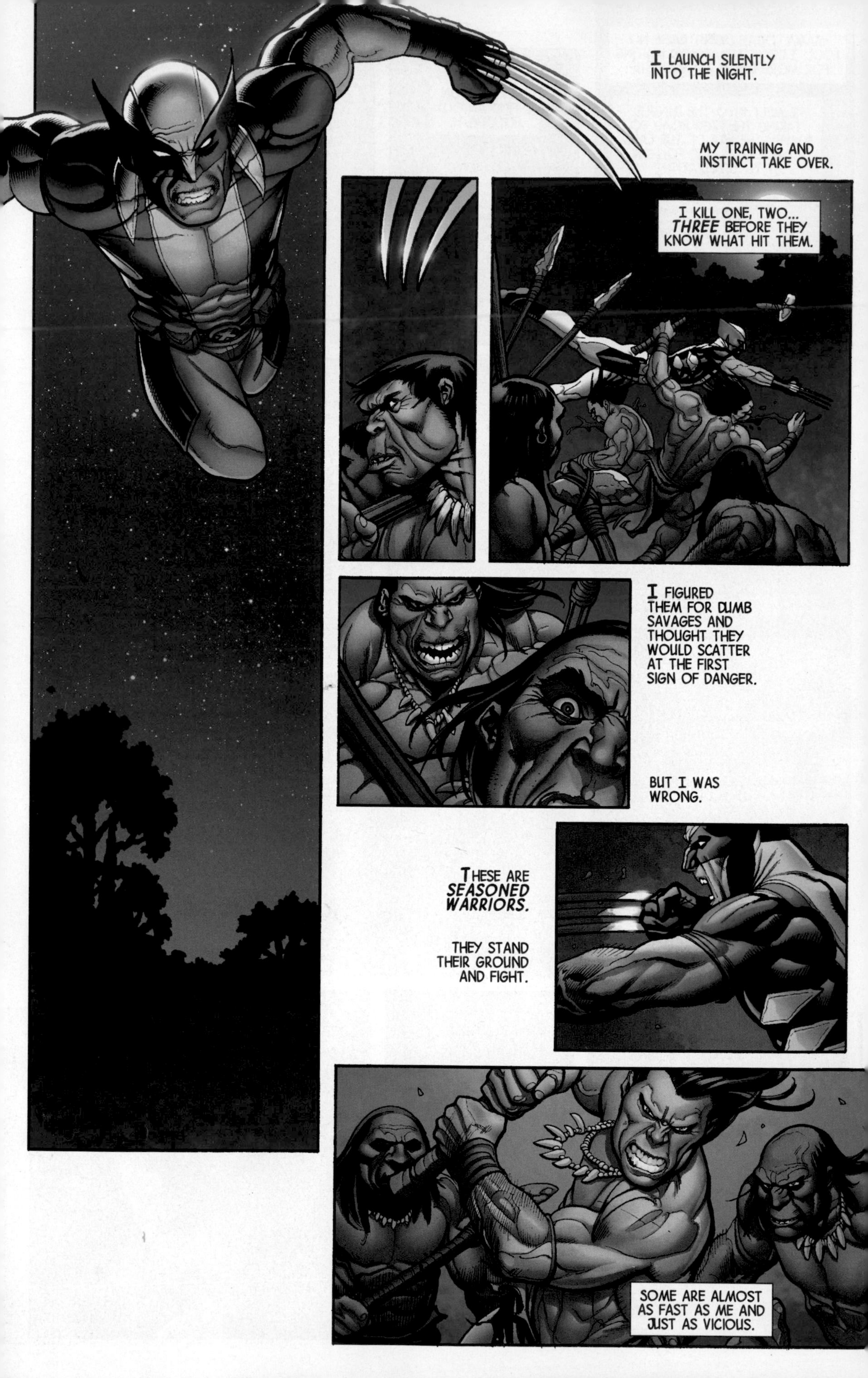
I LAUNCH SILENTLY INTO THE NIGHT.
MY TRAINING AND INSTINCT TAKE OVER.
I KILL ONE, TWO... *THREE* BEFORE THEY KNOW WHAT HIT THEM.
I FIGURED THEM FOR DUMB SAVAGES AND THOUGHT THEY WOULD SCATTER AT THE FIRST SIGN OF DANGER.
BUT I WAS WRONG.
THESE ARE *SEASONED WARRIORS.*
THEY STAND THEIR GROUND AND FIGHT.
SOME ARE ALMOST AS FAST AS ME AND JUST AS VICIOUS.

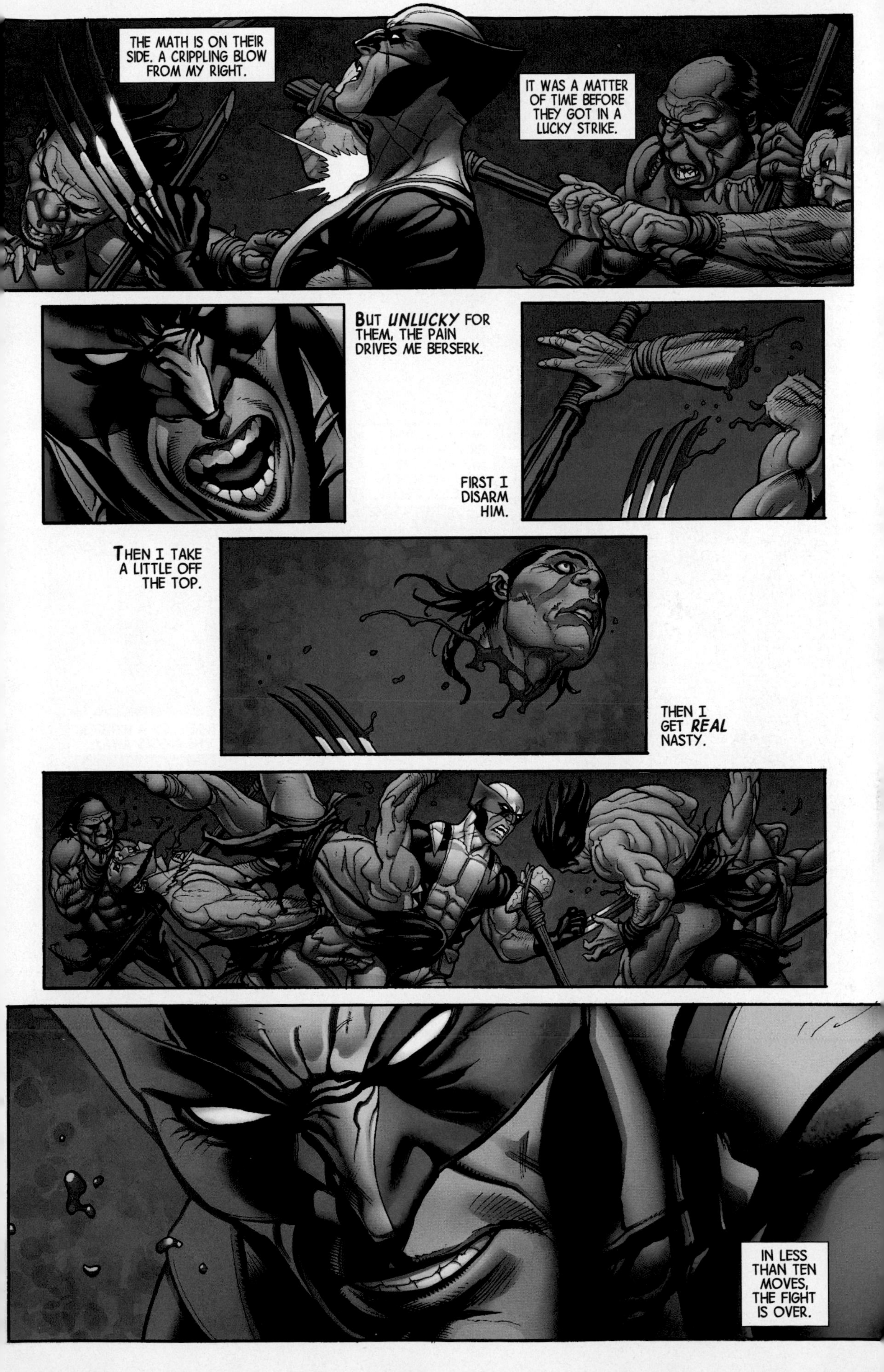
THE MATH IS ON THEIR SIDE. A CRIPPLING BLOW FROM MY RIGHT.
IT WAS A MATTER OF TIME BEFORE THEY GOT IN A LUCKY STRIKE.
BUT UNLUCKY FOR THEM, THE PAIN DRIVES ME BERSERK.
FIRST I DISARM HIM.
THEN I TAKE A LITTLE OFF THE TOP.
THEN I GET REAL NASTY.
IN LESS THAN TEN MOVES, THE FIGHT IS OVER.

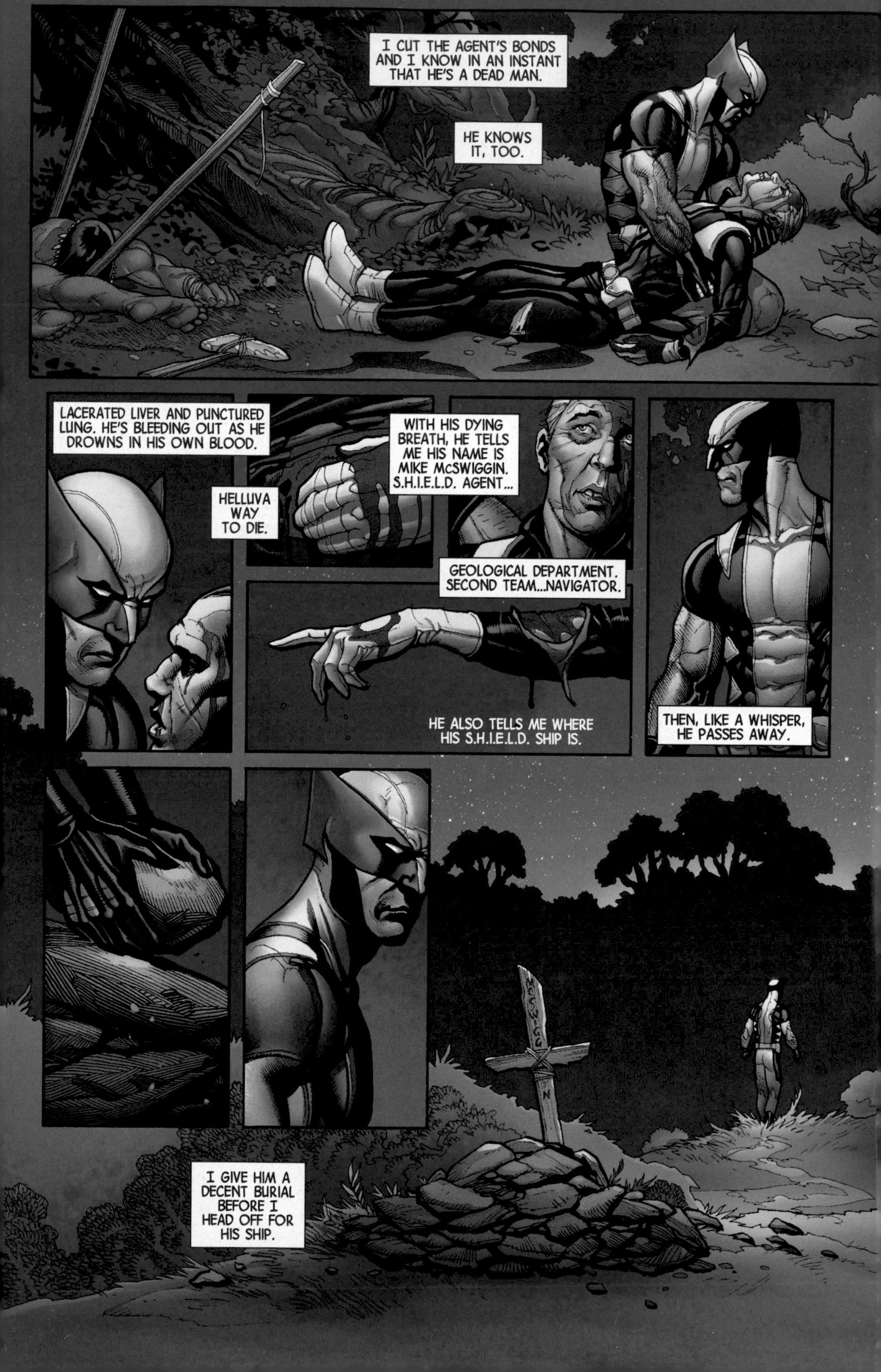
I CUT THE AGENT'S BONDS AND I KNOW IN AN INSTANT THAT HE'S A DEAD MAN.
HE KNOWS IT, TOO.
LACERATED LIVER AND PUNCTURED LUNG. HE'S BLEEDING OUT AS HE DROWNS IN HIS OWN BLOOD.
HELLUVA WAY TO DIE.
WITH HIS DYING BREATH, HE TELLS ME HIS NAME IS MIKE McSWIGGIN. S.H.I.E.L.D. AGENT...
GEOLOGICAL DEPARTMENT. SECOND TEAM...NAVIGATOR.
HE ALSO TELLS ME WHERE HIS S.H.I.E.L.D. SHIP IS.
THEN, LIKE A WHISPER, HE PASSES AWAY.
I GIVE HIM A DECENT BURIAL BEFORE I HEAD OFF FOR HIS SHIP.

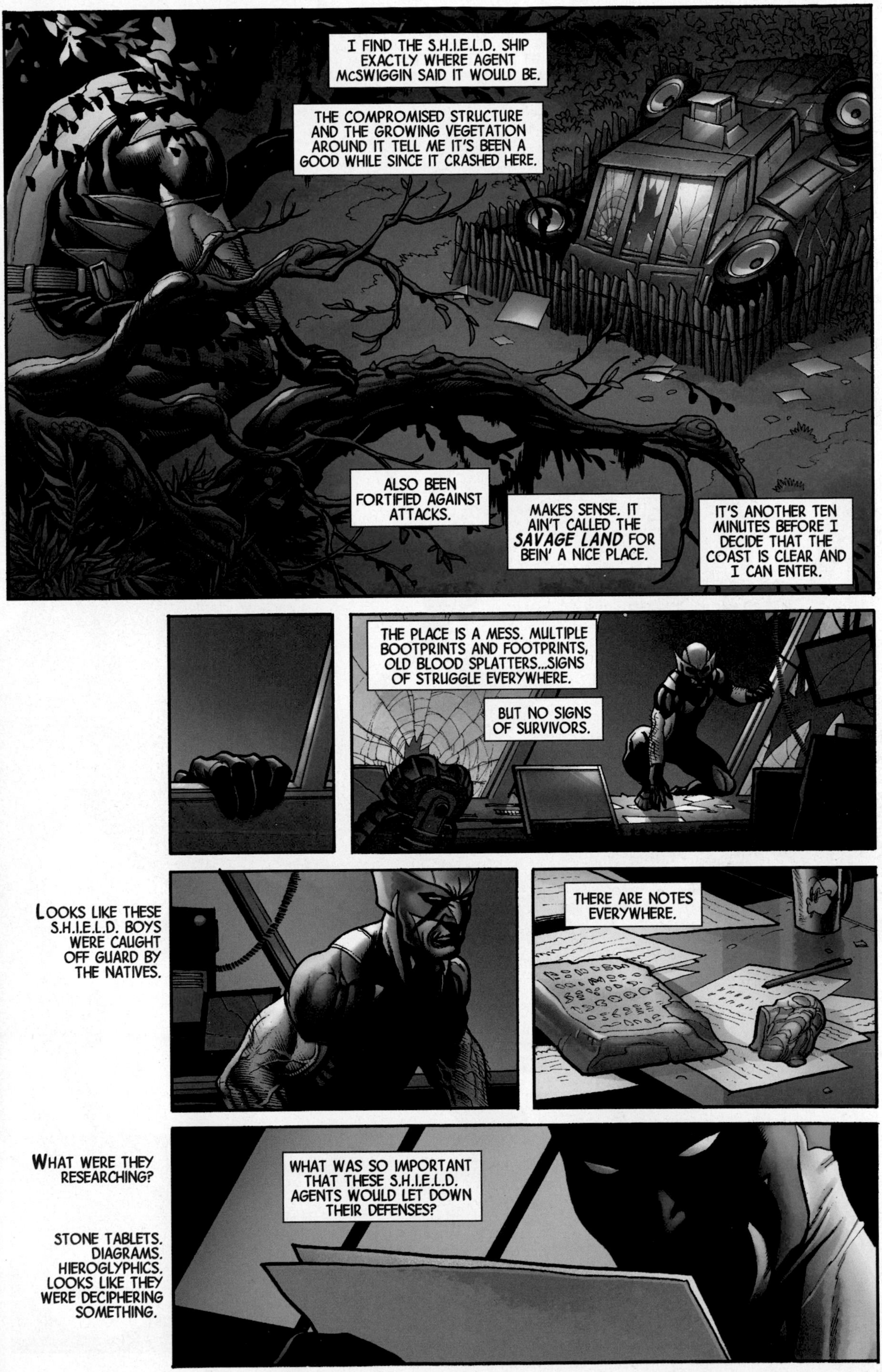
I FIND THE S.H.I.E.L.D. SHIP EXACTLY WHERE AGENT McSWIGGIN SAID IT WOULD BE.
THE COMPROMISED STRUCTURE AND THE GROWING VEGETATION AROUND IT TELL ME IT'S BEEN A GOOD WHILE SINCE IT CRASHED HERE.
ALSO BEEN FORTIFIED AGAINST ATTACKS.
MAKES SENSE. IT AIN'T CALLED THE *SAVAGE LAND* FOR BEIN' A NICE PLACE.
IT'S ANOTHER TEN MINUTES BEFORE I DECIDE THAT THE COAST IS CLEAR AND I CAN ENTER.
THE PLACE IS A MESS. MULTIPLE BOOTPRINTS AND FOOTPRINTS, OLD BLOOD SPLATTERS...SIGNS OF STRUGGLE EVERYWHERE.
BUT NO SIGNS OF SURVIVORS.
LOOKS LIKE THESE S.H.I.E.L.D. BOYS WERE CAUGHT OFF GUARD BY THE NATIVES.
THERE ARE NOTES EVERYWHERE.
WHAT WERE THEY RESEARCHING?
WHAT WAS SO IMPORTANT THAT THESE S.H.I.E.L.D. AGENTS WOULD LET DOWN THEIR DEFENSES?
STONE TABLETS. DIAGRAMS. HIEROGLYPHICS. LOOKS LIKE THEY WERE DECIPHERING SOMETHING.

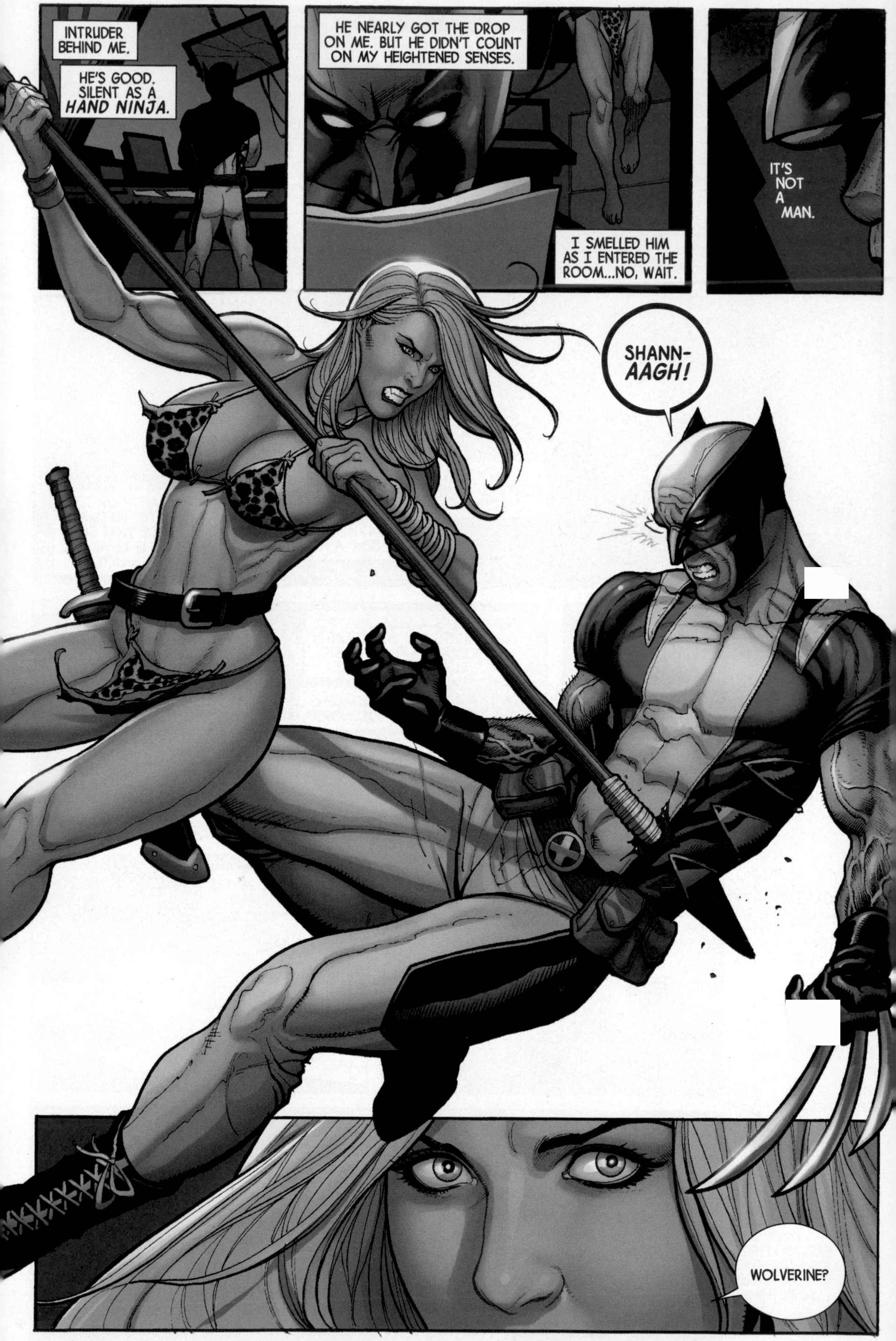
INTRUDER BEHIND ME.
HE'S GOOD. SILENT AS A HAND NINJA.
HE NEARLY GOT THE DROP ON ME. BUT HE DIDN'T COUNT ON MY HEIGHTENED SENSES.
I SMELLED HIM AS I ENTERED THE ROOM...NO, WAIT.
IT'S NOT A MAN.
SHANN-AAGH!
WOLVERINE?

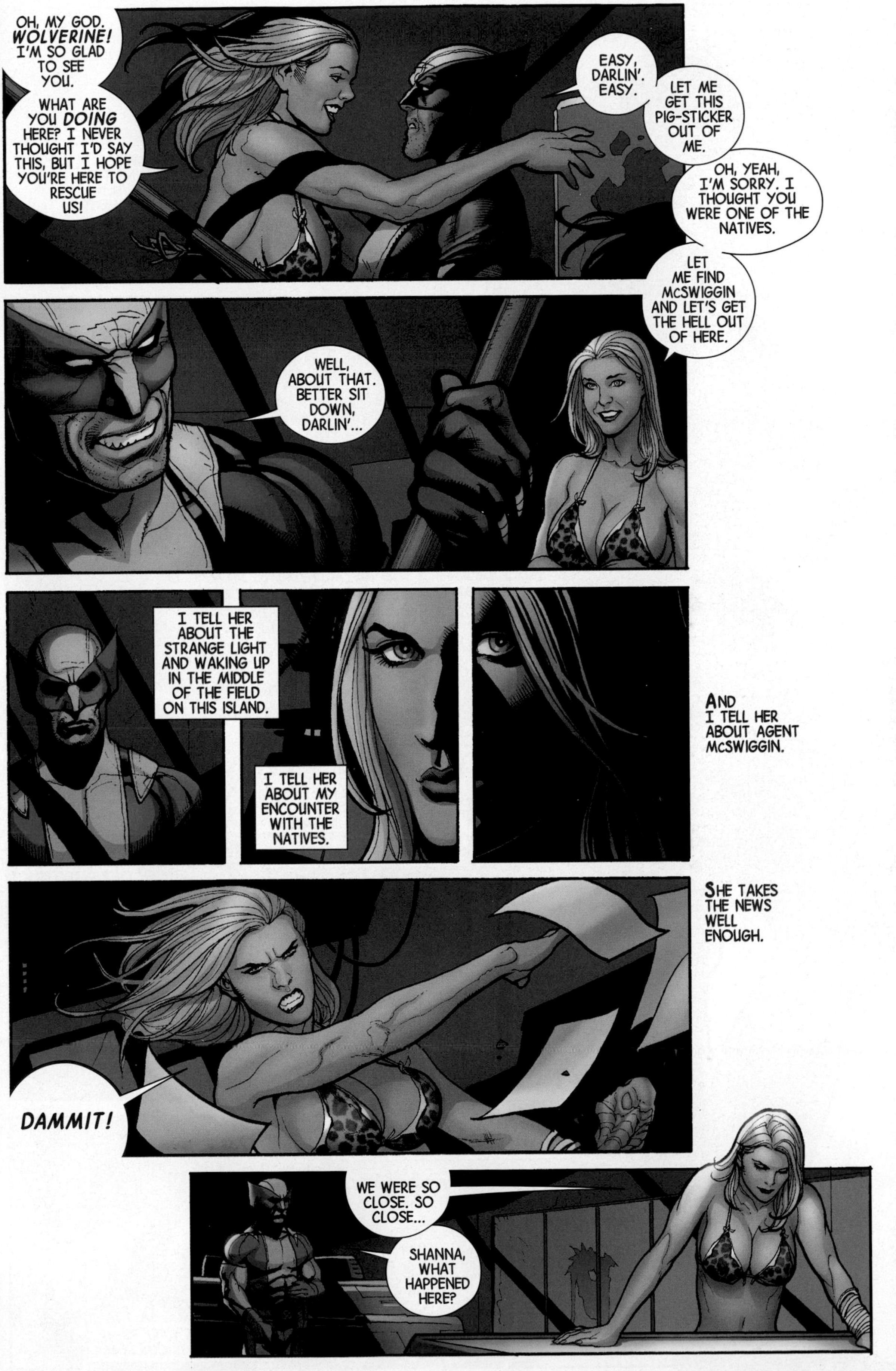
OH, MY GOD. WOLVERINE! I'M SO GLAD TO SEE YOU.
WHAT ARE YOU DOING HERE? I NEVER THOUGHT I'D SAY THIS, BUT I HOPE YOU'RE HERE TO RESCUE US!
EASY, DARLIN'. EASY.
LET ME GET THIS PIG-STICKER OUT OF ME.
OH, YEAH, I'M SORRY. I THOUGHT YOU WERE ONE OF THE NATIVES.
LET ME FIND McSWIGGIN AND LET'S GET THE HELL OUT OF HERE.
WELL, ABOUT THAT. BETTER SIT DOWN, DARLIN'...
I TELL HER ABOUT THE STRANGE LIGHT AND WAKING UP IN THE MIDDLE OF THE FIELD ON THIS ISLAND.
I TELL HER ABOUT MY ENCOUNTER WITH THE NATIVES.
AND I TELL HER ABOUT AGENT McSWIGGIN.
SHE TAKES THE NEWS WELL ENOUGH.
DAMMIT!
WE WERE SO CLOSE. SO CLOSE...
SHANNA, WHAT HAPPENED HERE?

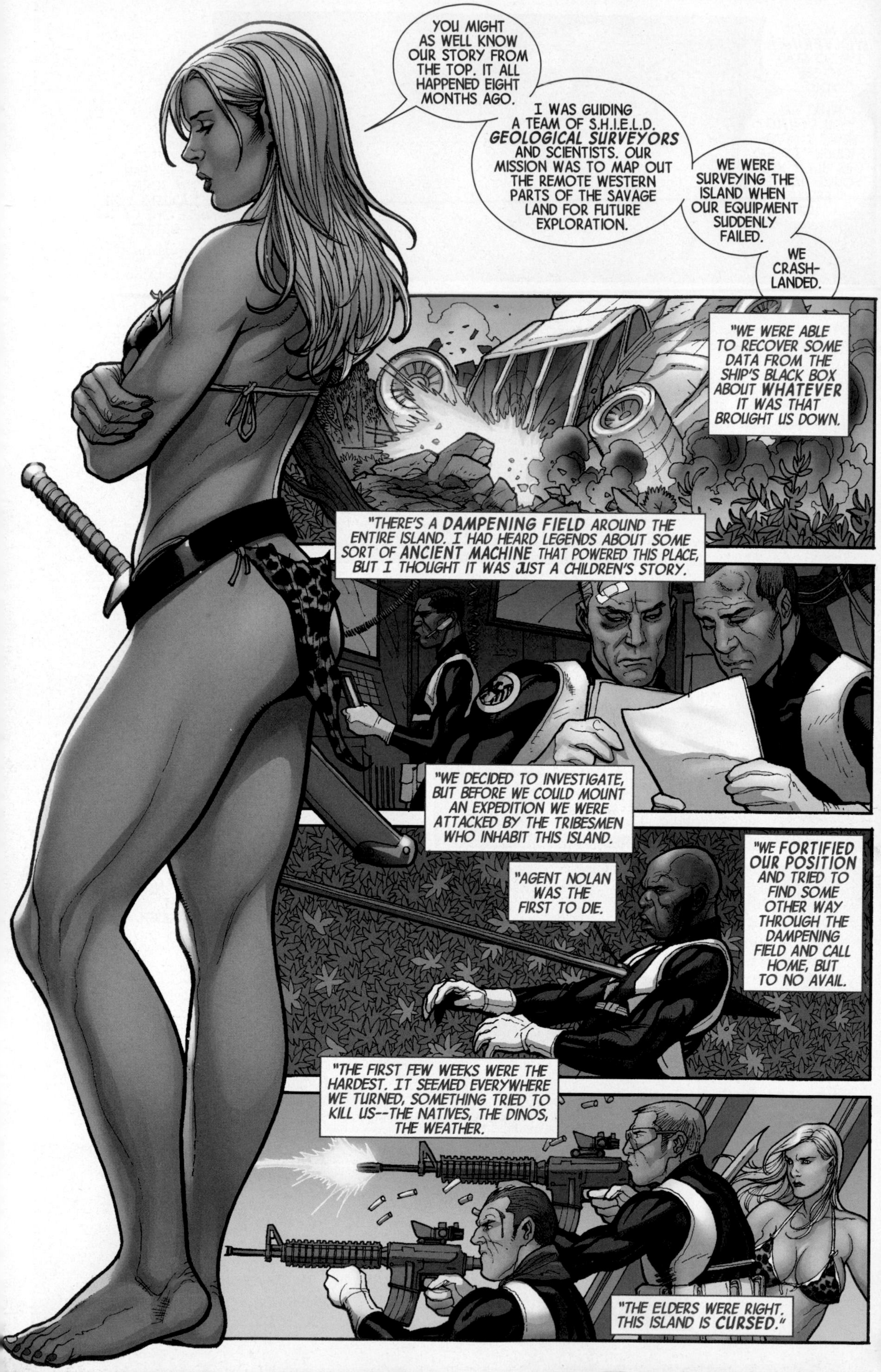
YOU MIGHT AS WELL KNOW OUR STORY FROM THE TOP. IT ALL HAPPENED EIGHT MONTHS AGO.
I WAS GUIDING A TEAM OF S.H.I.E.L.D. GEOLOGICAL SURVEYORS AND SCIENTISTS. OUR MISSION WAS TO MAP OUT THE REMOTE WESTERN PARTS OF THE SAVAGE LAND FOR FUTURE EXPLORATION.
WE WERE SURVEYING THE ISLAND WHEN OUR EQUIPMENT SUDDENLY FAILED.
WE CRASH-LANDED.
"WE WERE ABLE TO RECOVER SOME DATA FROM THE SHIP'S BLACK BOX ABOUT WHATEVER IT WAS THAT BROUGHT US DOWN.
"THERE'S A DAMPENING FIELD AROUND THE ENTIRE ISLAND. I HAD HEARD LEGENDS ABOUT SOME SORT OF ANCIENT MACHINE THAT POWERED THIS PLACE, BUT I THOUGHT IT WAS JUST A CHILDREN'S STORY.
"WE DECIDED TO INVESTIGATE, BUT BEFORE WE COULD MOUNT AN EXPEDITION WE WERE ATTACKED BY THE TRIBESMEN WHO INHABIT THIS ISLAND.
"AGENT NOLAN WAS THE FIRST TO DIE.
"WE FORTIFIED OUR POSITION AND TRIED TO FIND SOME OTHER WAY THROUGH THE DAMPENING FIELD AND CALL HOME, BUT TO NO AVAIL.
"THE FIRST FEW WEEKS WERE THE HARDEST. IT SEEMED EVERYWHERE WE TURNED, SOMETHING TRIED TO KILL US--THE NATIVES, THE DINOS, THE WEATHER.
"THE ELDERS WERE RIGHT. THIS ISLAND IS CURSED."

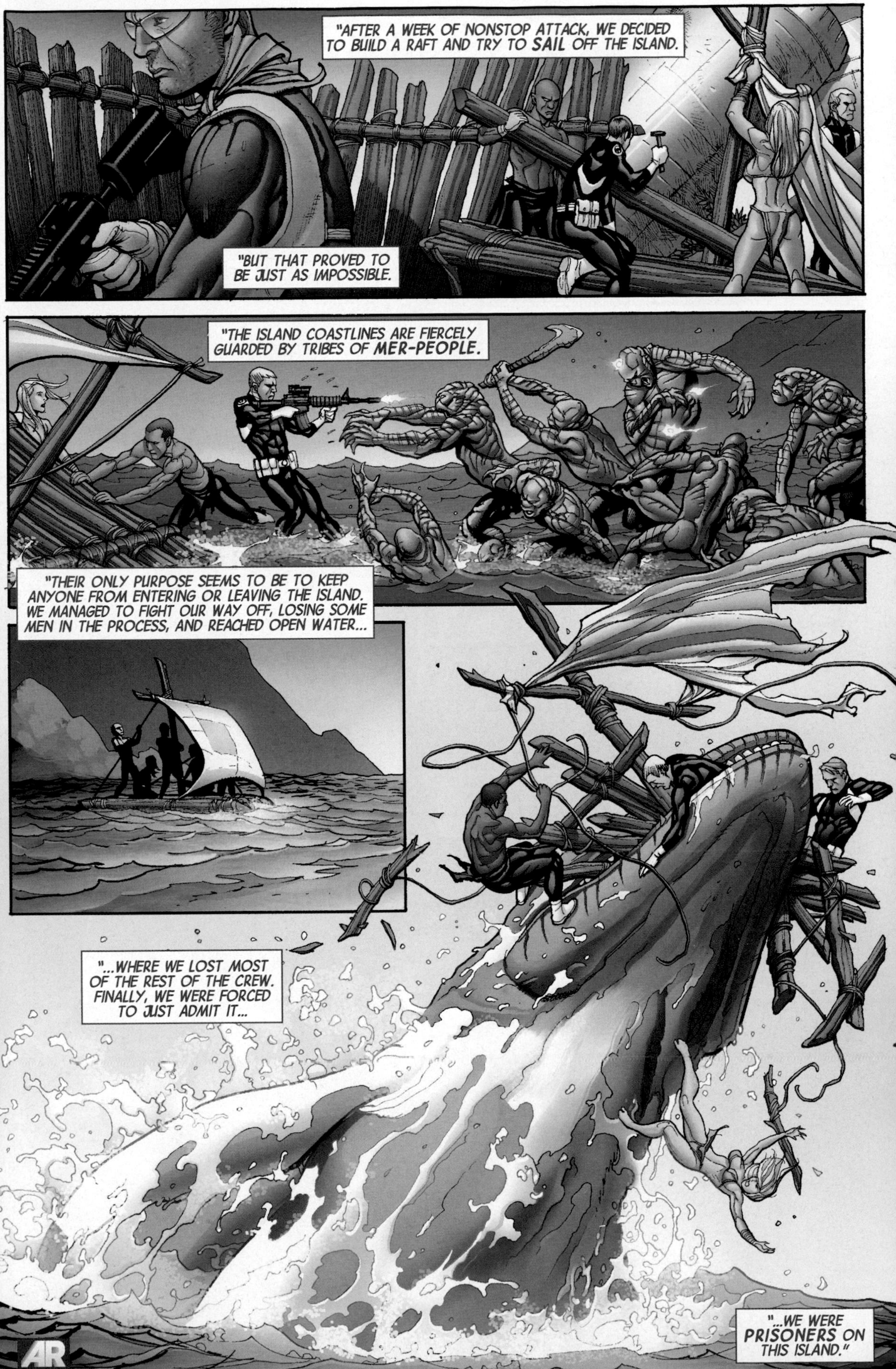
"AFTER A WEEK OF NONSTOP ATTACK, WE DECIDED TO BUILD A RAFT AND TRY TO SAIL OFF THE ISLAND.
"BUT THAT PROVED TO BE JUST AS IMPOSSIBLE.
"THE ISLAND COASTLINES ARE FIERCELY GUARDED BY TRIBES OF MER-PEOPLE.
"THEIR ONLY PURPOSE SEEMS TO BE TO KEEP ANYONE FROM ENTERING OR LEAVING THE ISLAND. WE MANAGED TO FIGHT OUR WAY OFF, LOSING SOME MEN IN THE PROCESS, AND REACHED OPEN WATER...
"...WHERE WE LOST MOST OF THE REST OF THE CREW. FINALLY, WE WERE FORCED TO JUST ADMIT IT...
"...WE WERE PRISONERS ON THIS ISLAND."
AR

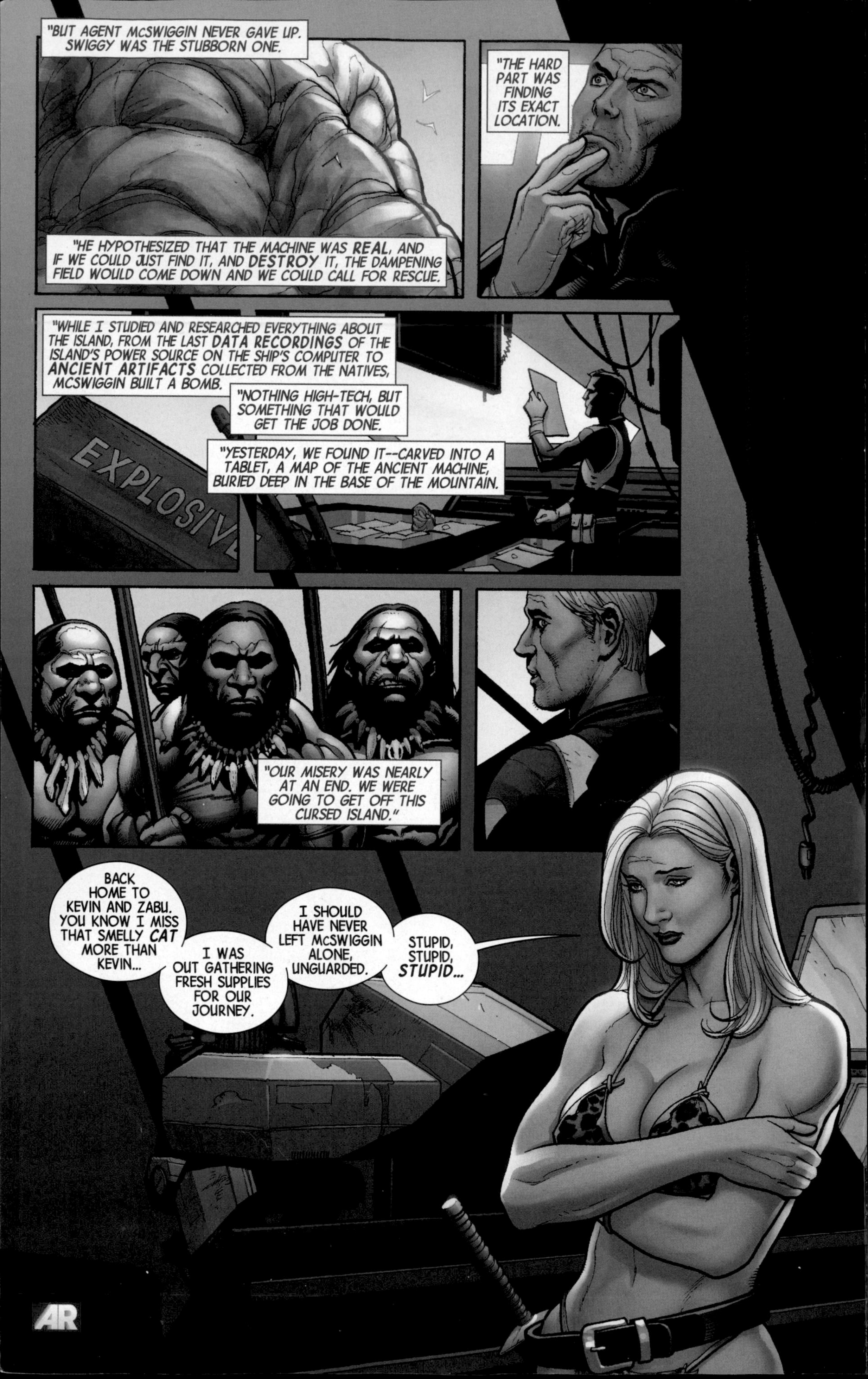
"BUT AGENT McSWIGGIN NEVER GAVE UP. SWIGGY WAS THE STUBBORN ONE.
"HE HYPOTHESIZED THAT THE MACHINE WAS REAL, AND IF WE COULD JUST FIND IT, AND DESTROY IT, THE DAMPENING FIELD WOULD COME DOWN AND WE COULD CALL FOR RESCUE.
"THE HARD PART WAS FINDING ITS EXACT LOCATION.
"WHILE I STUDIED AND RESEARCHED EVERYTHING ABOUT THE ISLAND, FROM THE LAST DATA RECORDINGS OF THE ISLAND'S POWER SOURCE ON THE SHIP'S COMPUTER TO ANCIENT ARTIFACTS COLLECTED FROM THE NATIVES, McSWIGGIN BUILT A BOMB.
"NOTHING HIGH-TECH, BUT SOMETHING THAT WOULD GET THE JOB DONE.
EXPLOSIVE
"YESTERDAY, WE FOUND IT--CARVED INTO A TABLET, A MAP OF THE ANCIENT MACHINE, BURIED DEEP IN THE BASE OF THE MOUNTAIN.
"OUR MISERY WAS NEARLY AT AN END. WE WERE GOING TO GET OFF THIS CURSED ISLAND."
BACK HOME TO KEVIN AND ZABU. YOU KNOW I MISS THAT SMELLY CAT MORE THAN KEVIN...
I WAS OUT GATHERING FRESH SUPPLIES FOR OUR JOURNEY.
I SHOULD HAVE NEVER LEFT McSWIGGIN ALONE, UNGUARDED.
STUPID, STUPID, STUPID...
AR

YOU HAD TO DO WHAT YOU HAD TO. DON'T BLAME YOURSELF, KID.

I WOULD HAVE DONE THE SAME THING.

RULES OF THE JUNGLE, HUH?

YEAH. SOMETHING LIKE THAT.

TELL ME MORE ABOUT THE BOMB. IS THAT IT?

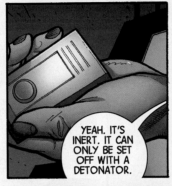

YEAH. IT'S INERT. IT CAN ONLY BE SET OFF WITH A DETONATOR.

GIMME. HOW DOES IT WORK?

THE EXPLOSIVE IS ENCASED IN THE BODY. JUST STICK THE BOMB ON THE WALL AND PUSH THE TWO BUTTONS ON THE TOP AND SIDE TO DETONATE IT. IT HAS A 20 SECOND FUSE.

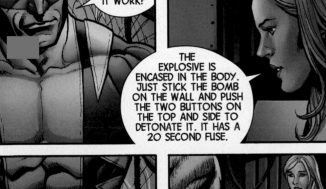

HAND ME THE RADIO.

WELL, WHAT DO YOU KNOW...

YOU GUYS DO USE THOSE POUCHES. I THOUGHT THEY WERE FOR SHOW.

WHERE DO YOU THINK I KEEP MY HOUSE KEYS?

SO WHAT'S THE PLAN?

SAME AS YOURS. FIND THE MACHINE, BLOW IT UP, CALL HOME...

...AND GET OFF THIS LOUSY ISLAND.

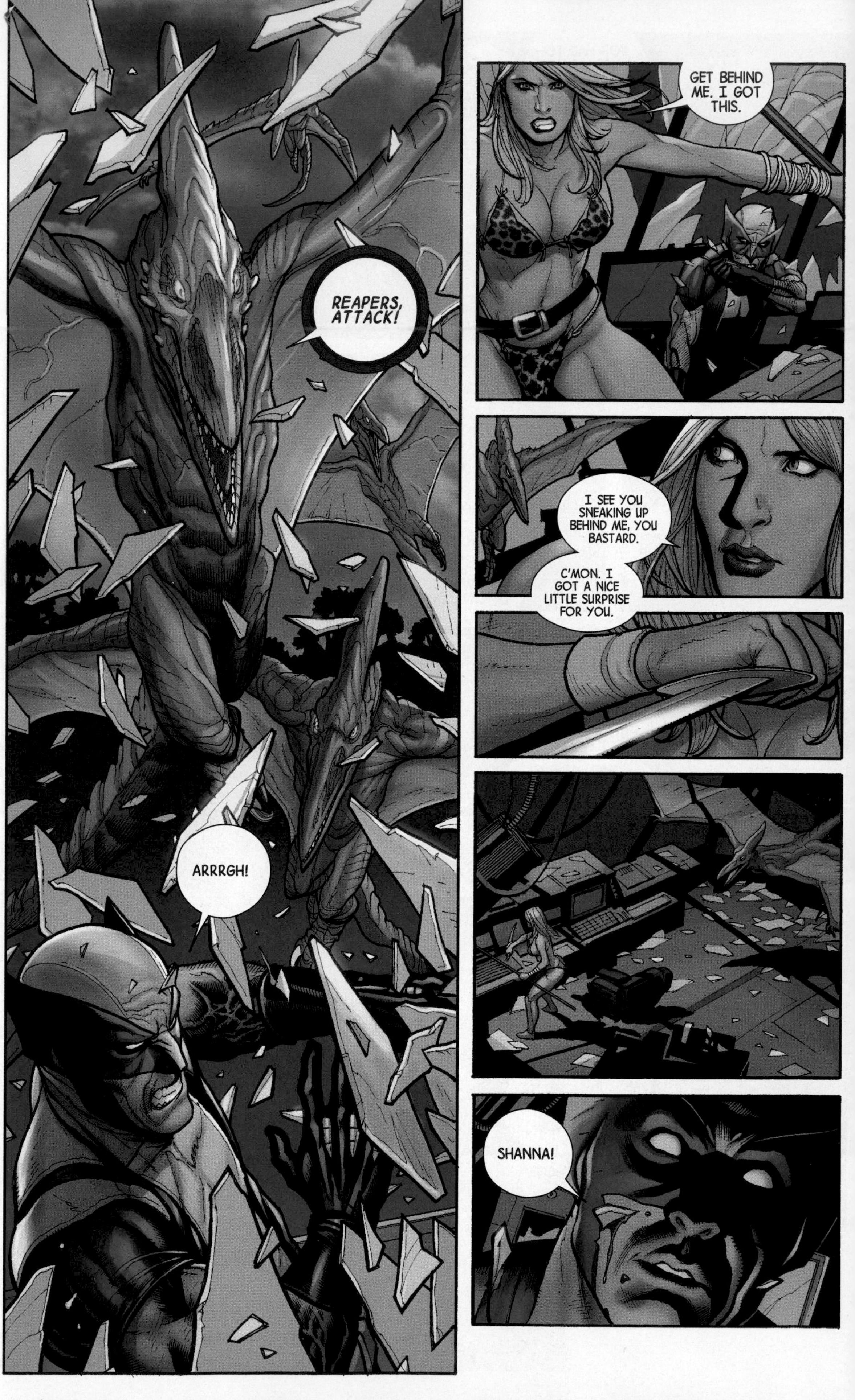
REAPERS, ATTACK!
ARRRGH!
GET BEHIND ME. I GOT THIS.
I SEE YOU SNEAKING UP BEHIND ME, YOU BASTARD.
C'MON. I GOT A NICE LITTLE SURPRISE FOR YOU.
SHANNA!

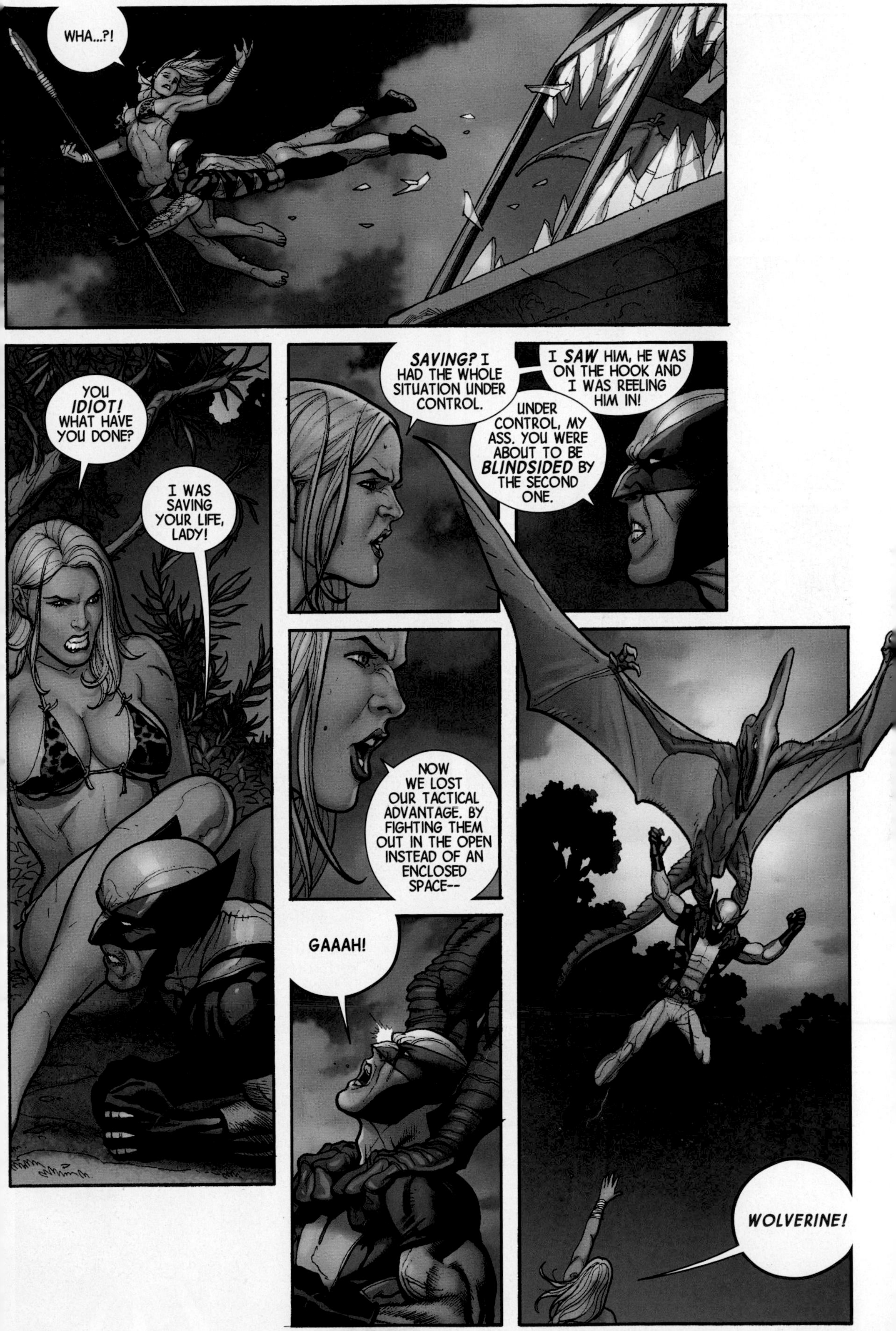
WHA...?!
YOU IDIOT! WHAT HAVE YOU DONE?
I WAS SAVING YOUR LIFE, LADY!
SAVING? I HAD THE WHOLE SITUATION UNDER CONTROL.
I SAW HIM, HE WAS ON THE HOOK AND I WAS REELING HIM IN!
UNDER CONTROL, MY ASS. YOU WERE ABOUT TO BE BLINDSIDED BY THE SECOND ONE.
NOW WE LOST OUR TACTICAL ADVANTAGE. BY FIGHTING THEM OUT IN THE OPEN INSTEAD OF AN ENCLOSED SPACE--
GAAAH!
WOLVERINE!

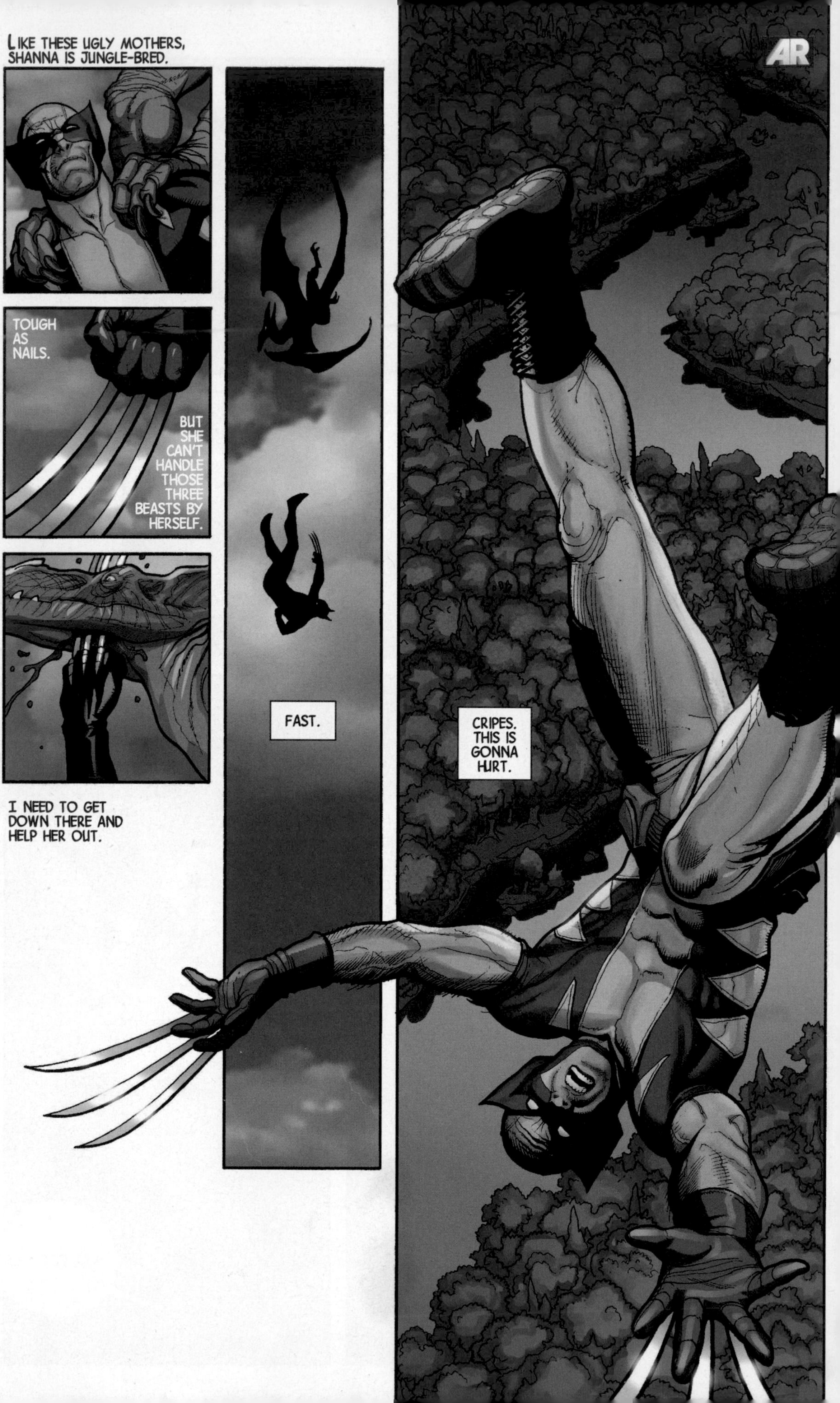

LIKE THESE UGLY MOTHERS, SHANNA IS JUNGLE-BRED.
TOUGH AS NAILS.
BUT SHE CAN'T HANDLE THOSE THREE BEASTS BY HERSELF.
I NEED TO GET DOWN THERE AND HELP HER OUT.
FAST.
CRIPES. THIS IS GONNA HURT.

THE CUTTING EDGE

Send e-mail to officex@marvel.com (please mark as OKAY TO PRINT)

Babes, BRAWLS AND *BRACHIOSAURS.*

THAT'S WHAT WE SAID TO **FRANK CHO** WHEN HE ASKED **EIC AXEL ALONSO** AND ME WHAT KIND OF A WOLVERINE PITCH WE WERE LOOKING FOR.

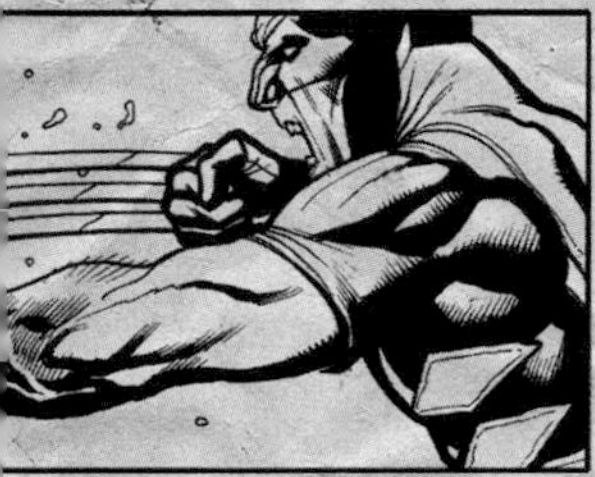

Okay, actually no one said that. I think we might have said, "whatever you want!" but that's not as good a story and alliteration makes everything better, so.

SO HE TOOK *the weekend,*

and he sent us back a massively detailed outline featuring an issue one that, almost to a scene, is exactly what you just read. A pulpy Wolverine in the Savage Land comic, but one that tilted everything just a little: the damsel isn't as in distress as you thought she'd be; the natives aren't as clueless as they're usually portrayed. So you're never really sure if you know where the story's going.

One Of The Things

that makes Wolverine so awesome is that Wolverine is a dude that you can drop into any situation and he sort of doesn't seem so out of place. Dinosaurs, mer-people, samurai, aliens, giant robots, World War II, that time he met the Devil...he'll roll with all of it, and still bounce back as the baddest-ass cranky-as-hell headmaster of a school you've ever met. And trust me when I say that Frank has got some stuff up his sleeve to rival all of that, including some huge guest stars! It's gonna get weird up in here, and you'll be so glad you're along for the ride.

ALSO, A FEW MORE QUICK SHOUT-OUTS:

Jason Keith, who is painstakingly coloring the hell out of this book, **Cory Petit,** who designed a really cool lettering style and layout to match the tone of the book, **Chris Eliopoulos,** who went all out on design pages (like the one you're reading now), and **Brian Overton,** our library supervisor, whose enthusiasm for pulp comics was a massive help in envisioning what the whole package could look like (also he introduced me to the awesomeness of Epic Illustrated, a gorgeously trippy piece of Marvel publishing history). And, of course, Axel Alonso, whose support has been integral to getting this book off the ground.

So buckle in, suit up, brace yourself, all those other things you don't when something's gonna blow you away, cos this is gonna be a great ride.

And make sure you write in and let us know what you think, at

officex@marvel.com

(or you can find our street address on the last page if you're old timey)! Make sure you mark everything OKAY TO PRINT, and Frank and the rest of Team Wolverine will answer all your burning questions.

See you next month!
Hugs and snikts,

J9

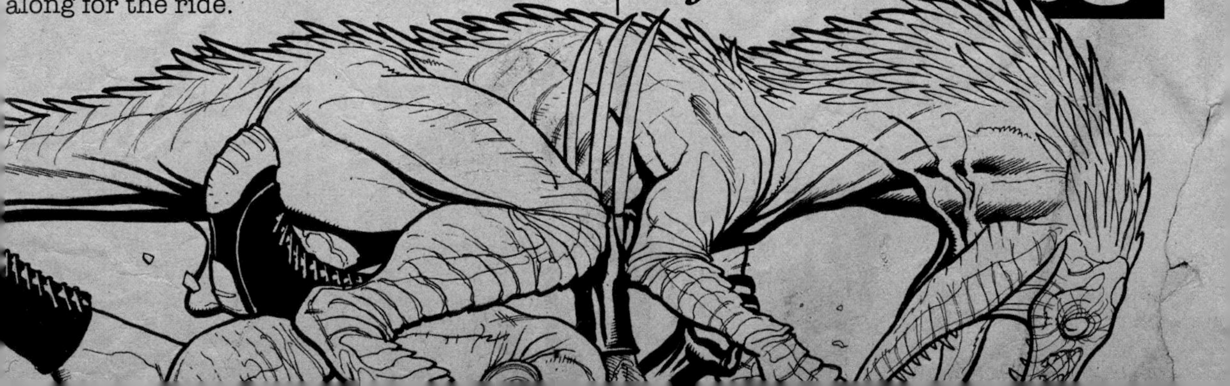

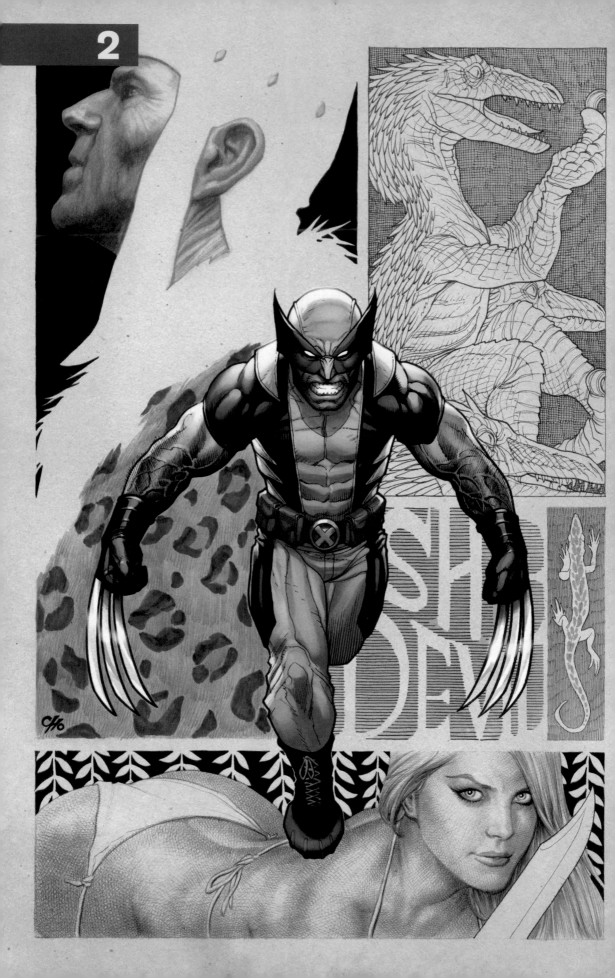

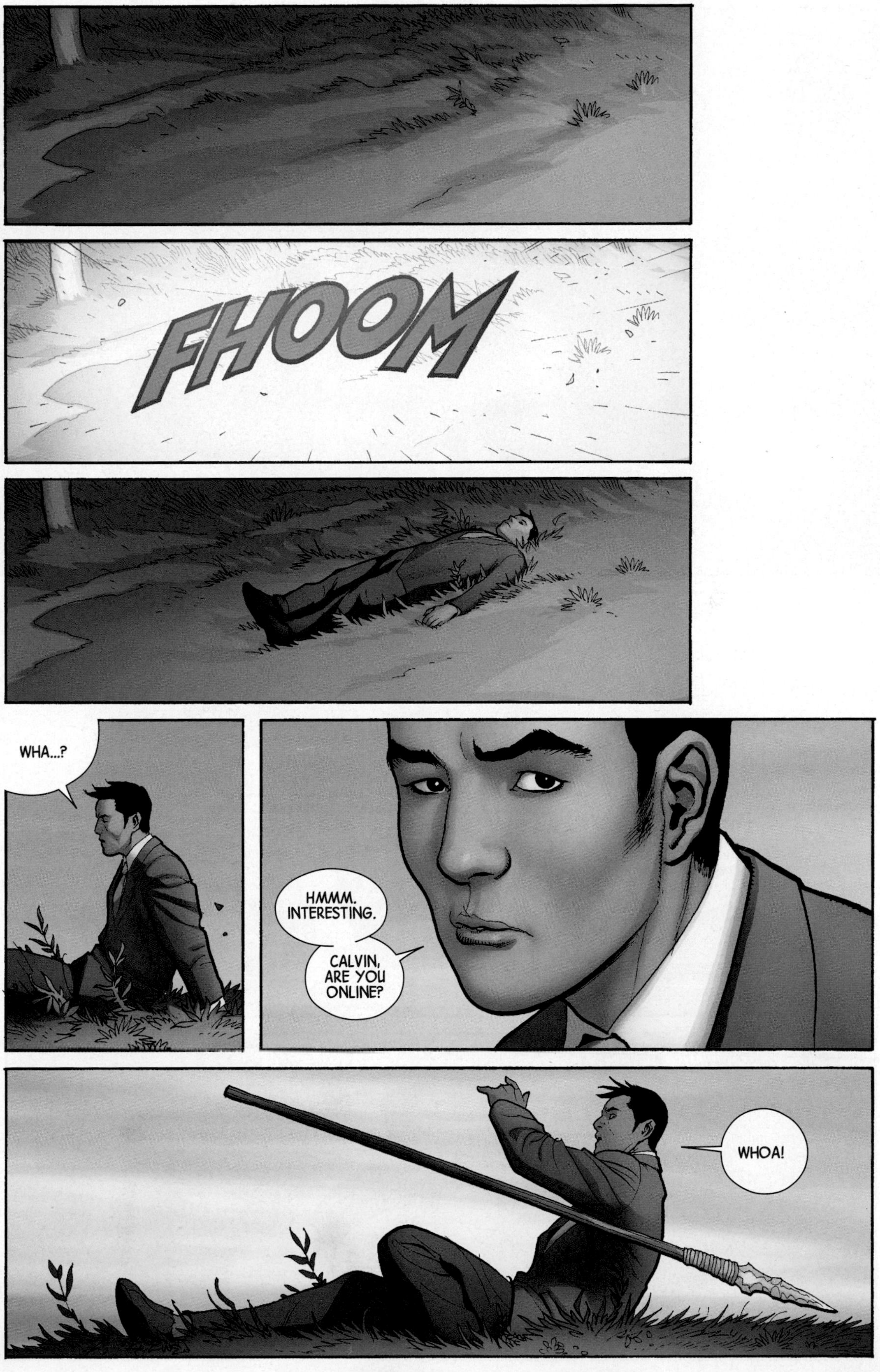
FHOOM
WHA...?
HMMM. INTERESTING.
CALVIN, ARE YOU ONLINE?
WHOA!

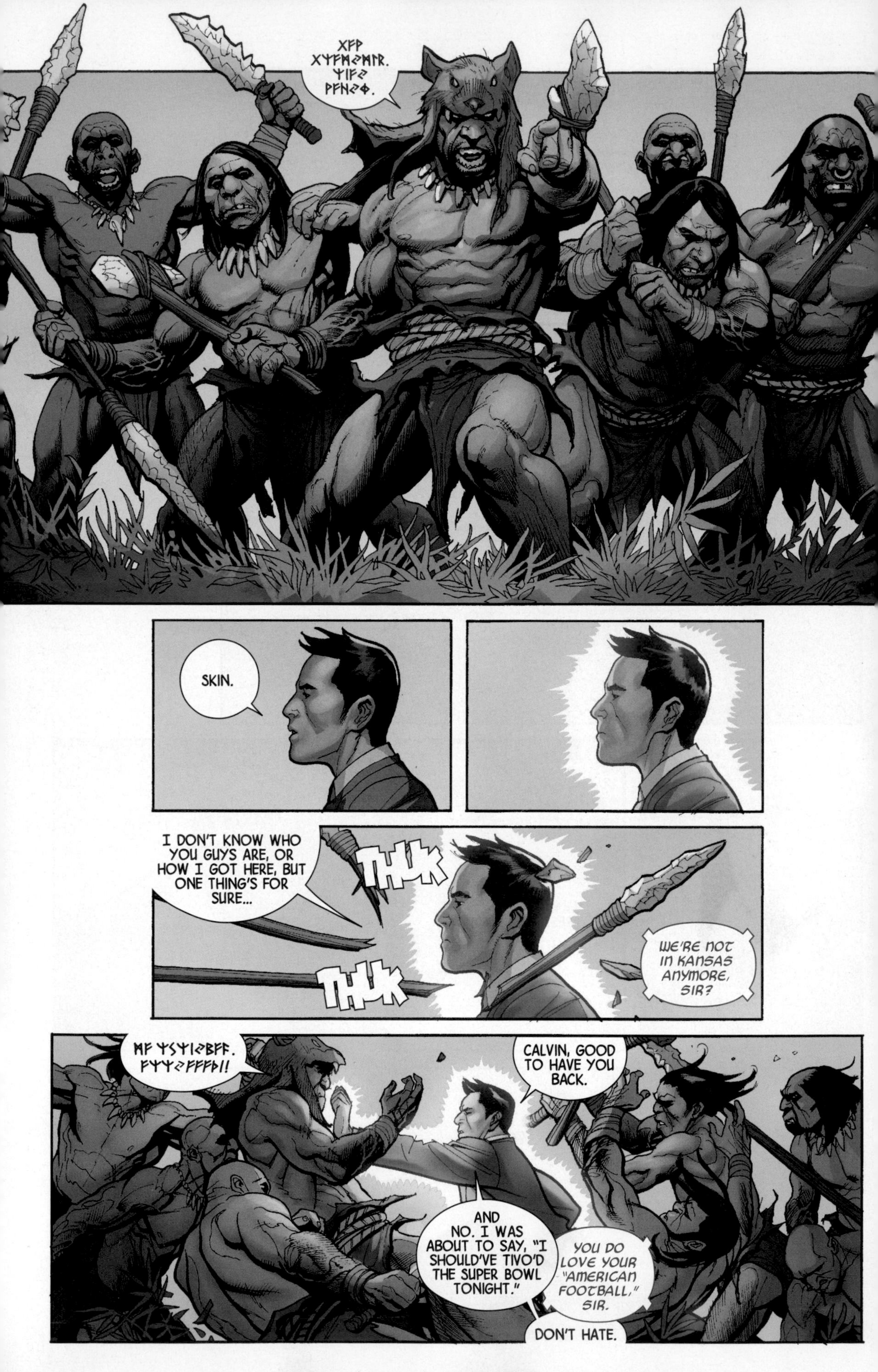
SKIN.
I DON'T KNOW WHO YOU GUYS ARE, OR HOW I GOT HERE, BUT ONE THING'S FOR SURE...
THUK
THUK
WE'RE NOT IN KANSAS ANYMORE, SIR?
CALVIN, GOOD TO HAVE YOU BACK.
AND NO. I WAS ABOUT TO SAY, "I SHOULD'VE TIVO'D THE SUPER BOWL TONIGHT."
YOU DO LOVE YOUR "AMERICAN FOOTBALL," SIR.
DON'T HATE.

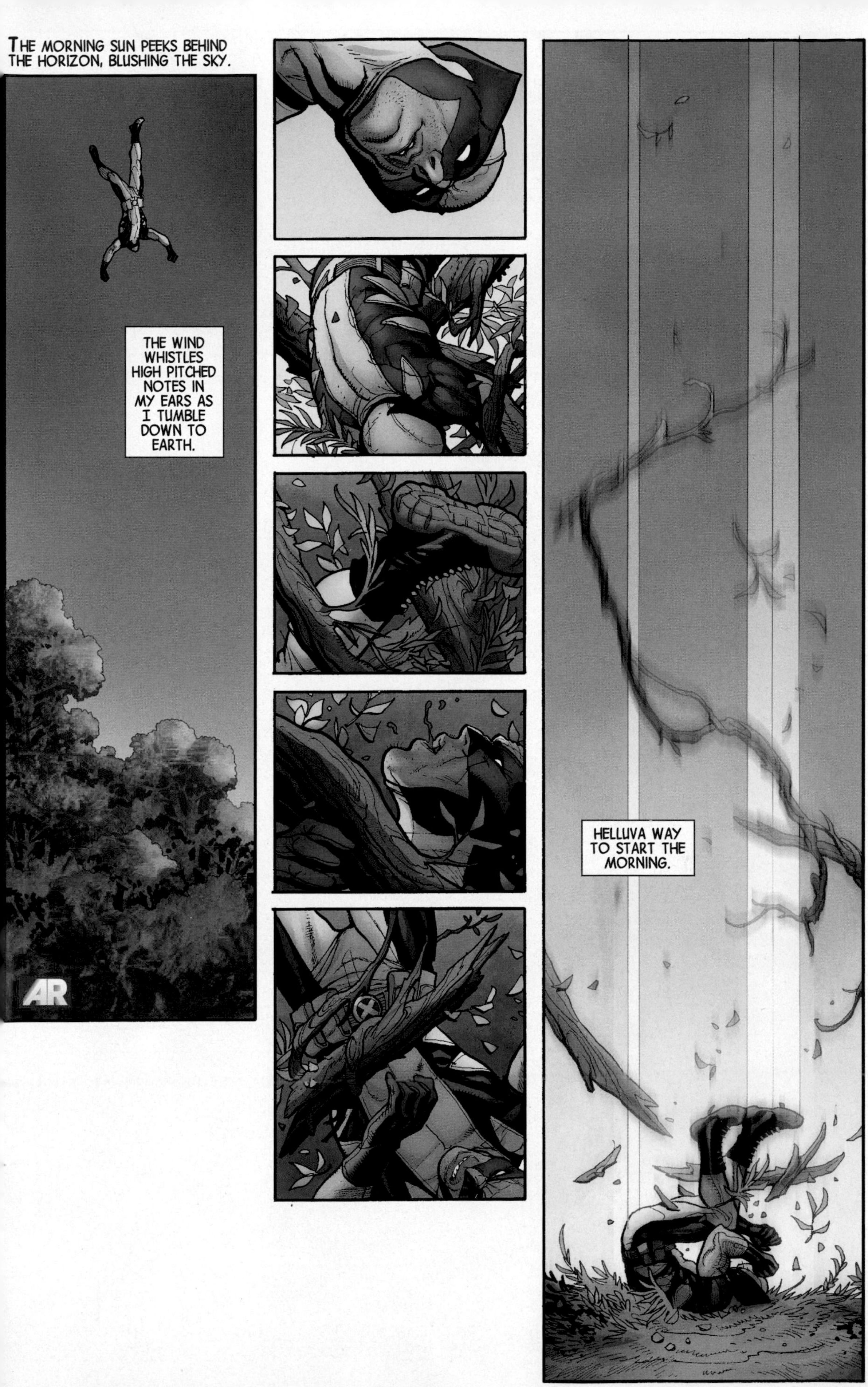
THE MORNING SUN PEEKS BEHIND THE HORIZON, BLUSHING THE SKY.
THE WIND WHISTLES HIGH PITCHED NOTES IN MY EARS AS I TUMBLE DOWN TO EARTH.
AR
HELLUVA WAY TO START THE MORNING.

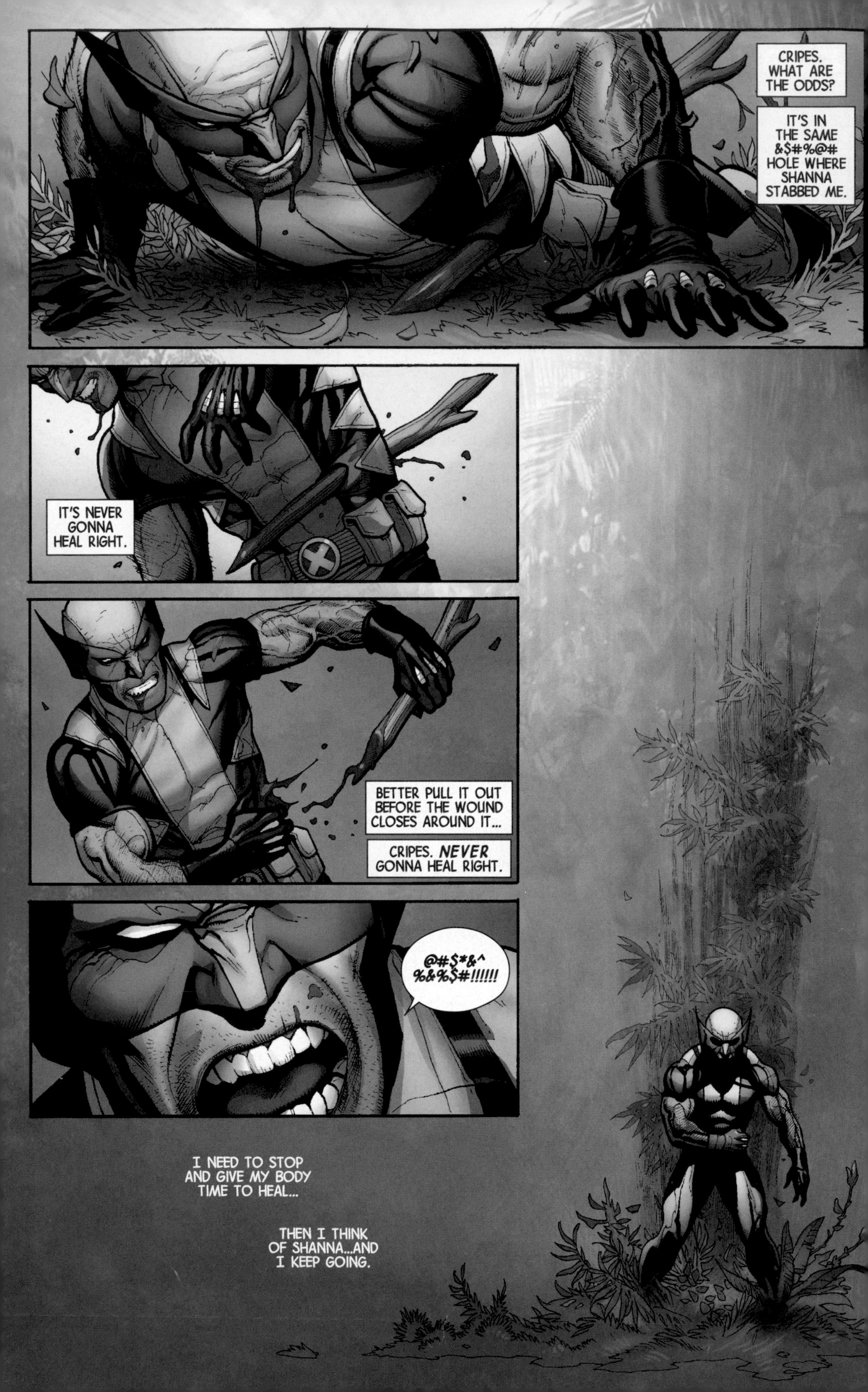
CRIPES. WHAT ARE THE ODDS?
IT'S IN THE SAME &$#%@# HOLE WHERE SHANNA STABBED ME.
IT'S NEVER GONNA HEAL RIGHT.
BETTER PULL IT OUT BEFORE THE WOUND CLOSES AROUND IT...
CRIPES. NEVER GONNA HEAL RIGHT.
@#$*&^ %&%$#!!!!!!
I NEED TO STOP AND GIVE MY BODY TIME TO HEAL...
THEN I THINK OF SHANNA...AND I KEEP GOING.

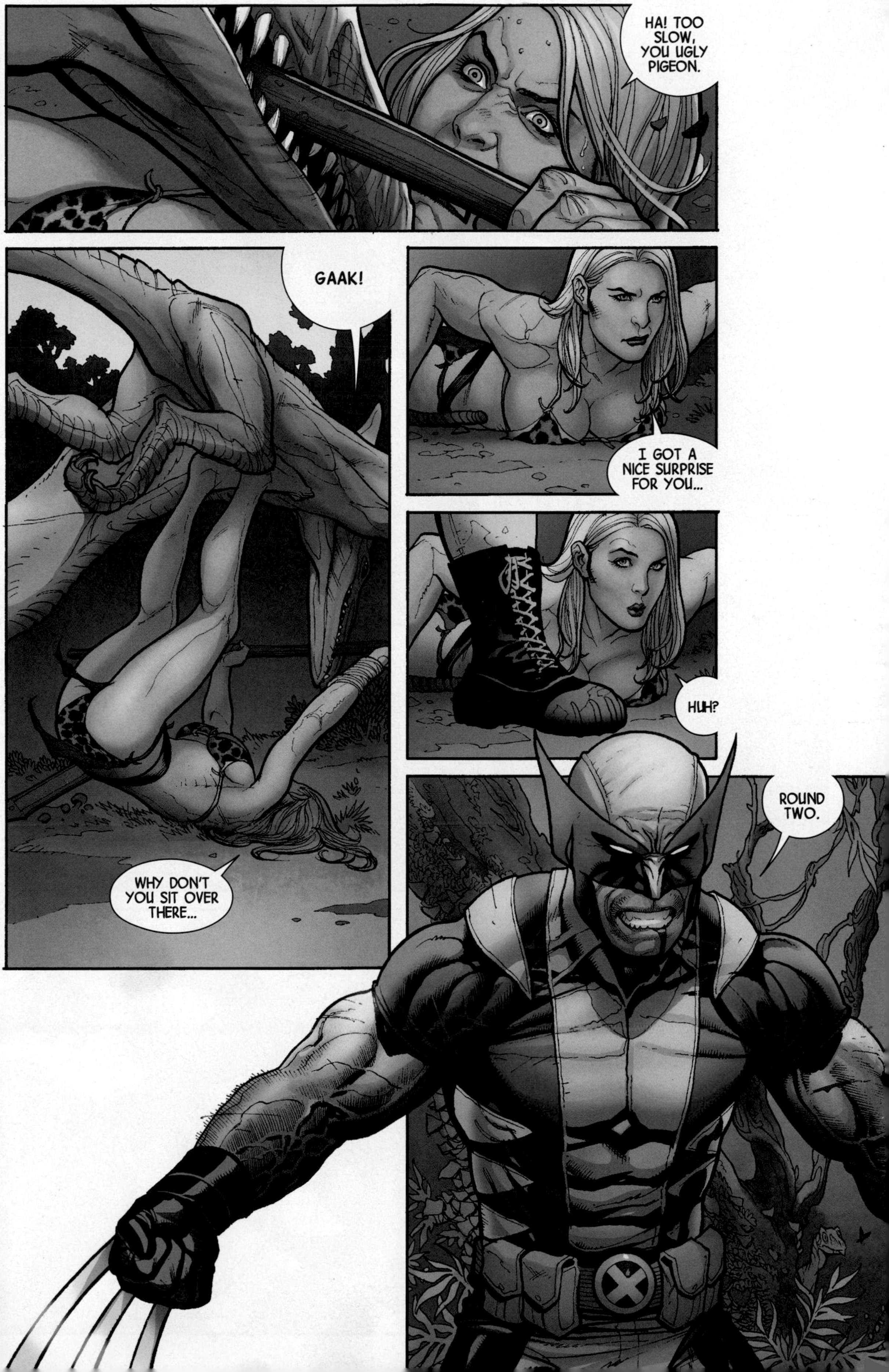
HA! TOO SLOW, YOU UGLY PIGEON.
GAAK!
WHY DON'T YOU SIT OVER THERE...
I GOT A NICE SURPRISE FOR YOU...
HUH?
ROUND TWO.

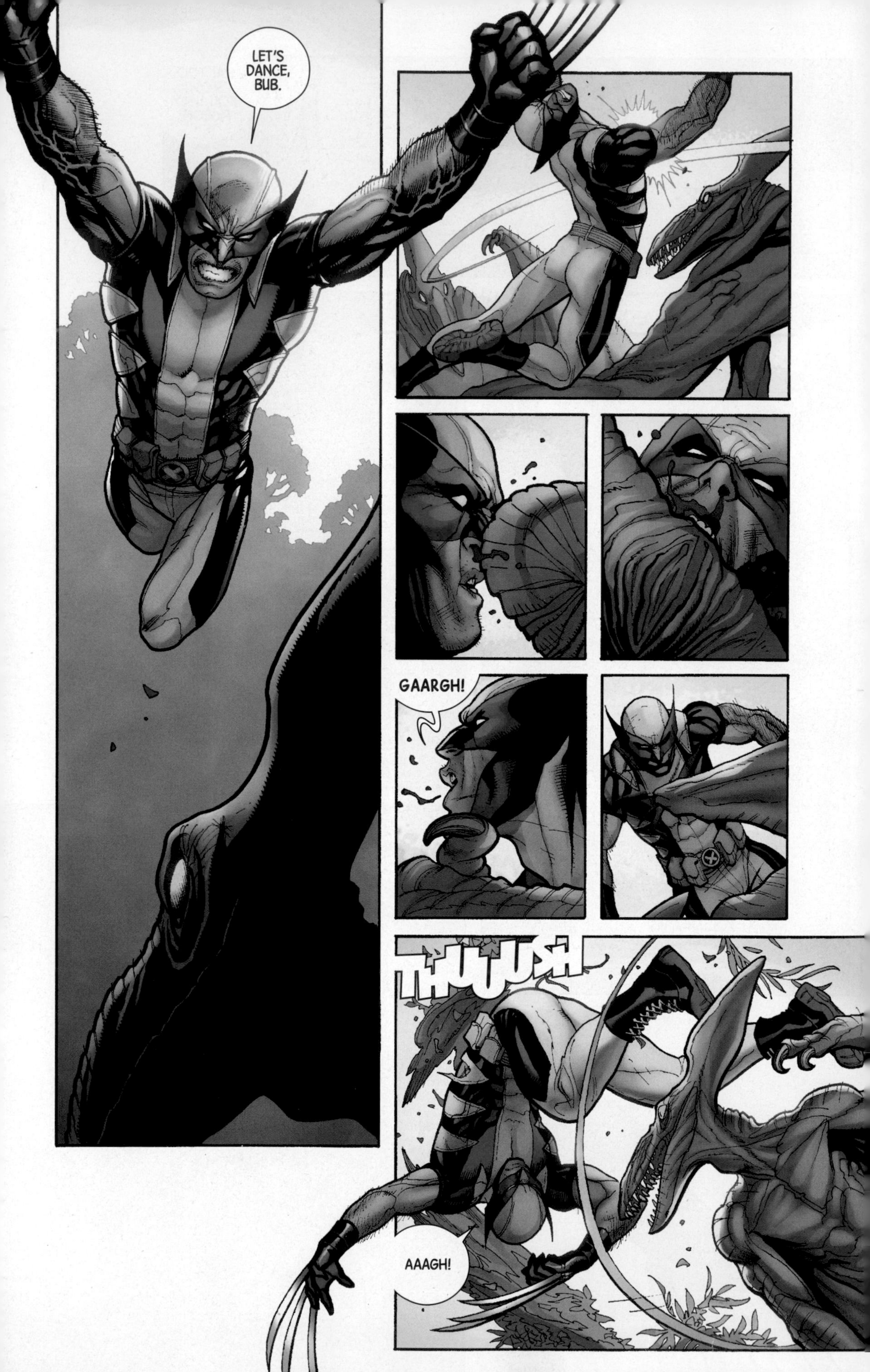
LET'S DANCE, BUB.
GAARGH!
THUUUSH
AAAGH!

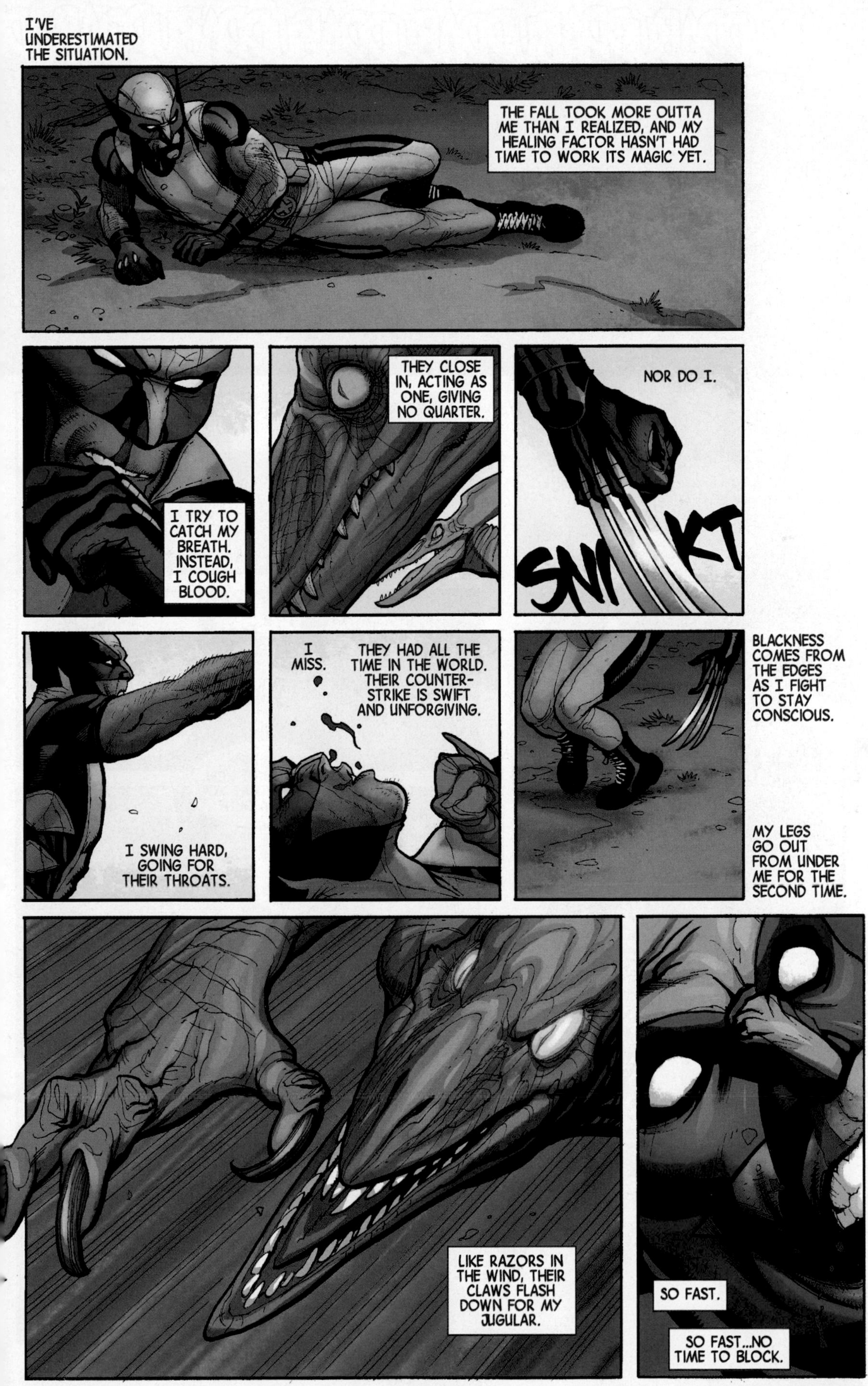
I'VE UNDERESTIMATED THE SITUATION.
THE FALL TOOK MORE OUTTA ME THAN I REALIZED, AND MY HEALING FACTOR HASN'T HAD TIME TO WORK ITS MAGIC YET.
I TRY TO CATCH MY BREATH. INSTEAD, I COUGH BLOOD.
THEY CLOSE IN, ACTING AS ONE, GIVING NO QUARTER.
NOR DO I.
SNIKT
I SWING HARD, GOING FOR THEIR THROATS.
I MISS.
THEY HAD ALL THE TIME IN THE WORLD. THEIR COUNTER-STRIKE IS SWIFT AND UNFORGIVING.
BLACKNESS COMES FROM THE EDGES AS I FIGHT TO STAY CONSCIOUS.
MY LEGS GO OUT FROM UNDER ME FOR THE SECOND TIME.
LIKE RAZORS IN THE WIND, THEIR CLAWS FLASH DOWN FOR MY JUGULAR.
SO FAST.
SO FAST...NO TIME TO BLOCK.

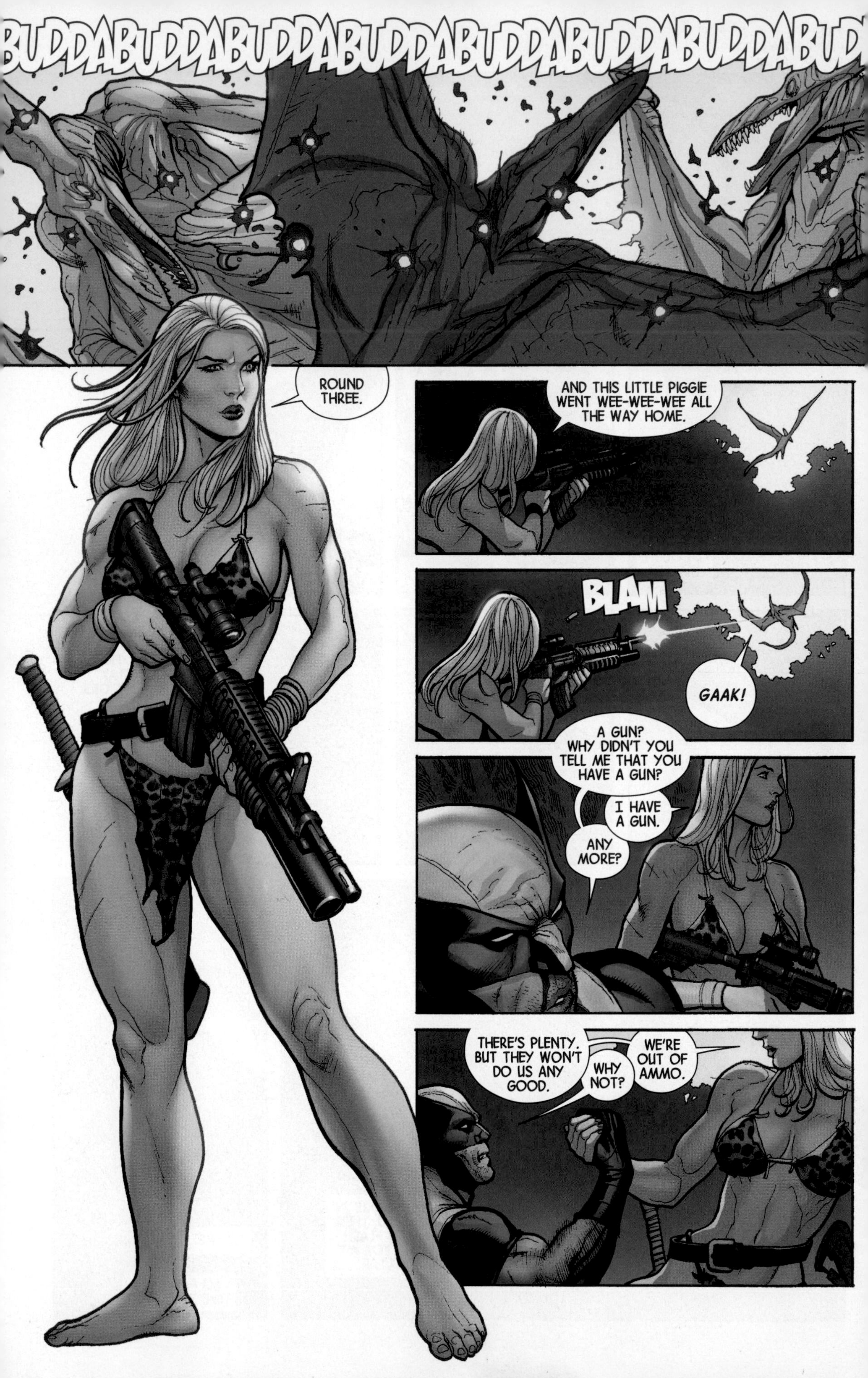
BUDDABUDDABUDDABUDDABUDDABUDDABUDDABUD
ROUND THREE.
AND THIS LITTLE PIGGIE WENT WEE-WEE-WEE ALL THE WAY HOME.
BLAM
GAAK!
A GUN? WHY DIDN'T YOU TELL ME THAT YOU HAVE A GUN?
I HAVE A GUN.
ANY MORE?
WE'RE OUT OF AMMO.
THERE'S PLENTY. BUT THEY WON'T DO US ANY GOOD.
WHY NOT?

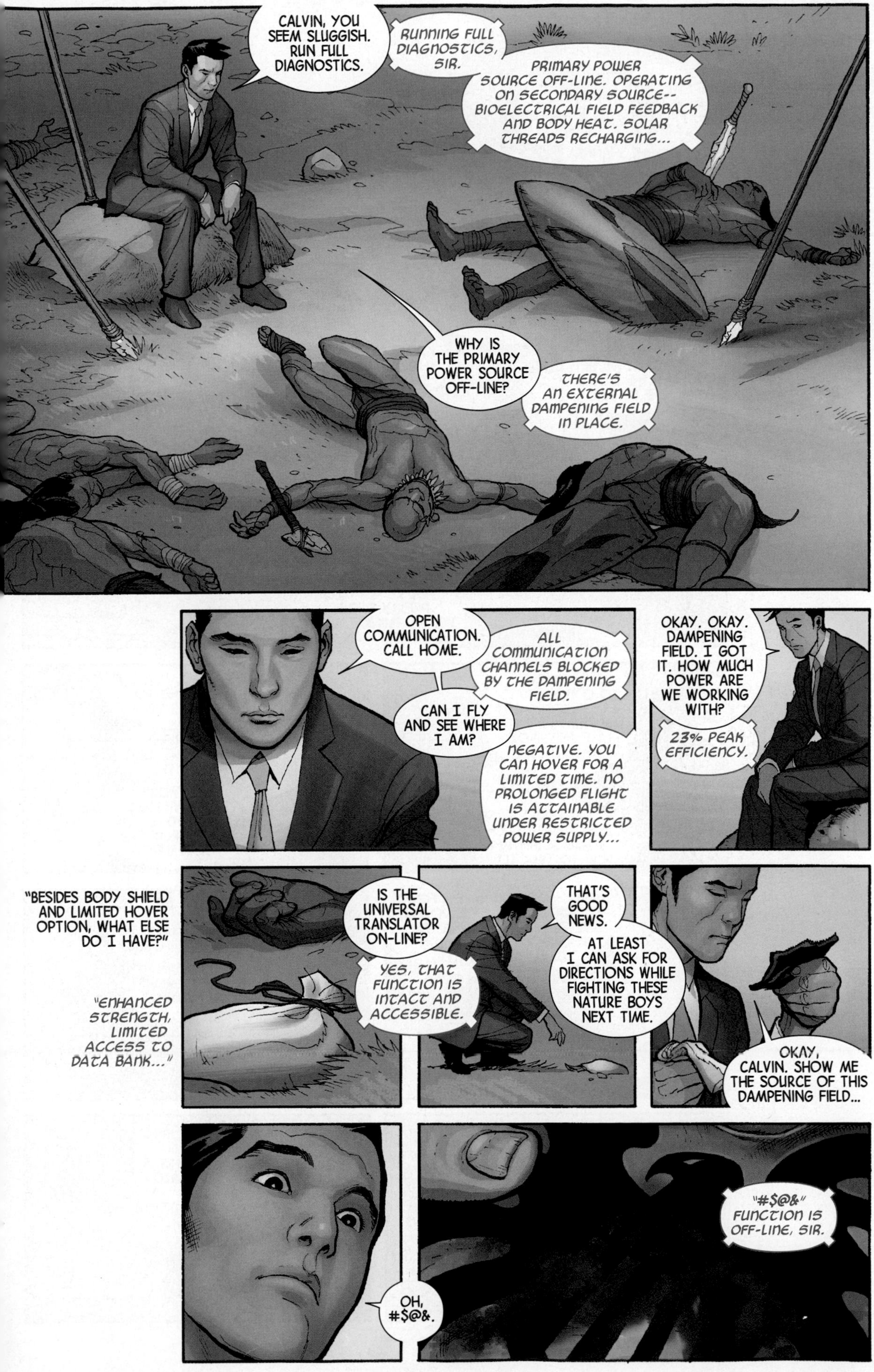
CALVIN, YOU SEEM SLUGGISH. RUN FULL DIAGNOSTICS.
RUNNING FULL DIAGNOSTICS, SIR.
PRIMARY POWER SOURCE OFF-LINE. OPERATING ON SECONDARY SOURCE-- BIOELECTRICAL FIELD FEEDBACK AND BODY HEAT. SOLAR THREADS RECHARGING...
WHY IS THE PRIMARY POWER SOURCE OFF-LINE?
THERE'S AN EXTERNAL DAMPENING FIELD IN PLACE.
OPEN COMMUNICATION. CALL HOME.
ALL COMMUNICATION CHANNELS BLOCKED BY THE DAMPENING FIELD.
CAN I FLY AND SEE WHERE I AM?
NEGATIVE. YOU CAN HOVER FOR A LIMITED TIME. NO PROLONGED FLIGHT IS ATTAINABLE UNDER RESTRICTED POWER SUPPLY...
OKAY. OKAY. DAMPENING FIELD. I GOT IT. HOW MUCH POWER ARE WE WORKING WITH?
23% PEAK EFFICIENCY.
"BESIDES BODY SHIELD AND LIMITED HOVER OPTION, WHAT ELSE DO I HAVE?"
"ENHANCED STRENGTH, LIMITED ACCESS TO DATA BANK..."
IS THE UNIVERSAL TRANSLATOR ON-LINE?
YES, THAT FUNCTION IS INTACT AND ACCESSIBLE.
THAT'S GOOD NEWS.
AT LEAST I CAN ASK FOR DIRECTIONS WHILE FIGHTING THESE NATURE BOYS NEXT TIME.
OKAY, CALVIN. SHOW ME THE SOURCE OF THIS DAMPENING FIELD...
"#$@&" FUNCTION IS OFF-LINE, SIR.
OH, #$@&.

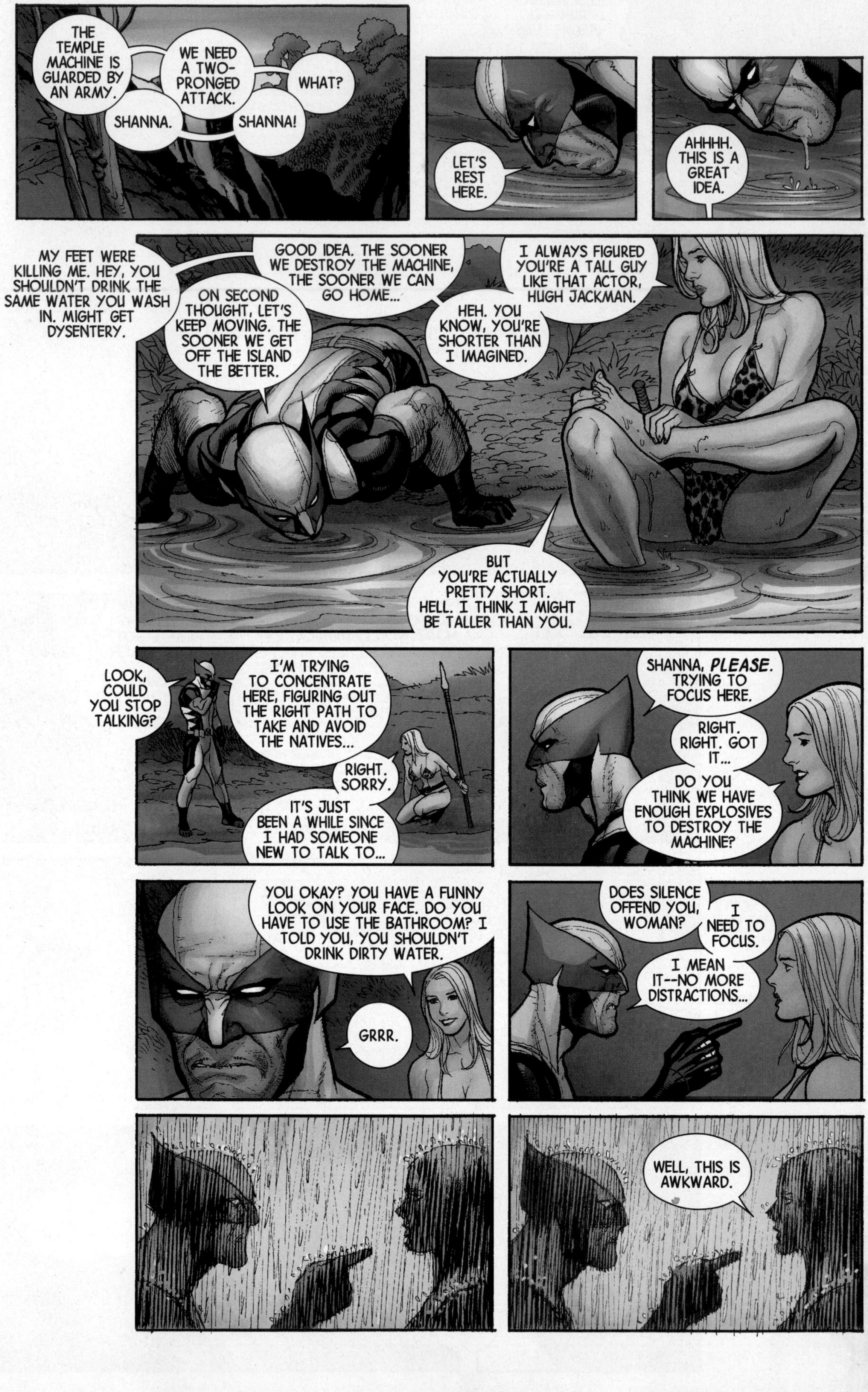
THE TEMPLE MACHINE IS GUARDED BY AN ARMY.
WE NEED A TWO-PRONGED ATTACK.
WHAT?
SHANNA.
SHANNA!
LET'S REST HERE.
AHHHH. THIS IS A GREAT IDEA.
MY FEET WERE KILLING ME. HEY, YOU SHOULDN'T DRINK THE SAME WATER YOU WASH IN. MIGHT GET DYSENTERY.
GOOD IDEA. THE SOONER WE DESTROY THE MACHINE, THE SOONER WE CAN GO HOME...
ON SECOND THOUGHT, LET'S KEEP MOVING. THE SOONER WE GET OFF THE ISLAND THE BETTER.
I ALWAYS FIGURED YOU'RE A TALL GUY LIKE THAT ACTOR, HUGH JACKMAN.
HEH. YOU KNOW, YOU'RE SHORTER THAN I IMAGINED.
BUT YOU'RE ACTUALLY PRETTY SHORT. HELL. I THINK I MIGHT BE TALLER THAN YOU.
LOOK, COULD YOU STOP TALKING?
I'M TRYING TO CONCENTRATE HERE, FIGURING OUT THE RIGHT PATH TO TAKE AND AVOID THE NATIVES...
RIGHT. SORRY.
IT'S JUST BEEN A WHILE SINCE I HAD SOMEONE NEW TO TALK TO...
SHANNA, *PLEASE*. TRYING TO FOCUS HERE.
RIGHT. RIGHT. GOT IT...
DO YOU THINK WE HAVE ENOUGH EXPLOSIVES TO DESTROY THE MACHINE?
YOU OKAY? YOU HAVE A FUNNY LOOK ON YOUR FACE. DO YOU HAVE TO USE THE BATHROOM? I TOLD YOU, YOU SHOULDN'T DRINK DIRTY WATER.
GRRR.
DOES SILENCE OFFEND YOU, WOMAN?
I NEED TO FOCUS.
I MEAN IT--NO MORE DISTRACTIONS...
WELL, THIS IS AWKWARD.

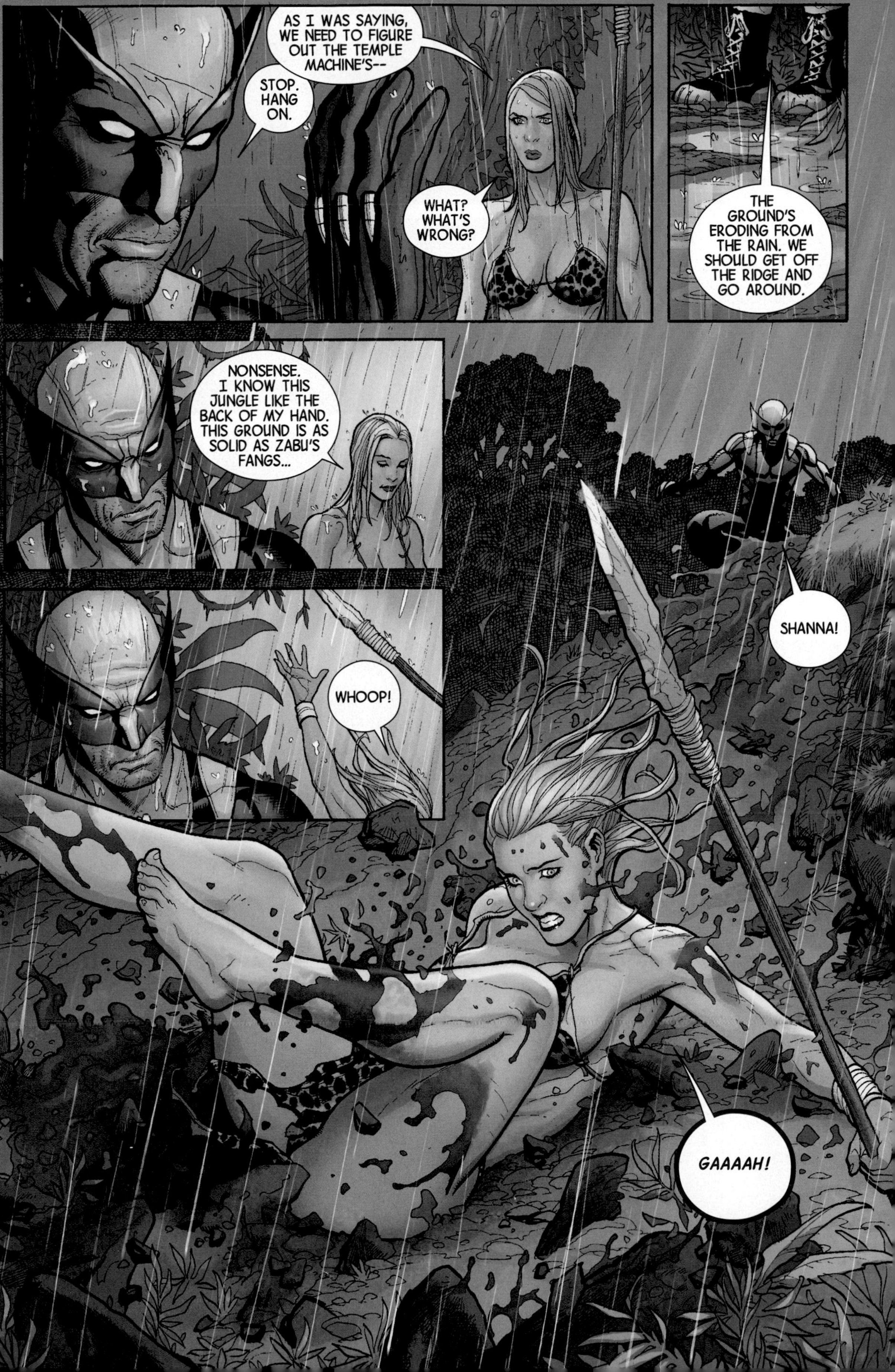
AS I WAS SAYING, WE NEED TO FIGURE OUT THE TEMPLE MACHINE'S--
STOP. HANG ON.
WHAT? WHAT'S WRONG?
THE GROUND'S ERODING FROM THE RAIN. WE SHOULD GET OFF THE RIDGE AND GO AROUND.
NONSENSE. I KNOW THIS JUNGLE LIKE THE BACK OF MY HAND. THIS GROUND IS AS SOLID AS ZABU'S FANGS...
WHOOP!
SHANNA!
GAAAAH!

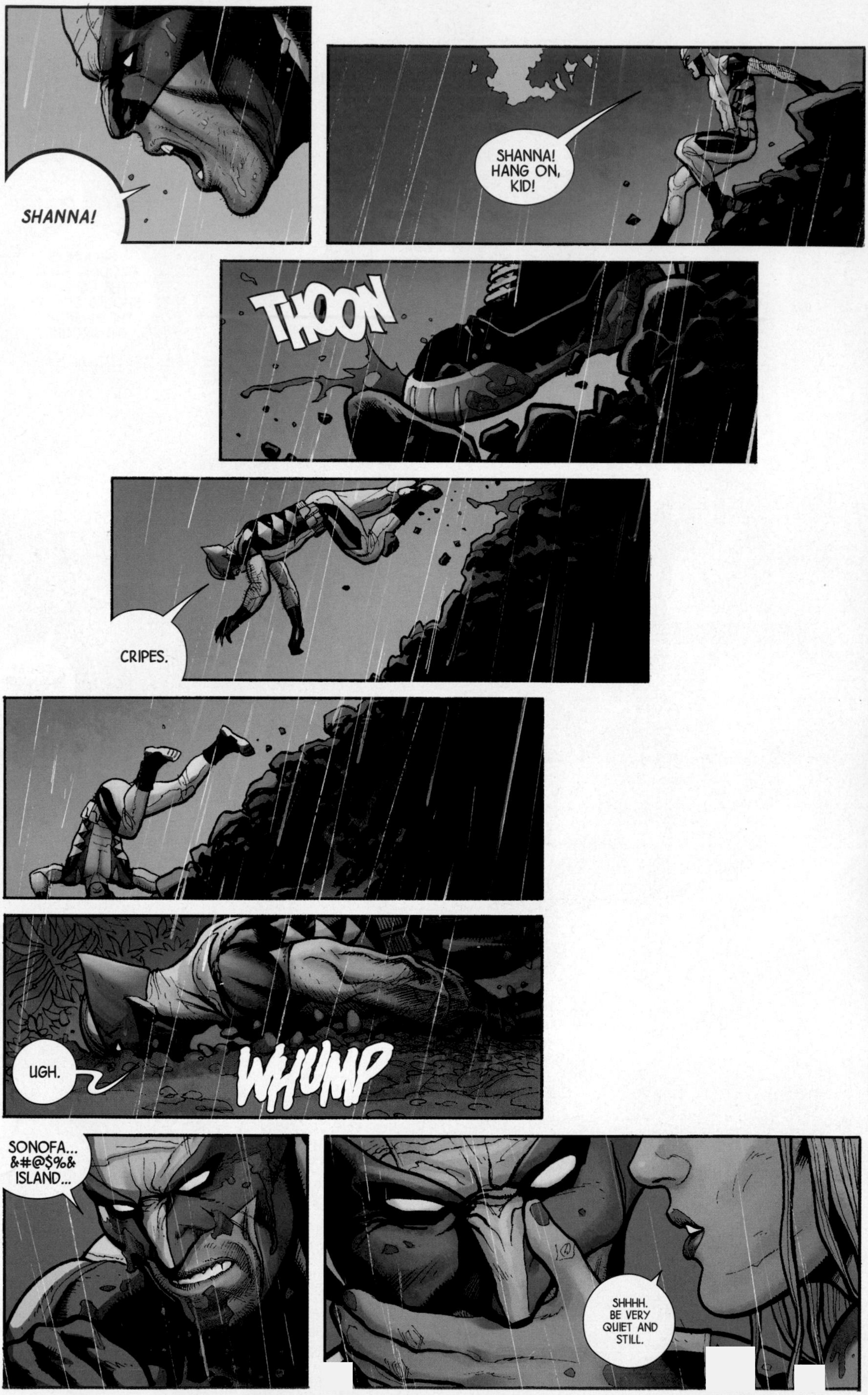
SHANNA!
SHANNA! HANG ON, KID!
THOON
CRIPES.
UGH.
WHUMP
SONOFA... &#@$%& ISLAND...
SHHHH. BE VERY QUIET AND STILL.

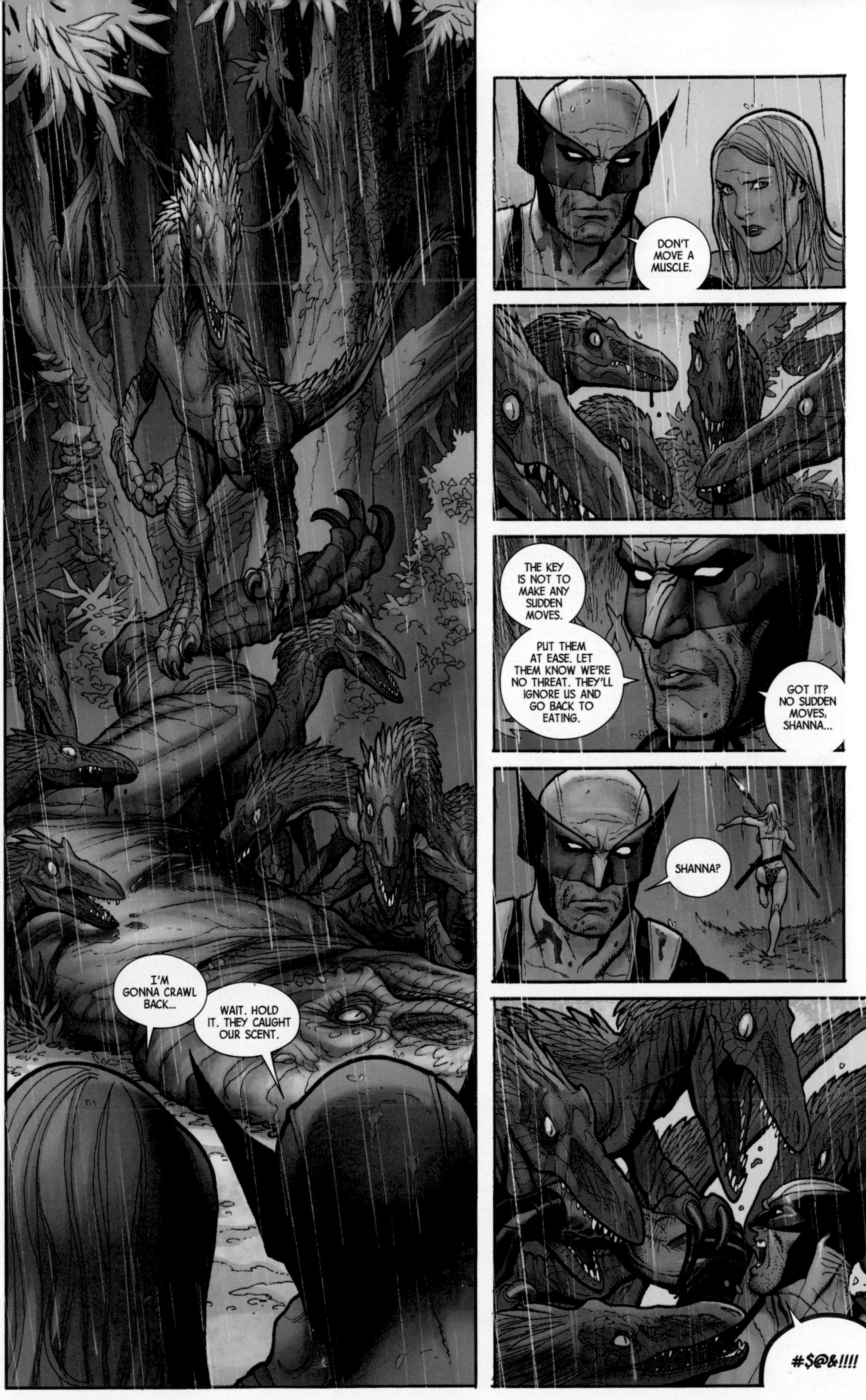
I'M GONNA CRAWL BACK...
WAIT. HOLD IT. THEY CAUGHT OUR SCENT.
DON'T MOVE A MUSCLE.
THE KEY IS NOT TO MAKE ANY SUDDEN MOVES.
PUT THEM AT EASE. LET THEM KNOW WE'RE NO THREAT. THEY'LL IGNORE US AND GO BACK TO EATING.
GOT IT? NO SUDDEN MOVES, SHANNA...
SHANNA?
#$@&!!!!

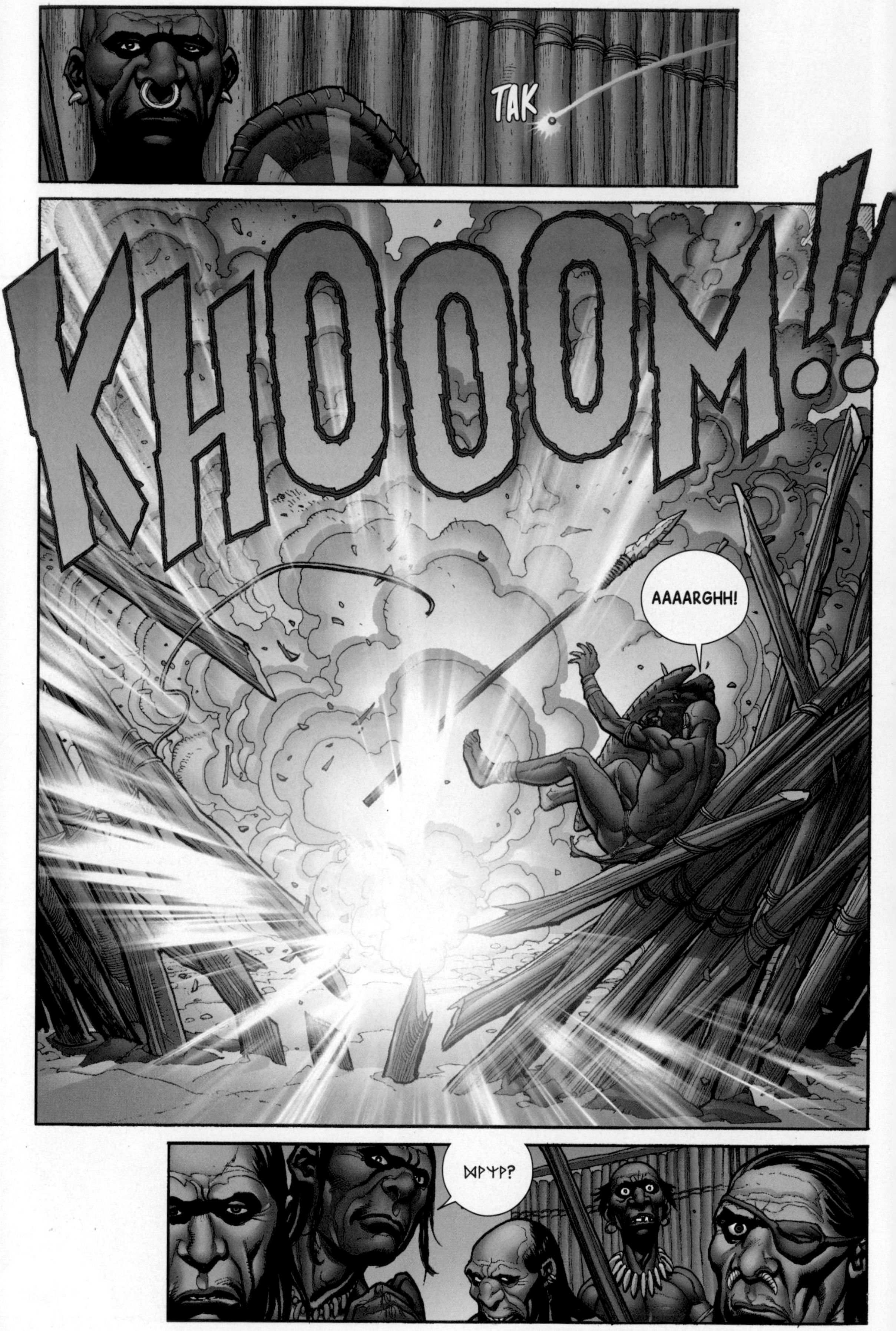
TAK
KHOOOM!!
AAAARGHH!
ᛞᚹᛉᚹ?

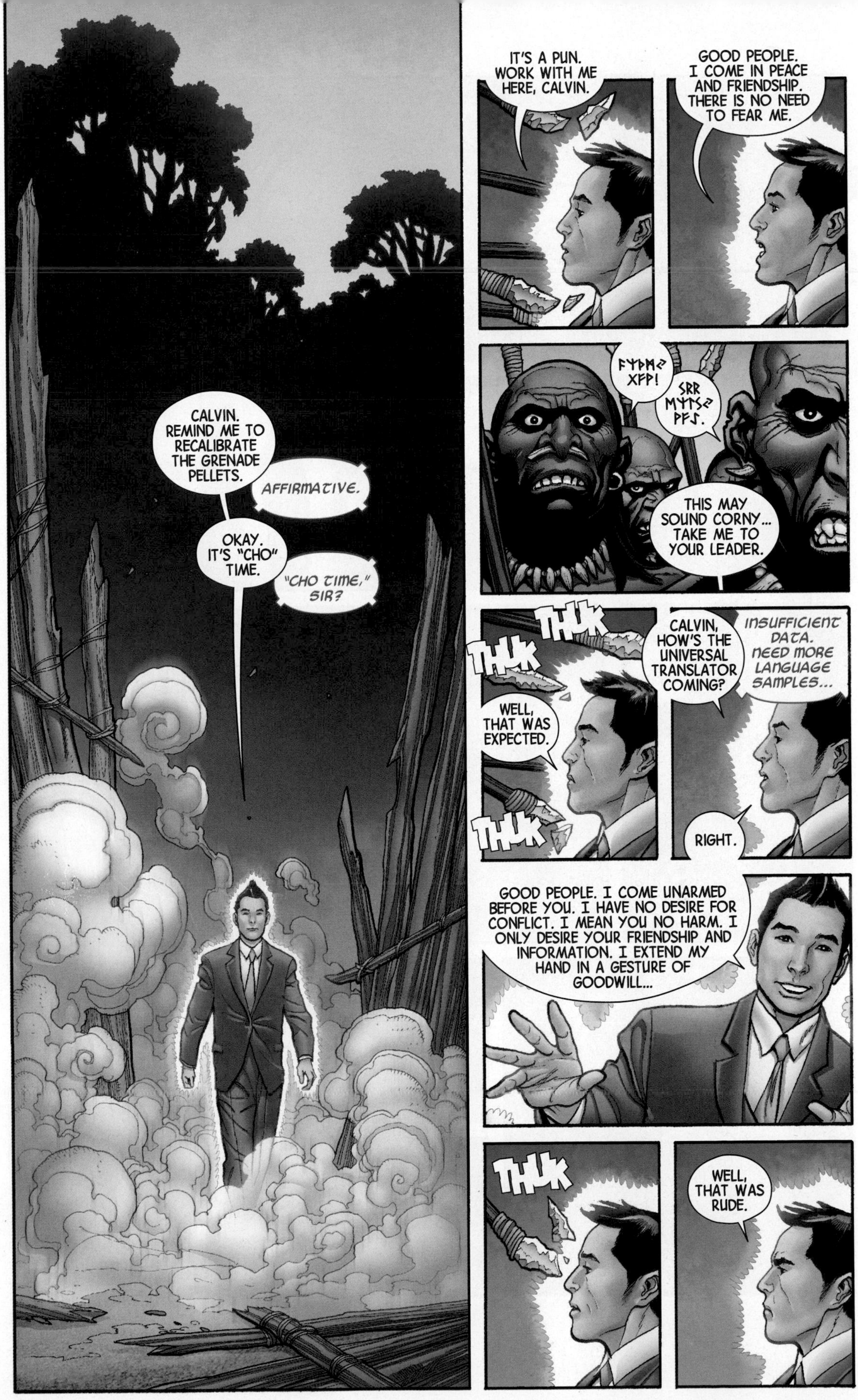
CALVIN. REMIND ME TO RECALIBRATE THE GRENADE PELLETS.
AFFIRMATIVE.
OKAY. IT'S "CHO" TIME.
"CHO TIME," SIR?
IT'S A PUN. WORK WITH ME HERE, CALVIN.
GOOD PEOPLE. I COME IN PEACE AND FRIENDSHIP. THERE IS NO NEED TO FEAR ME.
THIS MAY SOUND CORNY... TAKE ME TO YOUR LEADER.
THUK
THUK
CALVIN, HOW'S THE UNIVERSAL TRANSLATOR COMING?
INSUFFICIENT DATA. NEED MORE LANGUAGE SAMPLES...
WELL, THAT WAS EXPECTED.
THUK
RIGHT.
GOOD PEOPLE. I COME UNARMED BEFORE YOU. I HAVE NO DESIRE FOR CONFLICT. I MEAN YOU NO HARM. I ONLY DESIRE YOUR FRIENDSHIP AND INFORMATION. I EXTEND MY HAND IN A GESTURE OF GOODWILL...
THUK
WELL, THAT WAS RUDE.

ᐅᑭᑕᒥᖅ ᐱᖕᒥ!

HE APPEARS TO BE THE CHIEF, SIR.

YEAH, I GOT THAT. THANKS FOR THE HOT TIP, CALVIN.

ᒪᕓᖕ ᒥᐱᕆᐊᕝ.

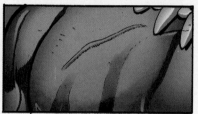

WELL, THERE'S SOMETHING YOU DON'T SEE EVERY DAY.

I SAW WHAT YOU DID THERE, CHIEF. BY HEALING THE MAN, YOU DEMONSTRATED YOUR AUTHORITY AND SHOWED ME YOUR POWER OVER LIFE AND DEATH. VERY CLEVER.

CALVIN, DID YOU ANALYZE WHAT THAT GREEN SUBSTANCE WAS?

NEGATIVE. NEED THE ACTUAL SAMPLE FOR ANALYSIS.

ᚺᛟᚾᛁᚱᛒᛟᚱ ᛁᛒᚱᚠᚱᛞᛟᚺᚱᛞ �

ᛟᚠᛈ ᚦᛇᚲᚲᚱ ᚦᚠᛁᚱᛗ ᛚ ᚦᛇᚲᚲᚱ ᛟᚠᛈᛈ

I COULD REALLY USE THAT UNIVERSAL TRANSLATOR NOW, CALVIN.

STILL NEED MORE LANGUAGE SAMPLES.

CAL-BEEN? CAL-BEEN ᛗᛇᚲᛟᛏᚱ ᚠᚱᛋᛒᚱᛖᛖᚱᛒ ᛈᛋᛋ. ᚠᛇᛋ ᛗᛇᛏᛗᛇᚠᚠ ᛗᛇᛏᛒᛖᚲᛋᚱᛖᛗ ᚦᛟᛇᛗᚱᚠ ᛇᚲᚲ ᚲᛇᛇᛗ ᛗᛇᛇᛒᛒᛟ CAL-BEEN?

KEEP HIM TALKING, SIR. UNIVERSAL TRANSLATOR 76% COMPLETE.

NO. NO. NOT CALVIN. I'M AMADEUS. I MEAN YOU NO HARM. I JUST NEED INFORMATION ON WHERE I AM...ME, AMADEUS. LIKE, "ROCK ME, AMADEUS."

AH-MAH-DEY-OSS? ᛗᚺᛇᛇᛟ ᛚᛇᚺᛈᛇᛒᚴ ᛗᛒᚺᛇ ᚠᛒᚱ ᚠᛇᛒᛒᚺᛞᛇᚱ AH-MAH-DEY-OSS, ᚠᛇᛗᛇᛇᛒ ᛗᛞᚠᛇᛟᛗ ᚲᚠᛋᚱ ᚺᛗ ᚠᛟ ᚠᛇᛇ ᚦᚺᛋ ᚠᛇ

I THINK I'M GETTING THROUGH TO HIM. I NEED THE UNIVERSAL TRANSLATOR, CALVIN.

ᚱᚠᛗᛟᛇᛏᛒ ᛋᛇᚺᚠᚺᛇᛗ ᛗᛇᚠᚠᛟ

TIME FOR SOME SHOCK AND AWE.

CALVIN, BOOST.

HOVER OPTION ENABLED. UNIVERSAL TRANSLATOR AT 89%.

ᚠᛇᚠᚠᛇᚠ ᚷᛟᛇᛞᛟᛞᛟ ᛋᛇᚲᛞᚱᛗ ᛈᚱ ᚺᚠᚺᚱᛗ ᚷᛇᛇᚠ?

UNIVERSAL TRANSLATOR AT 97%.

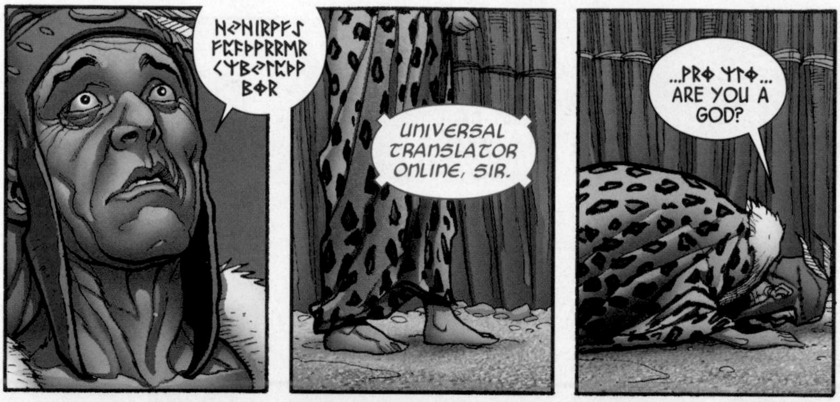
UNIVERSAL TRANSLATOR ONLINE, SIR.
ARE YOU A GOD?

"AM I...

"...A GOD?"

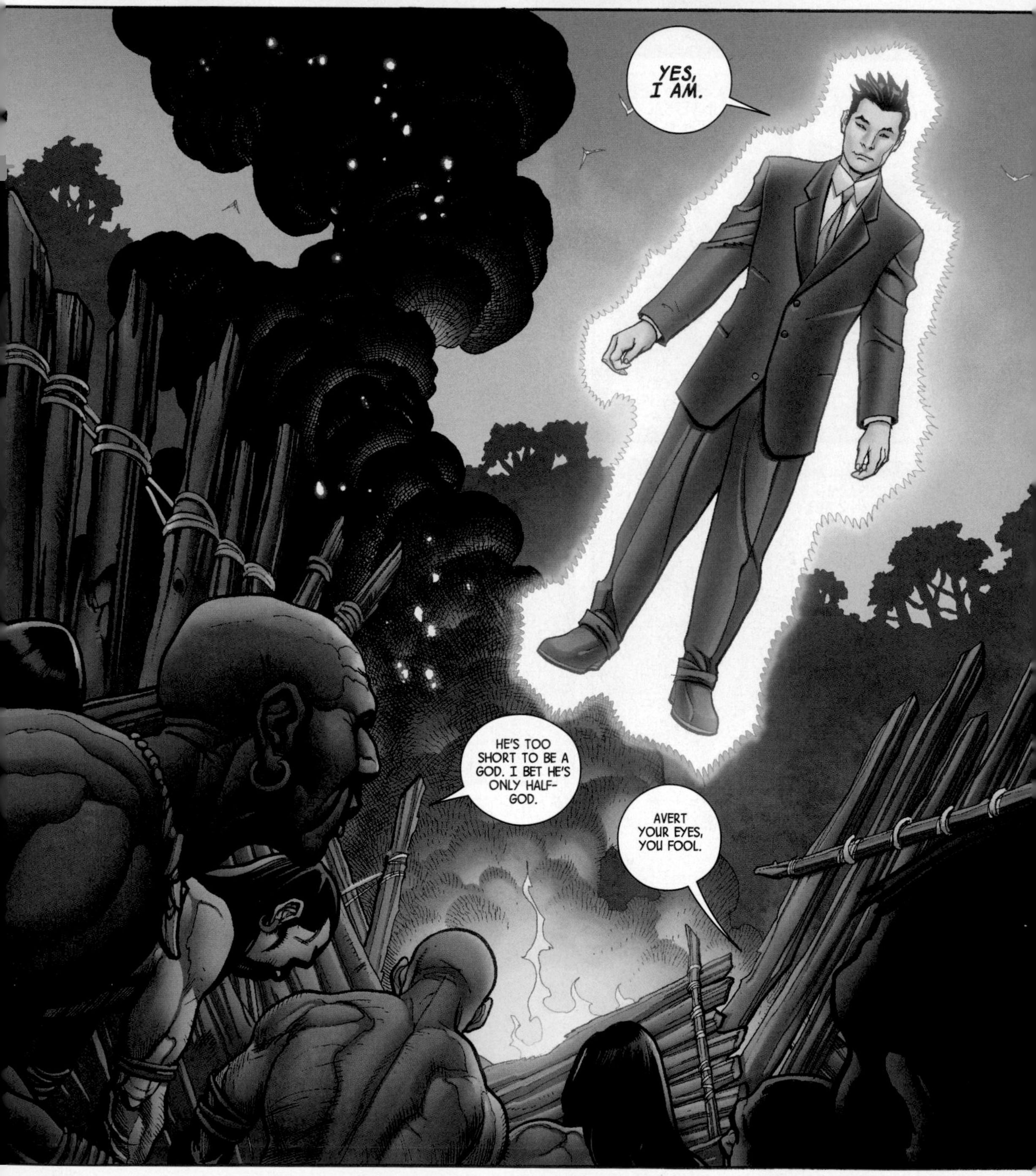
YES, I AM.
HE'S TOO SHORT TO BE A GOD. I BET HE'S ONLY HALF-GOD.
AVERT YOUR EYES, YOU FOOL.

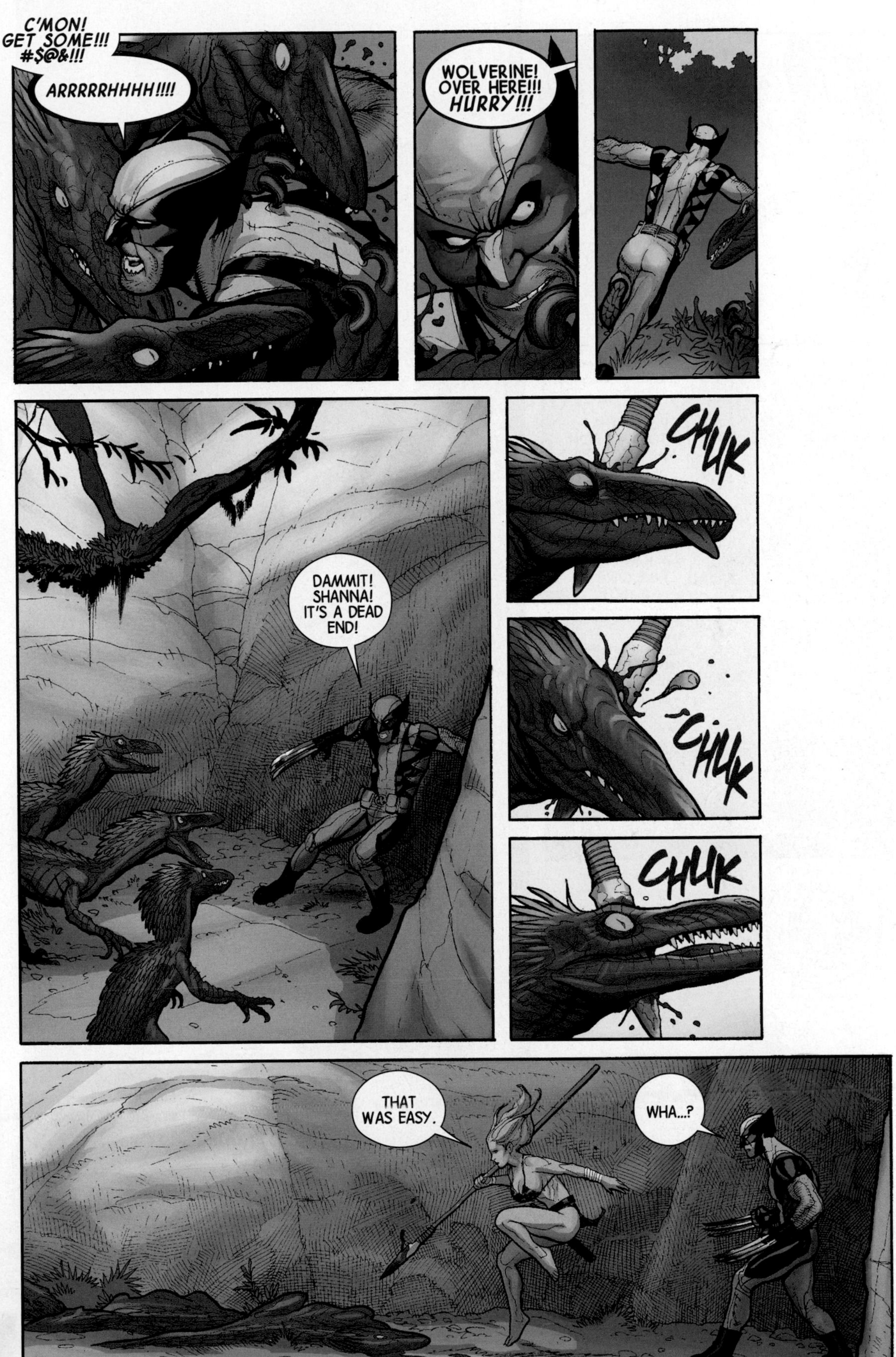
C'MON! GET SOME!!! #$@&!!!
ARRRRRHHHH!!!!
WOLVERINE! OVER HERE!!! HURRY!!!
DAMMIT! SHANNA! IT'S A DEAD END!
CHUK
CHUK
CHUK
THAT WAS EASY.
WHA...?

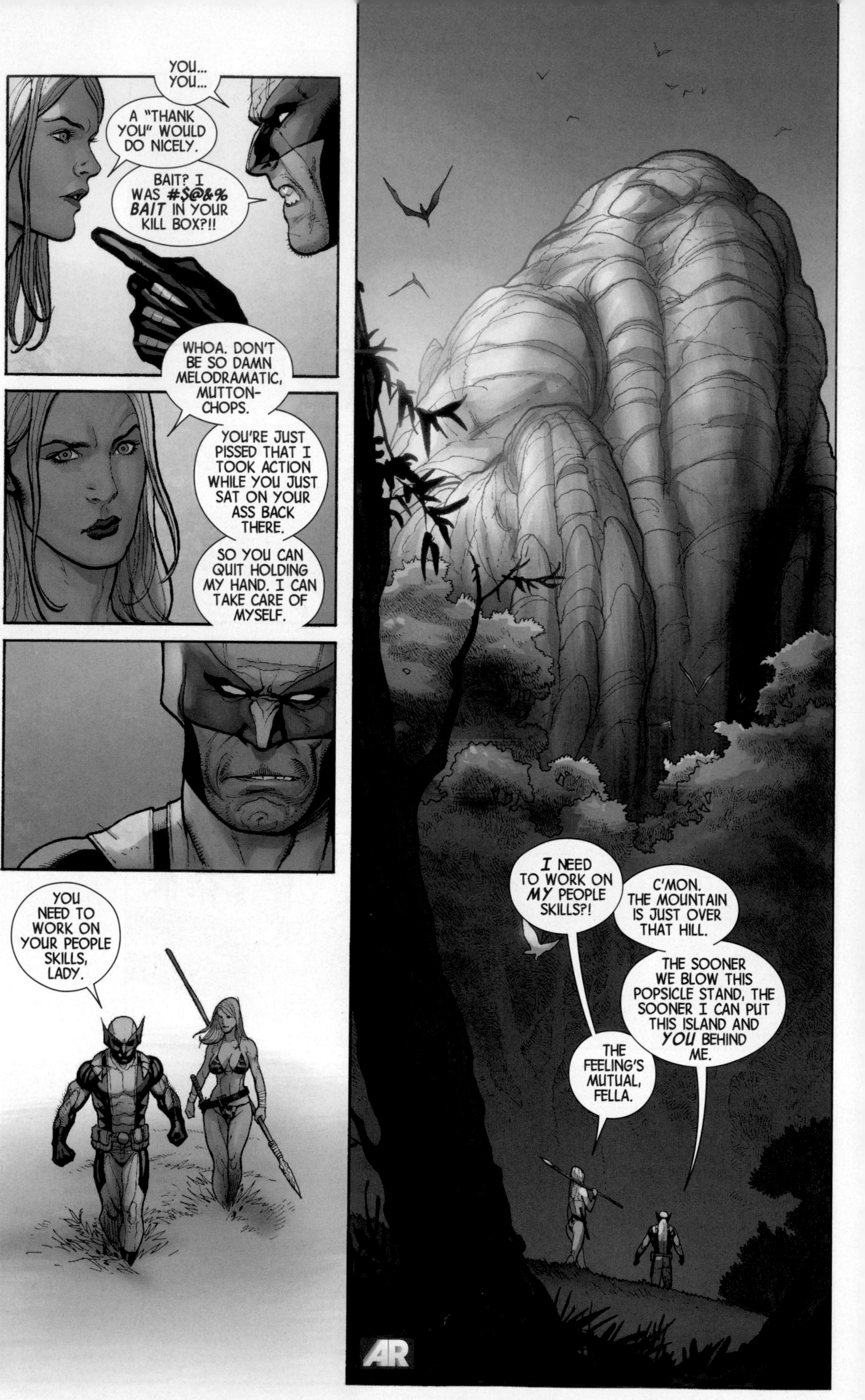
YOU... YOU...
A "THANK YOU" WOULD DO NICELY.
BAIT? I WAS #$@&% BAIT IN YOUR KILL BOX?!!
WHOA. DON'T BE SO DAMN MELODRAMATIC, MUTTON-CHOPS.
YOU'RE JUST PISSED THAT I TOOK ACTION WHILE YOU JUST SAT ON YOUR ASS BACK THERE.
SO YOU CAN QUIT HOLDING MY HAND. I CAN TAKE CARE OF MYSELF.
YOU NEED TO WORK ON YOUR PEOPLE SKILLS, LADY.
I NEED TO WORK ON MY PEOPLE SKILLS?!
C'MON. THE MOUNTAIN IS JUST OVER THAT HILL.
THE SOONER WE BLOW THIS POPSICLE STAND, THE SOONER I CAN PUT THIS ISLAND AND YOU BEHIND ME.
THE FEELING'S MUTUAL, FELLA.
AR

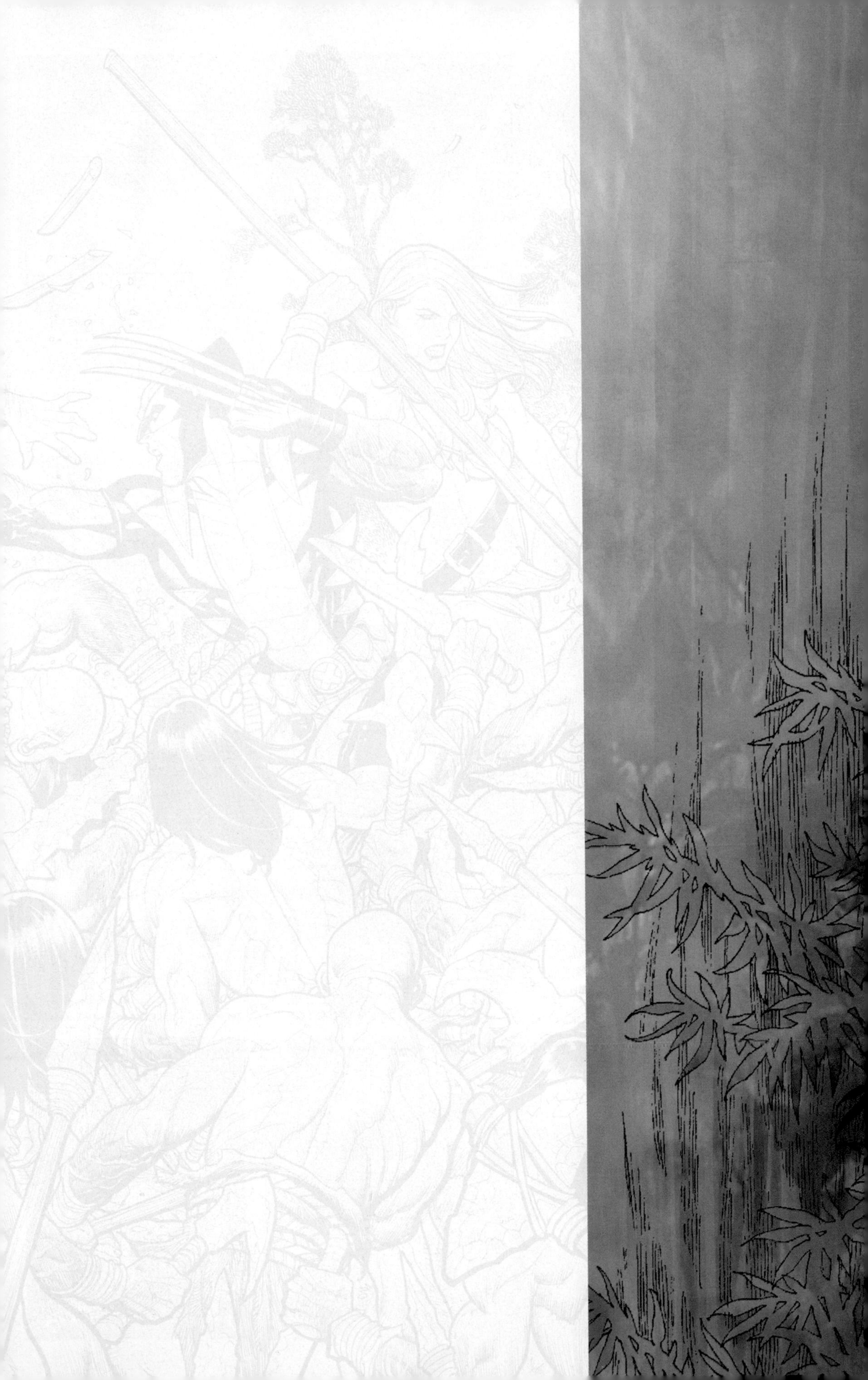

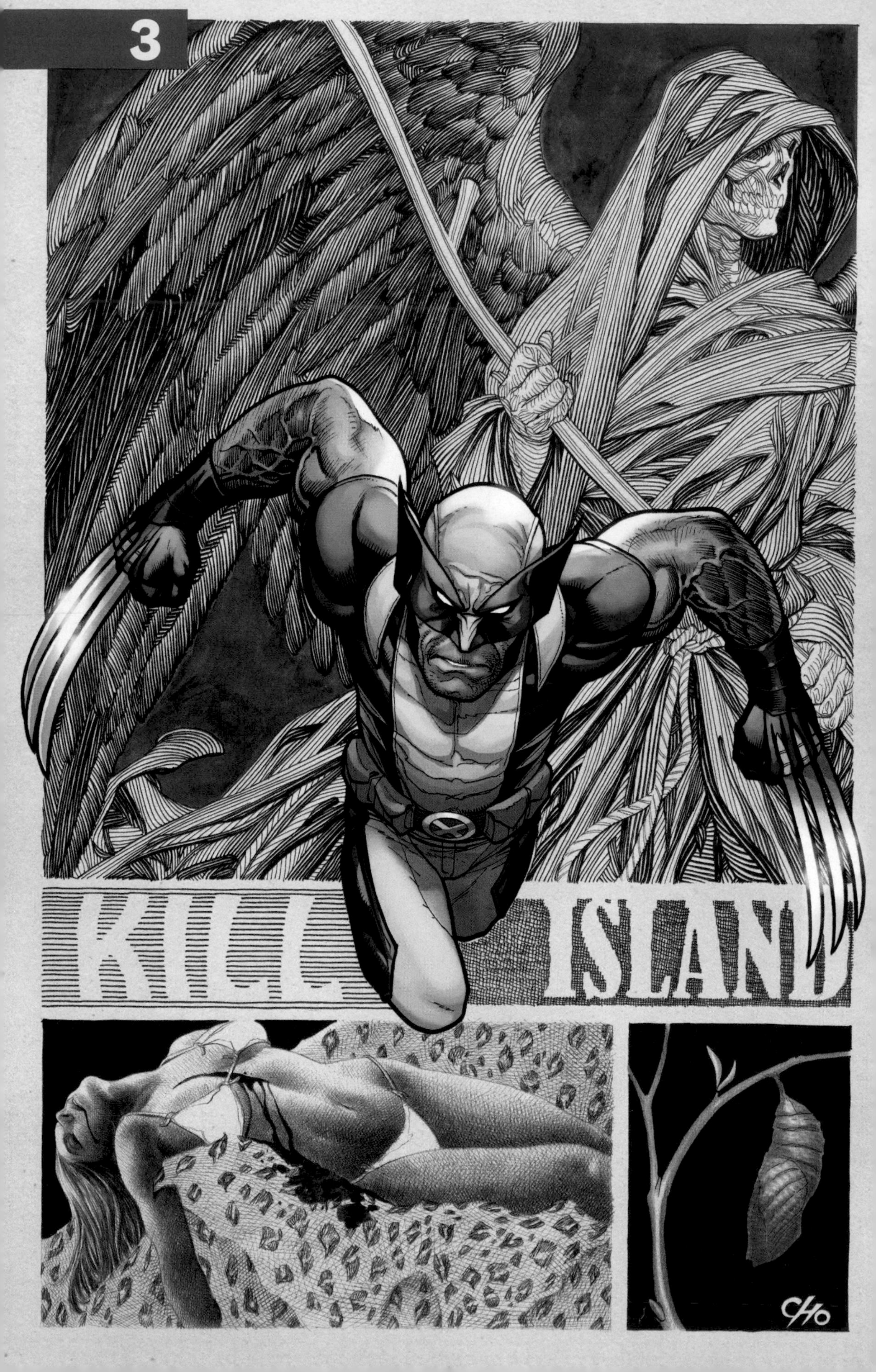

3
KILL ISLAND
CHO

COME IN, LADIES.

IN CELEBRATION OF YOUR ARRIVAL FROM THE HEAVENS, AMADEUS CHO...

...THESE ARE THE FINEST MAIDENS IN THE VILLAGE.

I HAVE PERSONALLY SELECTED THEM FOR THEIR BEAUTY AND THEIR SKILLS. THEY ARE HERE TO SERVE YOU IN ANY WAY YOU WISH.

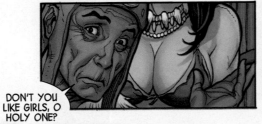

DON'T YOU LIKE GIRLS, O HOLY ONE?

YES...I LIKE THEM A LOT.

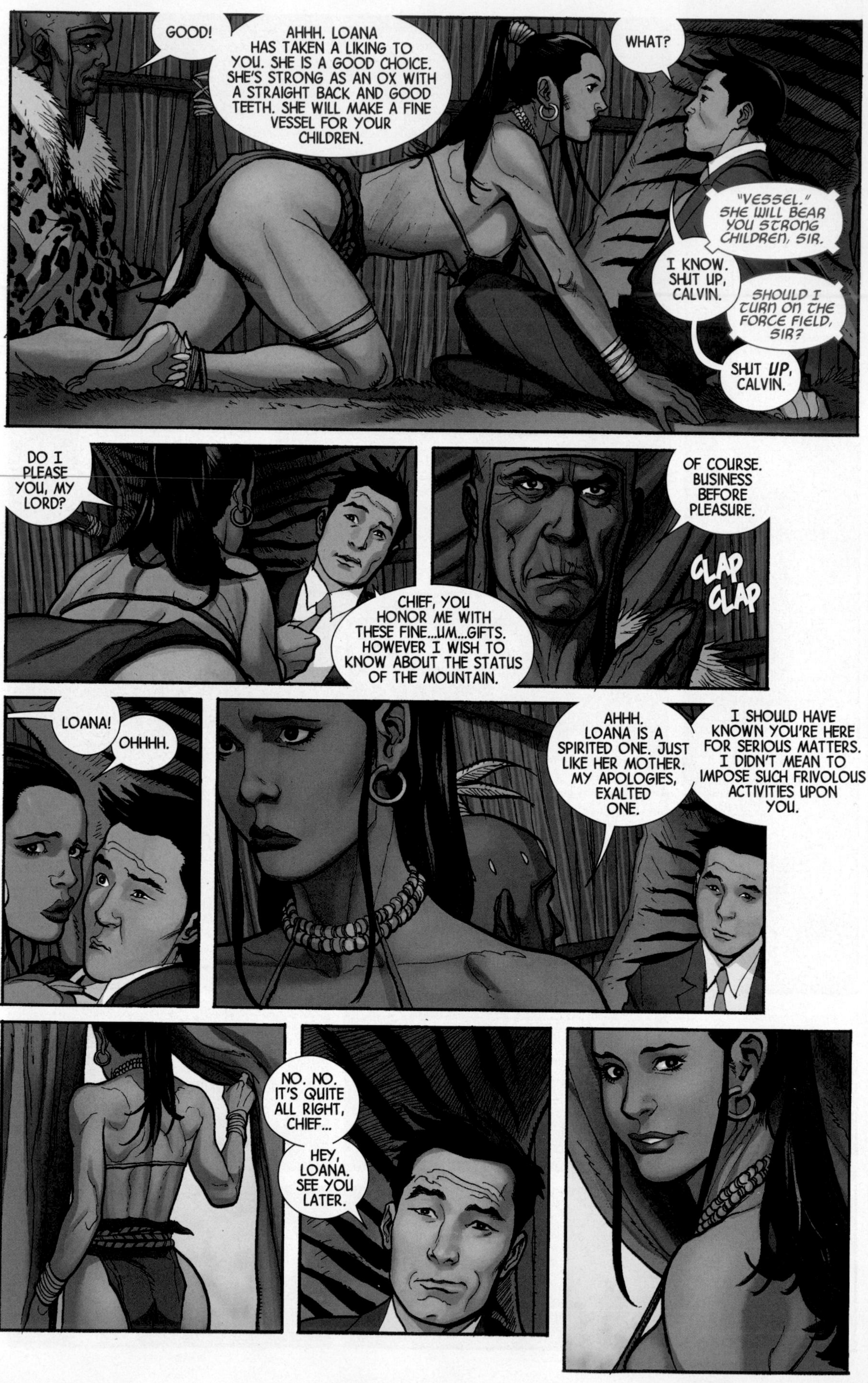
GOOD!
AHHH. LOANA HAS TAKEN A LIKING TO YOU. SHE IS A GOOD CHOICE. SHE'S STRONG AS AN OX WITH A STRAIGHT BACK AND GOOD TEETH. SHE WILL MAKE A FINE VESSEL FOR YOUR CHILDREN.
WHAT?
"VESSEL." SHE WILL BEAR YOU STRONG CHILDREN, SIR.
I KNOW. SHUT UP, CALVIN.
SHOULD I TURN ON THE FORCE FIELD, SIR?
SHUT UP, CALVIN.
DO I PLEASE YOU, MY LORD?
CHIEF, YOU HONOR ME WITH THESE FINE...UM...GIFTS. HOWEVER I WISH TO KNOW ABOUT THE STATUS OF THE MOUNTAIN.
OF COURSE. BUSINESS BEFORE PLEASURE.
CLAP CLAP
LOANA!
OHHHH.
AHHH. LOANA IS A SPIRITED ONE. JUST LIKE HER MOTHER. MY APOLOGIES, EXALTED ONE.
I SHOULD HAVE KNOWN YOU'RE HERE FOR SERIOUS MATTERS. I DIDN'T MEAN TO IMPOSE SUCH FRIVOLOUS ACTIVITIES UPON YOU.
NO. NO. IT'S QUITE ALL RIGHT, CHIEF...
HEY, LOANA. SEE YOU LATER.

SO, O HOLY ONE. WHAT DO YOU WANT TO KNOW?

I'VE READ YOUR STONE TABLETS BUT I WANT TO KNOW MORE ABOUT THE MOUNTAIN FROM YOU.

OF COURSE. WE'VE BEEN FOLLOWING THE HOLY TEXT. THE MOUNTAIN STRONGHOLD IS INTACT AND THE "DARK WALKER" SLUMBERS.

UM... GOOD. VERY GOOD. I AM PLEASED THAT THE "DARK WALKER" SLUMBERS.

HOW IS THE...?

THE ANCIENT MACHINE IS ALSO INTACT AND WORKING.

CROSS REFERENCING "DARK WALKER" AND "ANCIENT MACHINE" AGAINST THE STONE TABLETS...

GOOD. GOOD. TELL ME ABOUT THE MACHINE FROM THE BEGINNING.

FROM THE BEGINNING?

YES, FROM THE VERY BEGINNING.

AHH. I SEE. YOU WANT TO TEST ME. TO SEE IF I KNOW THE SACRED STAR TEXT, THE HISTORY OF OUR PEOPLE AND OUR RESPONSIBILITY.

YES.

YOU ARE VERY WISE, O HOLY ONE. VERY WELL...

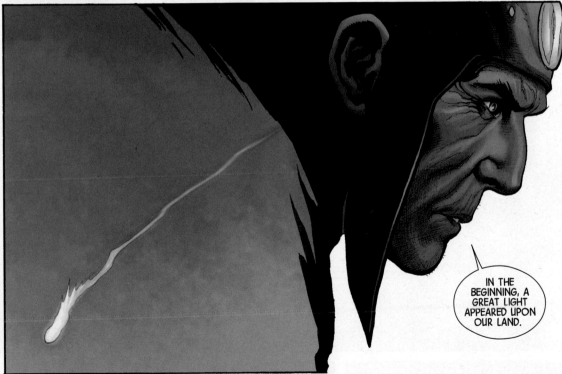

IN THE BEGINNING, A GREAT LIGHT APPEARED UPON OUR LAND.

"AS BRIGHT AS A HUNDRED SUNS.

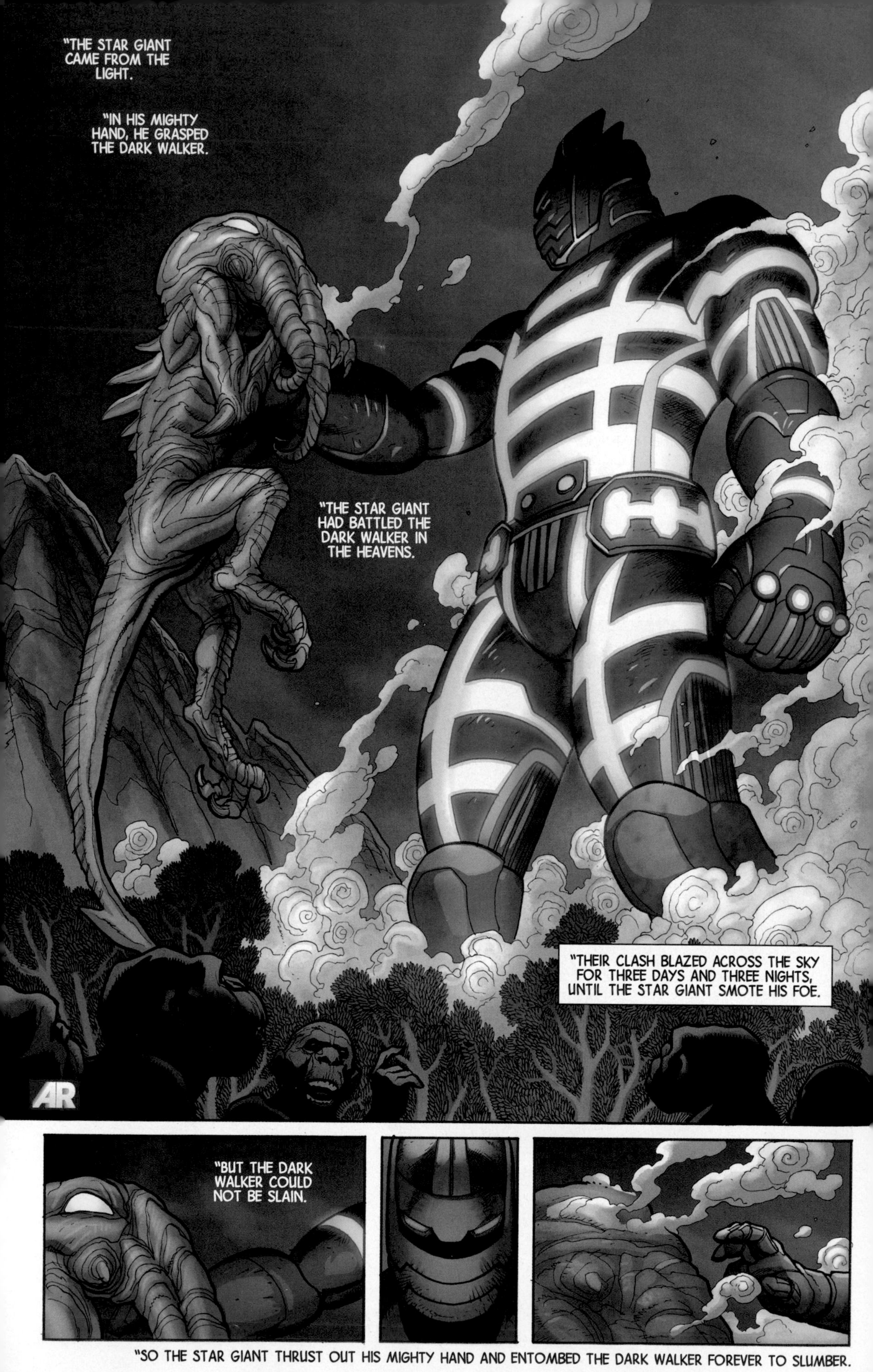
"THE STAR GIANT CAME FROM THE LIGHT.
"IN HIS MIGHTY HAND, HE GRASPED THE DARK WALKER.
"THE STAR GIANT HAD BATTLED THE DARK WALKER IN THE HEAVENS.
"THEIR CLASH BLAZED ACROSS THE SKY FOR THREE DAYS AND THREE NIGHTS, UNTIL THE STAR GIANT SMOTE HIS FOE.
AR
"BUT THE DARK WALKER COULD NOT BE SLAIN.
"SO THE STAR GIANT THRUST OUT HIS MIGHTY HAND AND ENTOMBED THE DARK WALKER FOREVER TO SLUMBER.

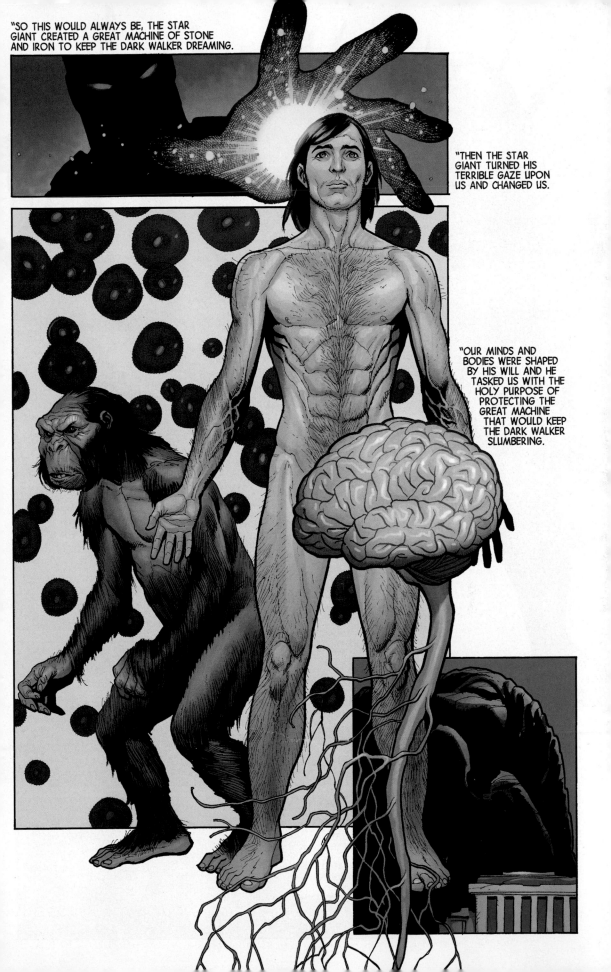

"SO THIS WOULD ALWAYS BE, THE STAR GIANT CREATED A GREAT MACHINE OF STONE AND IRON TO KEEP THE DARK WALKER DREAMING.

"THEN THE STAR GIANT TURNED HIS TERRIBLE GAZE UPON US AND CHANGED US.

"OUR MINDS AND BODIES WERE SHAPED BY HIS WILL AND HE TASKED US WITH THE HOLY PURPOSE OF PROTECTING THE GREAT MACHINE THAT WOULD KEEP THE DARK WALKER SLUMBERING.

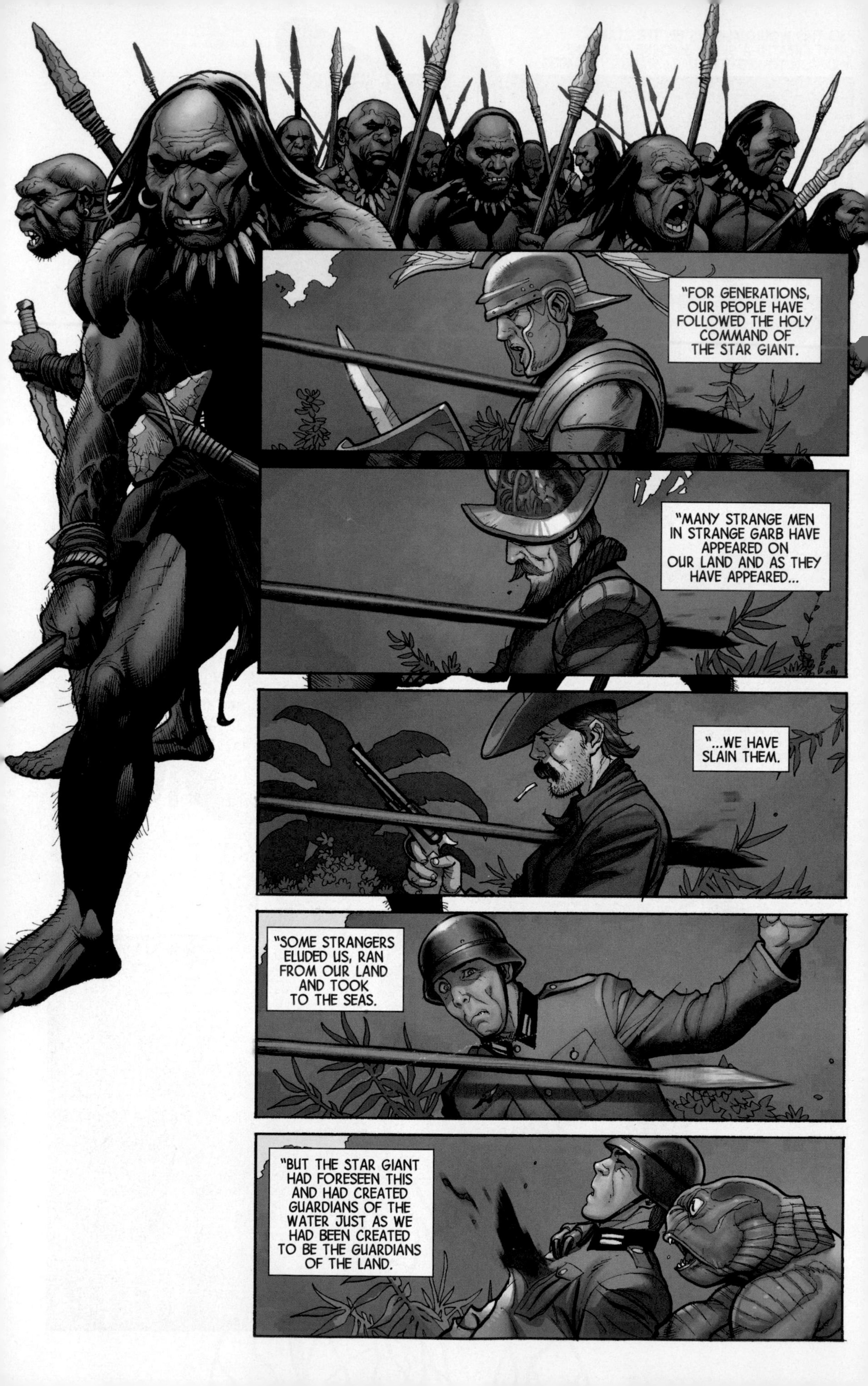
"FOR GENERATIONS, OUR PEOPLE HAVE FOLLOWED THE HOLY COMMAND OF THE STAR GIANT.
"MANY STRANGE MEN IN STRANGE GARB HAVE APPEARED ON OUR LAND AND AS THEY HAVE APPEARED...
"...WE HAVE SLAIN THEM.
"SOME STRANGERS ELUDED US, RAN FROM OUR LAND AND TOOK TO THE SEAS.
"BUT THE STAR GIANT HAD FORESEEN THIS AND HAD CREATED GUARDIANS OF THE WATER JUST AS WE HAD BEEN CREATED TO BE THE GUARDIANS OF THE LAND.

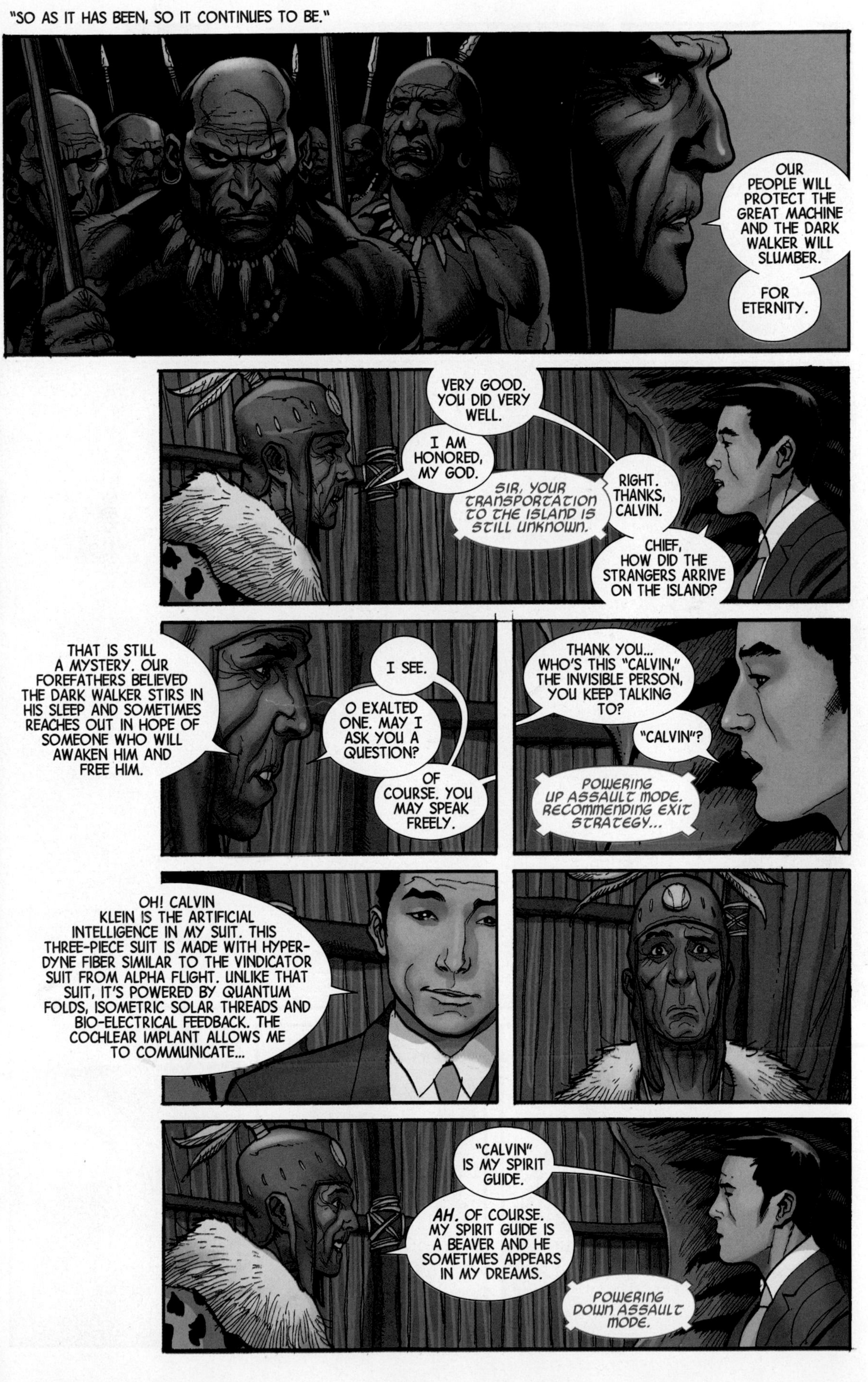
"SO AS IT HAS BEEN, SO IT CONTINUES TO BE."
OUR PEOPLE WILL PROTECT THE GREAT MACHINE AND THE DARK WALKER WILL SLUMBER.
FOR ETERNITY.
VERY GOOD. YOU DID VERY WELL.
I AM HONORED, MY GOD.
SIR, YOUR TRANSPORTATION TO THE ISLAND IS STILL UNKNOWN.
RIGHT. THANKS, CALVIN.
CHIEF, HOW DID THE STRANGERS ARRIVE ON THE ISLAND?
THAT IS STILL A MYSTERY. OUR FOREFATHERS BELIEVED THE DARK WALKER STIRS IN HIS SLEEP AND SOMETIMES REACHES OUT IN HOPE OF SOMEONE WHO WILL AWAKEN HIM AND FREE HIM.
I SEE.
O EXALTED ONE. MAY I ASK YOU A QUESTION?
OF COURSE. YOU MAY SPEAK FREELY.
THANK YOU... WHO'S THIS "CALVIN," THE INVISIBLE PERSON, YOU KEEP TALKING TO?
"CALVIN"?
POWERING UP ASSAULT MODE. RECOMMENDING EXIT STRATEGY...
OH! CALVIN KLEIN IS THE ARTIFICIAL INTELLIGENCE IN MY SUIT. THIS THREE-PIECE SUIT IS MADE WITH HYPER-DYNE FIBER SIMILAR TO THE VINDICATOR SUIT FROM ALPHA FLIGHT. UNLIKE THAT SUIT, IT'S POWERED BY QUANTUM FOLDS, ISOMETRIC SOLAR THREADS AND BIO-ELECTRICAL FEEDBACK. THE COCHLEAR IMPLANT ALLOWS ME TO COMMUNICATE...
"CALVIN" IS MY SPIRIT GUIDE.
AH. OF COURSE. MY SPIRIT GUIDE IS A BEAVER AND HE SOMETIMES APPEARS IN MY DREAMS.
POWERING DOWN ASSAULT MODE.

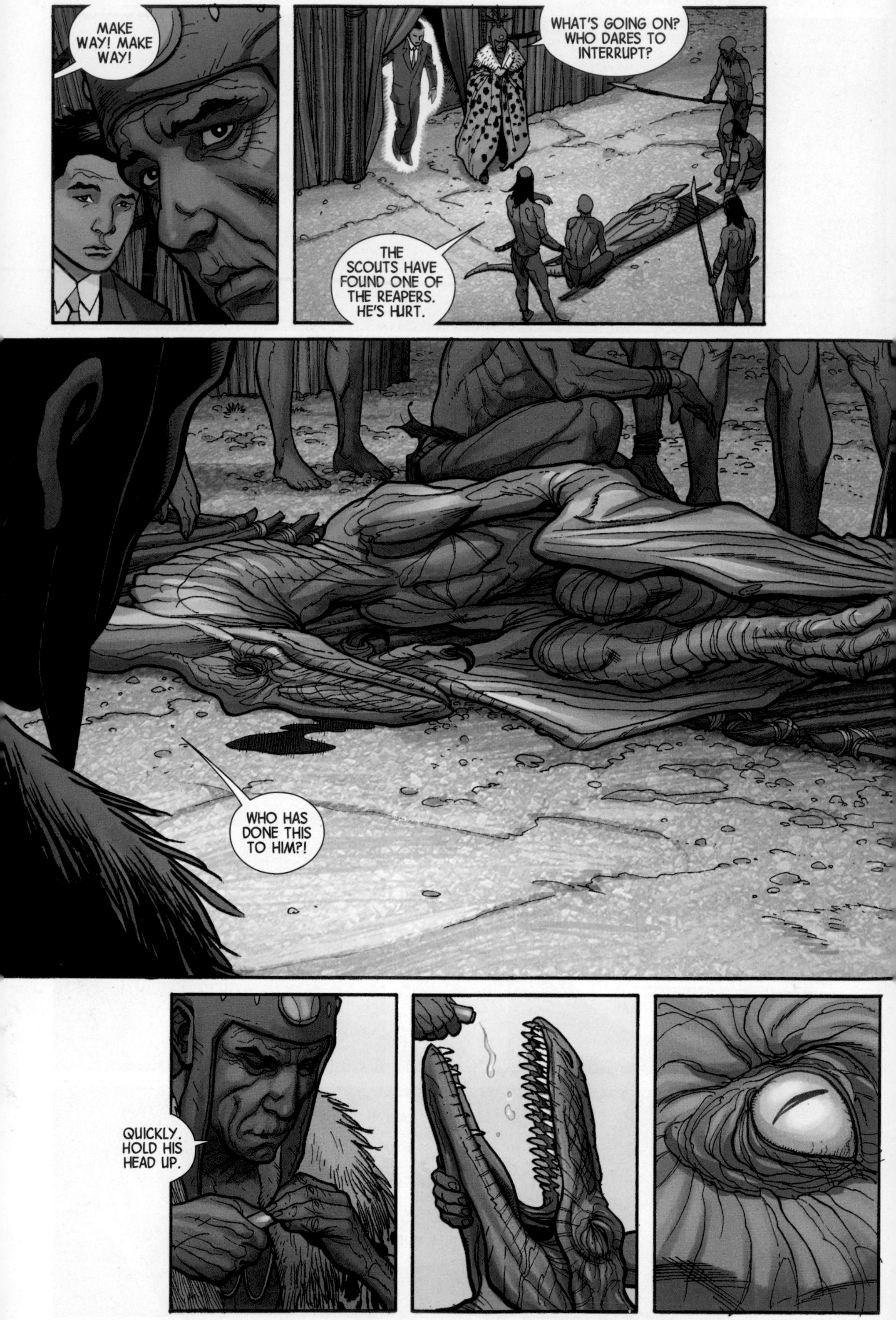
MAKE WAY! MAKE WAY!
WHAT'S GOING ON? WHO DARES TO INTERRUPT?
THE SCOUTS HAVE FOUND ONE OF THE REAPERS. HE'S HURT.
WHO HAS DONE THIS TO HIM?!
QUICKLY. HOLD HIS HEAD UP.

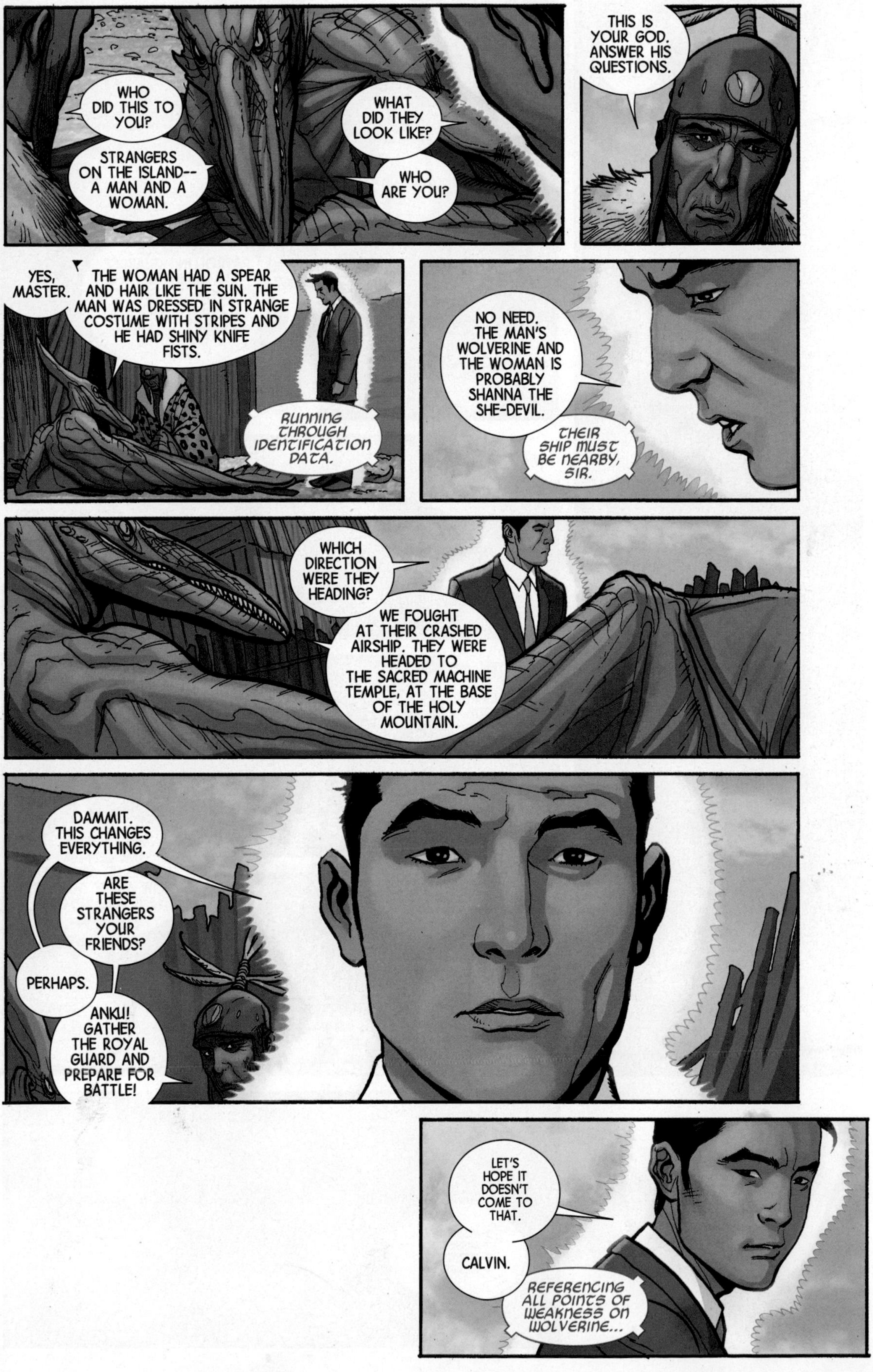
WHO DID THIS TO YOU?
STRANGERS ON THE ISLAND-- A MAN AND A WOMAN.
WHAT DID THEY LOOK LIKE?
WHO ARE YOU?
THIS IS YOUR GOD. ANSWER HIS QUESTIONS.
YES, MASTER.
THE WOMAN HAD A SPEAR AND HAIR LIKE THE SUN. THE MAN WAS DRESSED IN STRANGE COSTUME WITH STRIPES AND HE HAD SHINY KNIFE FISTS.
RUNNING THROUGH IDENTIFICATION DATA.
NO NEED. THE MAN'S WOLVERINE AND THE WOMAN IS PROBABLY SHANNA THE SHE-DEVIL.
THEIR SHIP MUST BE NEARBY, SIR.
WHICH DIRECTION WERE THEY HEADING?
WE FOUGHT AT THEIR CRASHED AIRSHIP. THEY WERE HEADED TO THE SACRED MACHINE TEMPLE, AT THE BASE OF THE HOLY MOUNTAIN.
DAMMIT. THIS CHANGES EVERYTHING.
ARE THESE STRANGERS YOUR FRIENDS?
PERHAPS.
ANKU! GATHER THE ROYAL GUARD AND PREPARE FOR BATTLE!
LET'S HOPE IT DOESN'T COME TO THAT.
CALVIN.
REFERENCING ALL POINTS OF WEAKNESS ON WOLVERINE...

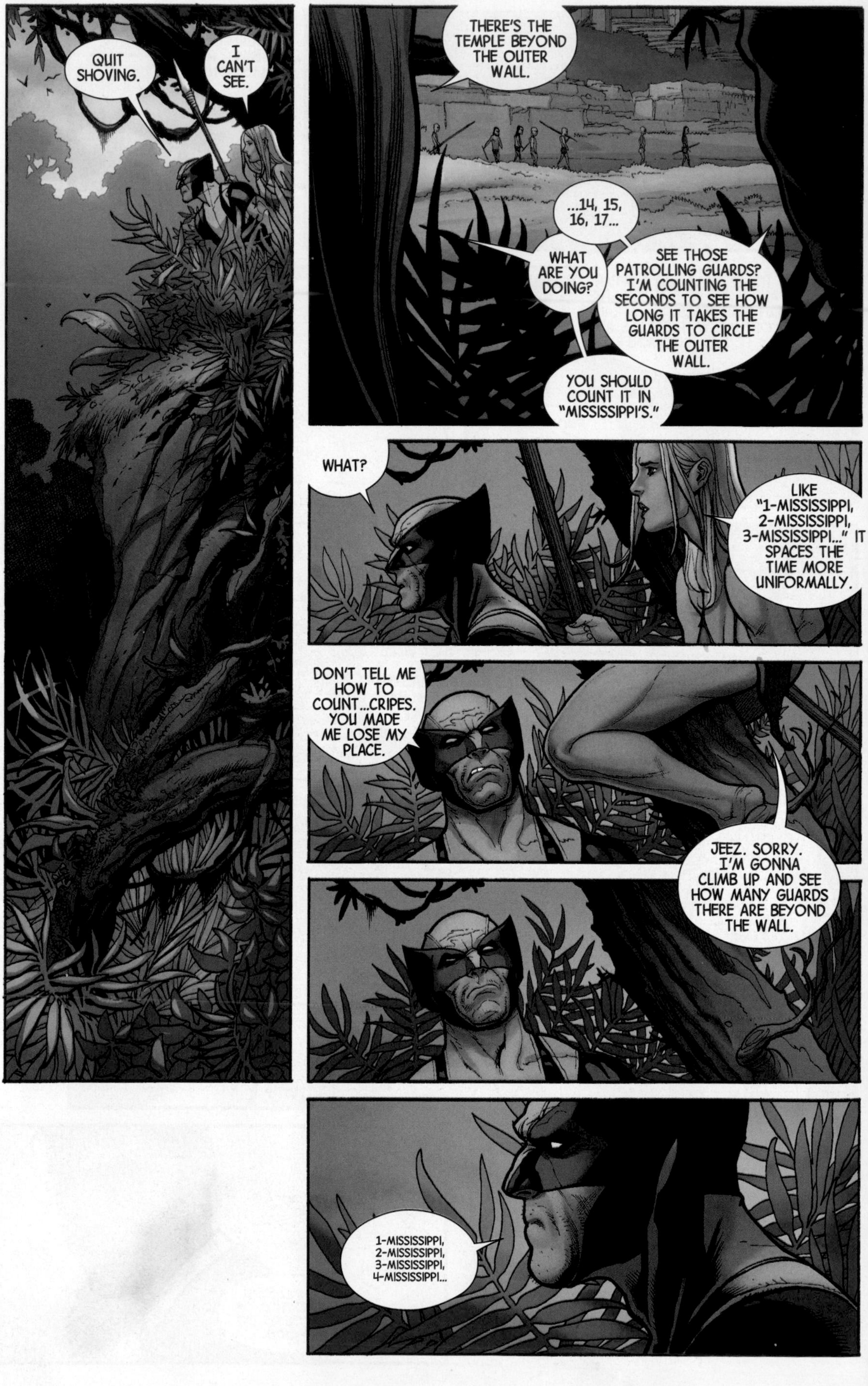
QUIT SHOVING.
I CAN'T SEE.
THERE'S THE TEMPLE BEYOND THE OUTER WALL.
...14, 15, 16, 17...
WHAT ARE YOU DOING?
SEE THOSE PATROLLING GUARDS? I'M COUNTING THE SECONDS TO SEE HOW LONG IT TAKES THE GUARDS TO CIRCLE THE OUTER WALL.
YOU SHOULD COUNT IT IN "MISSISSIPPI'S."
WHAT?
LIKE "1-MISSISSIPPI, 2-MISSISSIPPI, 3-MISSISSIPPI..." IT SPACES THE TIME MORE UNIFORMALLY.
DON'T TELL ME HOW TO COUNT...CRIPES. YOU MADE ME LOSE MY PLACE.
JEEZ. SORRY. I'M GONNA CLIMB UP AND SEE HOW MANY GUARDS THERE ARE BEYOND THE WALL.
1-MISSISSIPPI, 2-MISSISSIPPI, 3-MISSISSIPPI, 4-MISSISSIPPI...

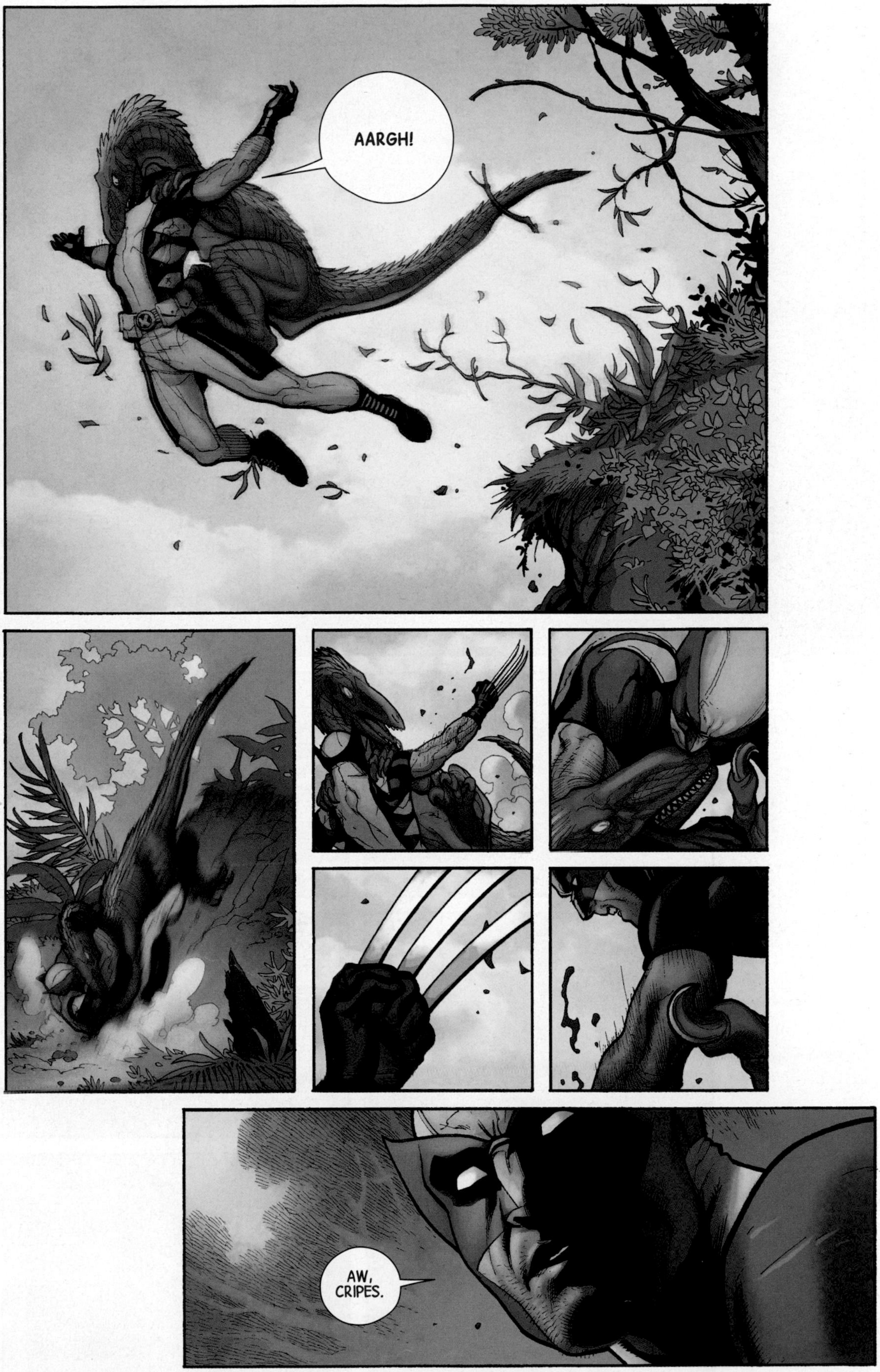
AARGH!
AW, CRIPES.

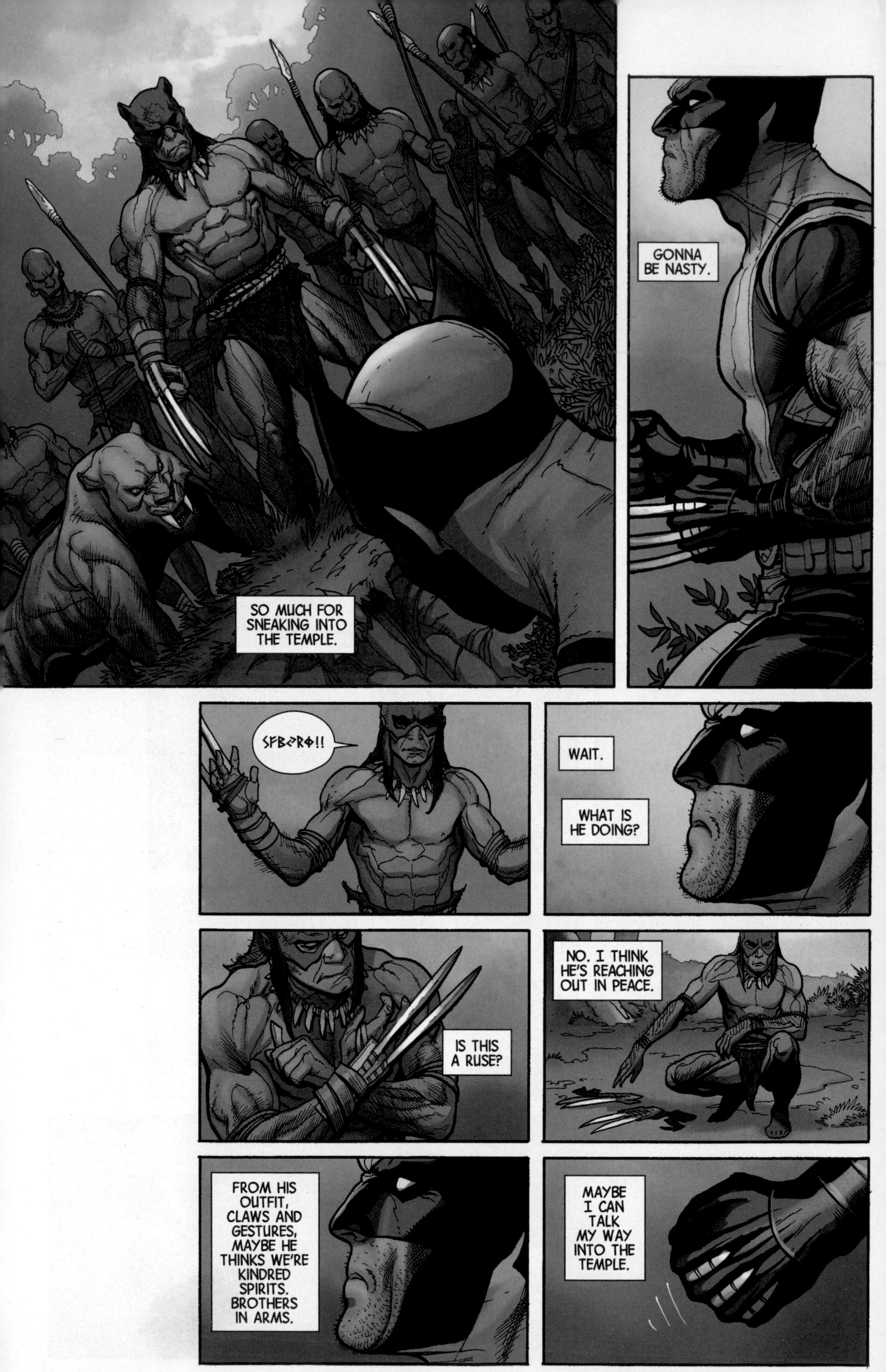
SO MUCH FOR SNEAKING INTO THE TEMPLE.
GONNA BE NASTY.
WAIT.
WHAT IS HE DOING?
IS THIS A RUSE?
NO. I THINK HE'S REACHING OUT IN PEACE.
FROM HIS OUTFIT, CLAWS AND GESTURES, MAYBE HE THINKS WE'RE KINDRED SPIRITS. BROTHERS IN ARMS.
MAYBE I CAN TALK MY WAY INTO THE TEMPLE.

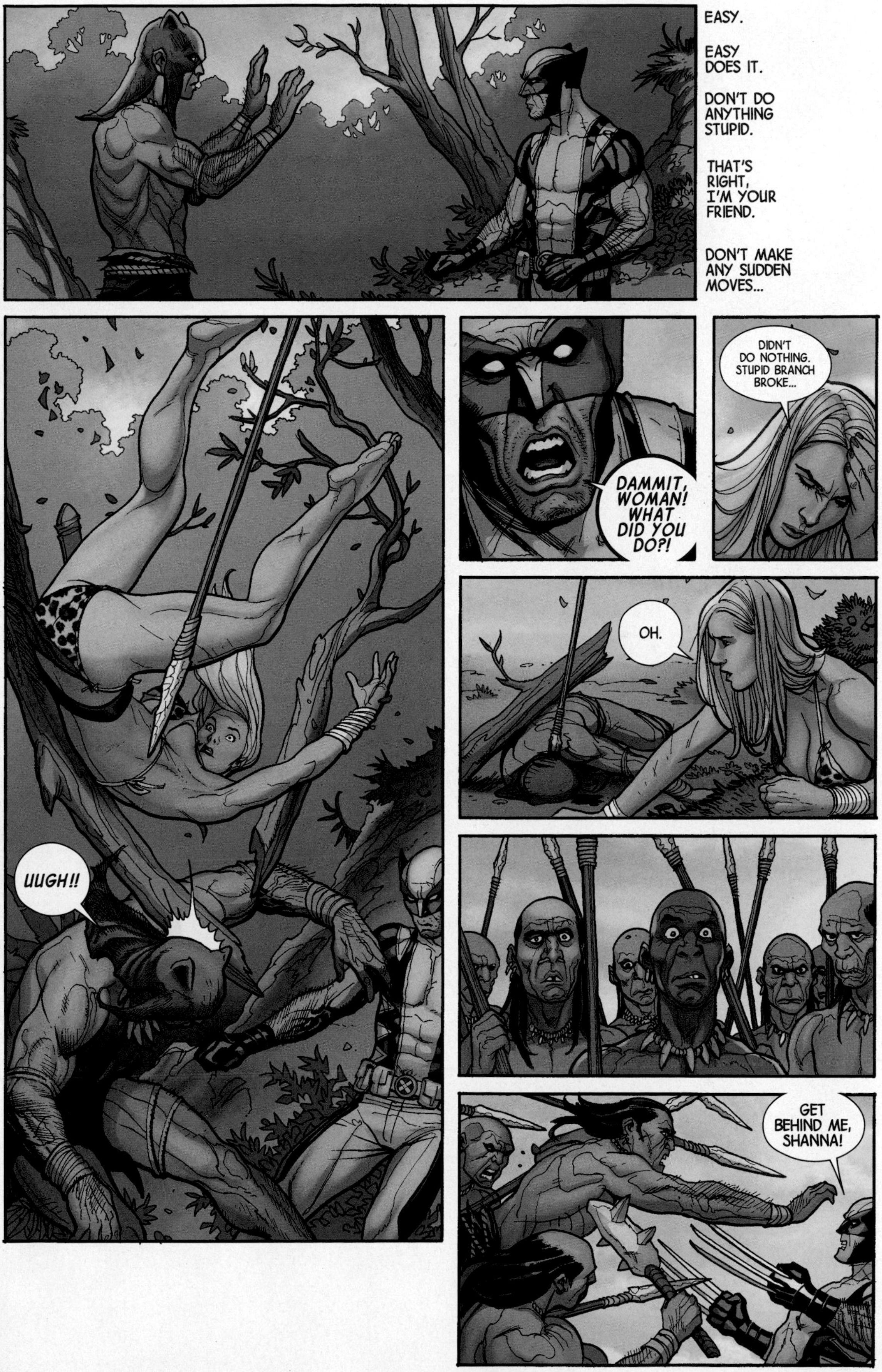

EASY.
EASY DOES IT.
DON'T DO ANYTHING STUPID.
THAT'S RIGHT, I'M YOUR FRIEND.
DON'T MAKE ANY SUDDEN MOVES...
UUGH!!
DAMMIT, WOMAN! WHAT DID YOU DO?!
DIDN'T DO NOTHING. STUPID BRANCH BROKE...
OH.
GET BEHIND ME, SHANNA!

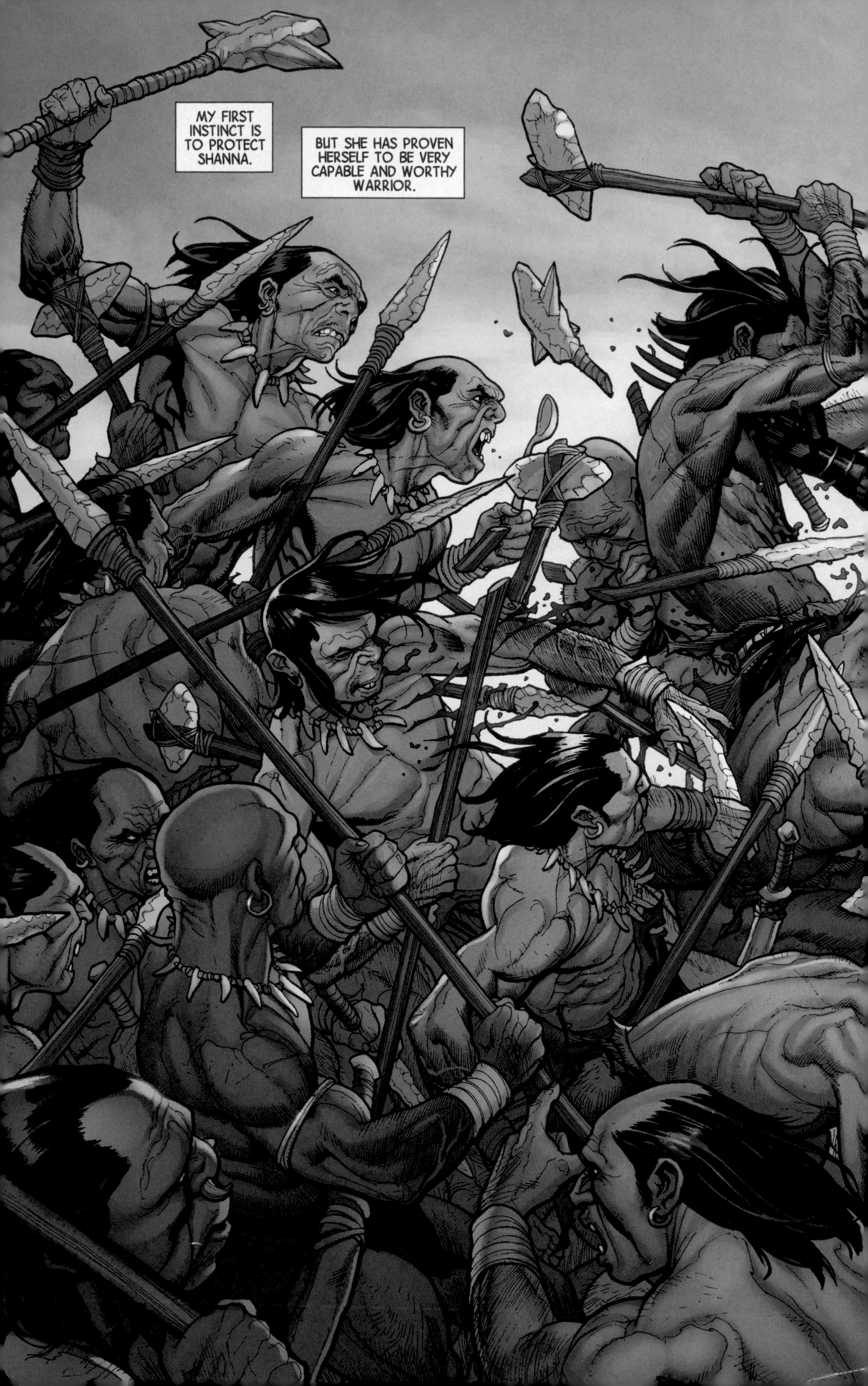
MY FIRST INSTINCT IS TO PROTECT SHANNA.
BUT SHE HAS PROVEN HERSELF TO BE VERY CAPABLE AND WORTHY WARRIOR.

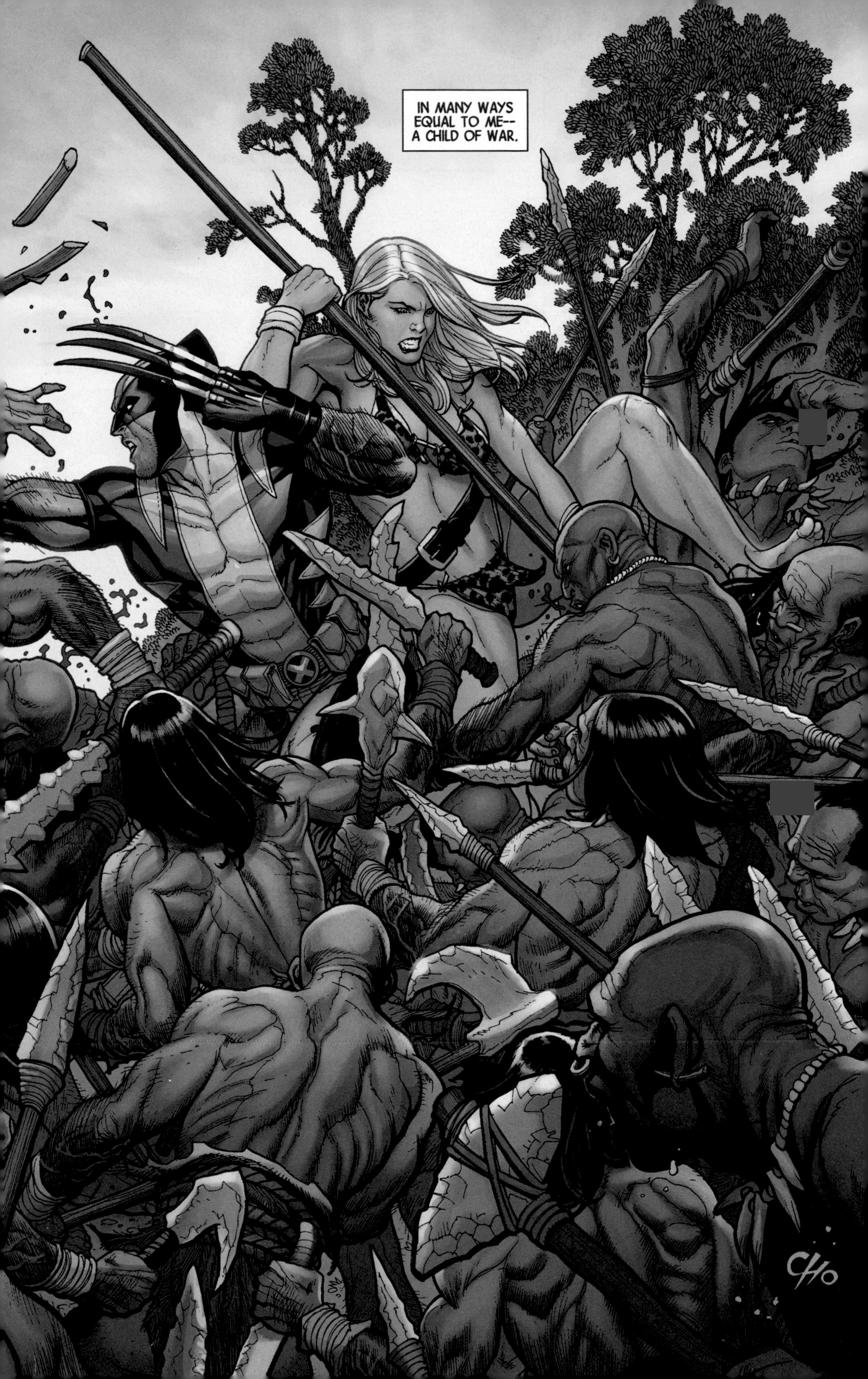
IN MANY WAYS EQUAL TO ME-- A CHILD OF WAR.
CHO

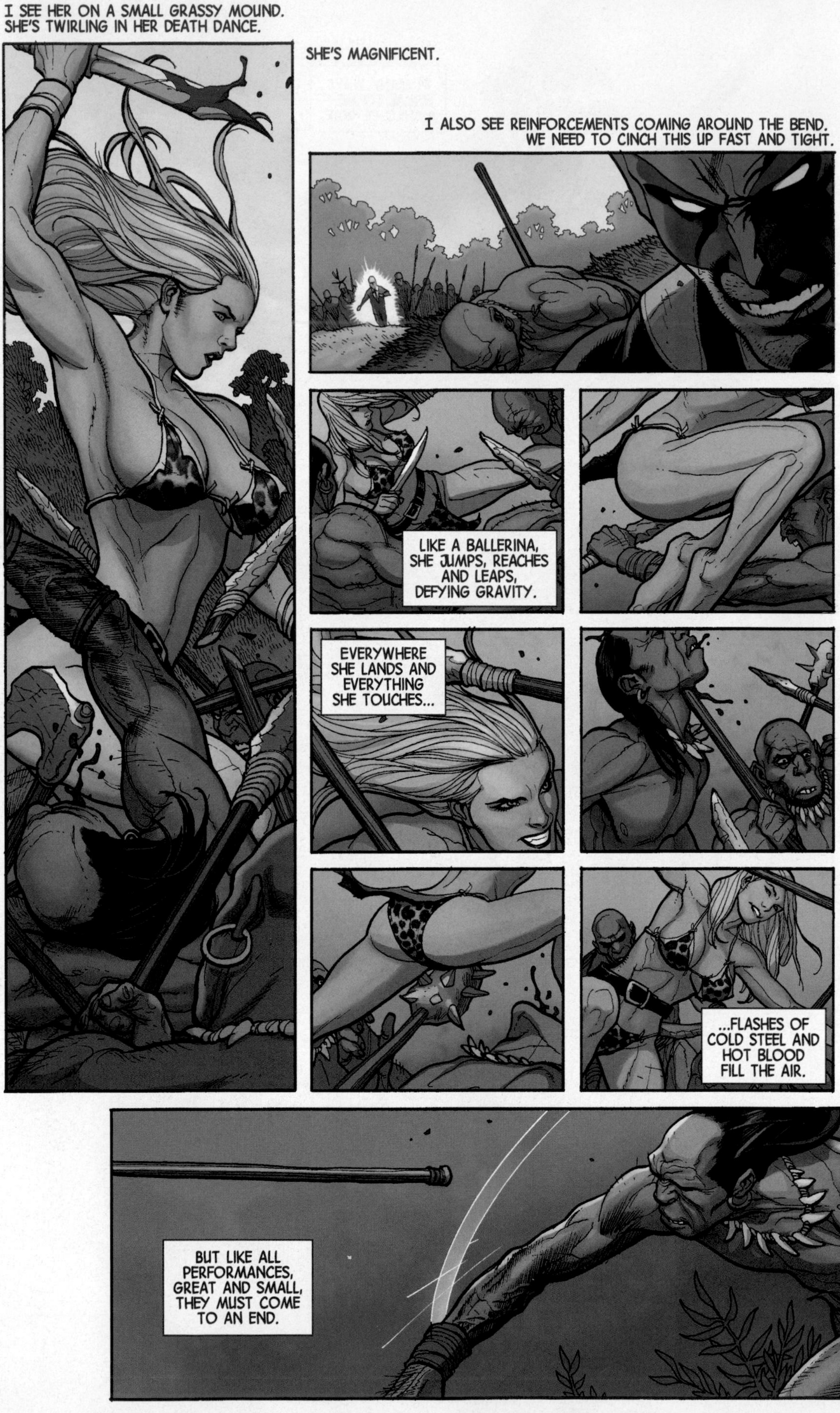
I SEE HER ON A SMALL GRASSY MOUND.
SHE'S TWIRLING IN HER DEATH DANCE.
SHE'S MAGNIFICENT.
I ALSO SEE REINFORCEMENTS COMING AROUND THE BEND.
WE NEED TO CINCH THIS UP FAST AND TIGHT.
LIKE A BALLERINA, SHE JUMPS, REACHES AND LEAPS, DEFYING GRAVITY.
EVERYWHERE SHE LANDS AND EVERYTHING SHE TOUCHES...
...FLASHES OF COLD STEEL AND HOT BLOOD FILL THE AIR.
BUT LIKE ALL PERFORMANCES, GREAT AND SMALL, THEY MUST COME TO AN END.

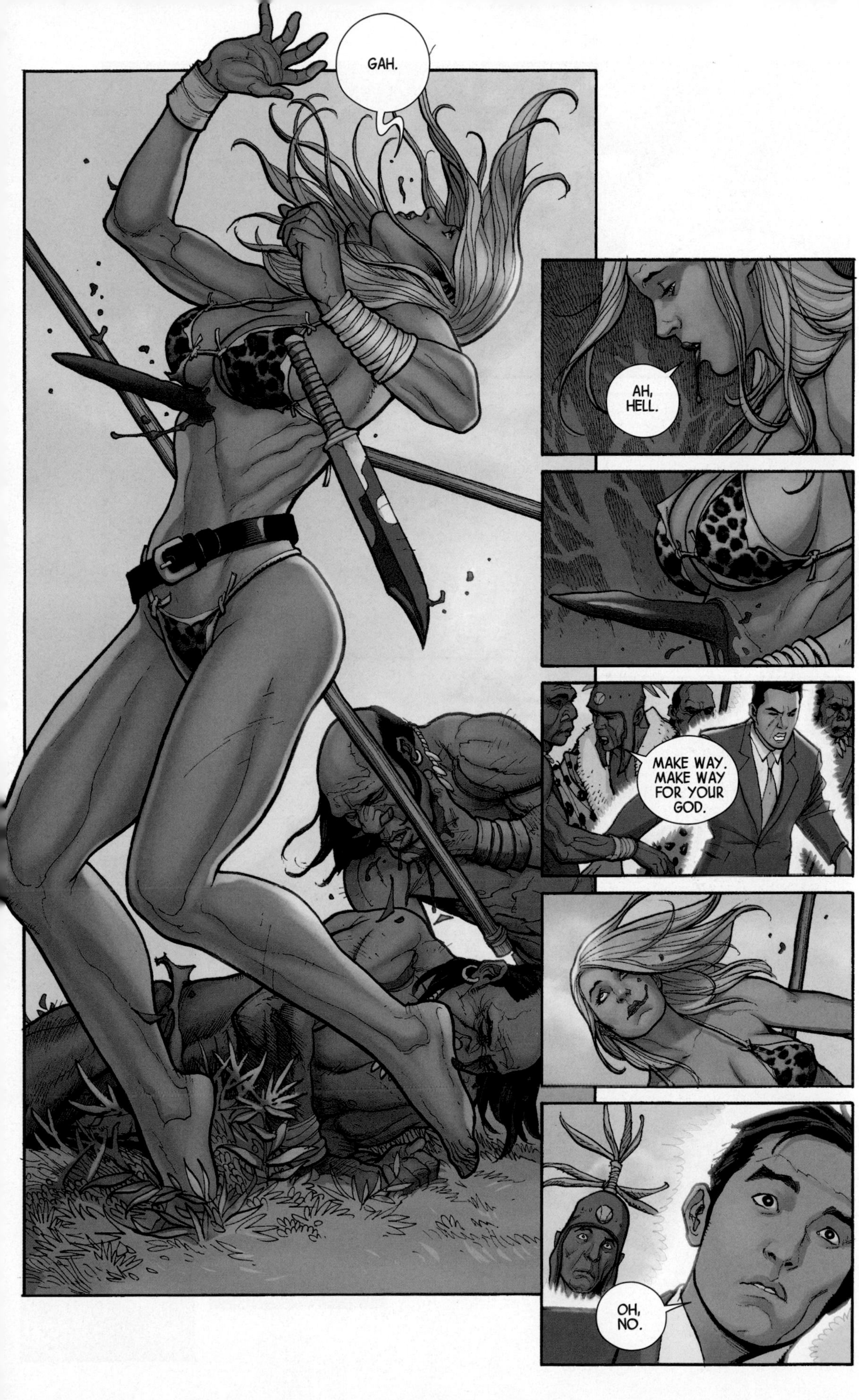
GAH.
AH, HELL.
MAKE WAY. MAKE WAY FOR YOUR GOD.
OH, NO.

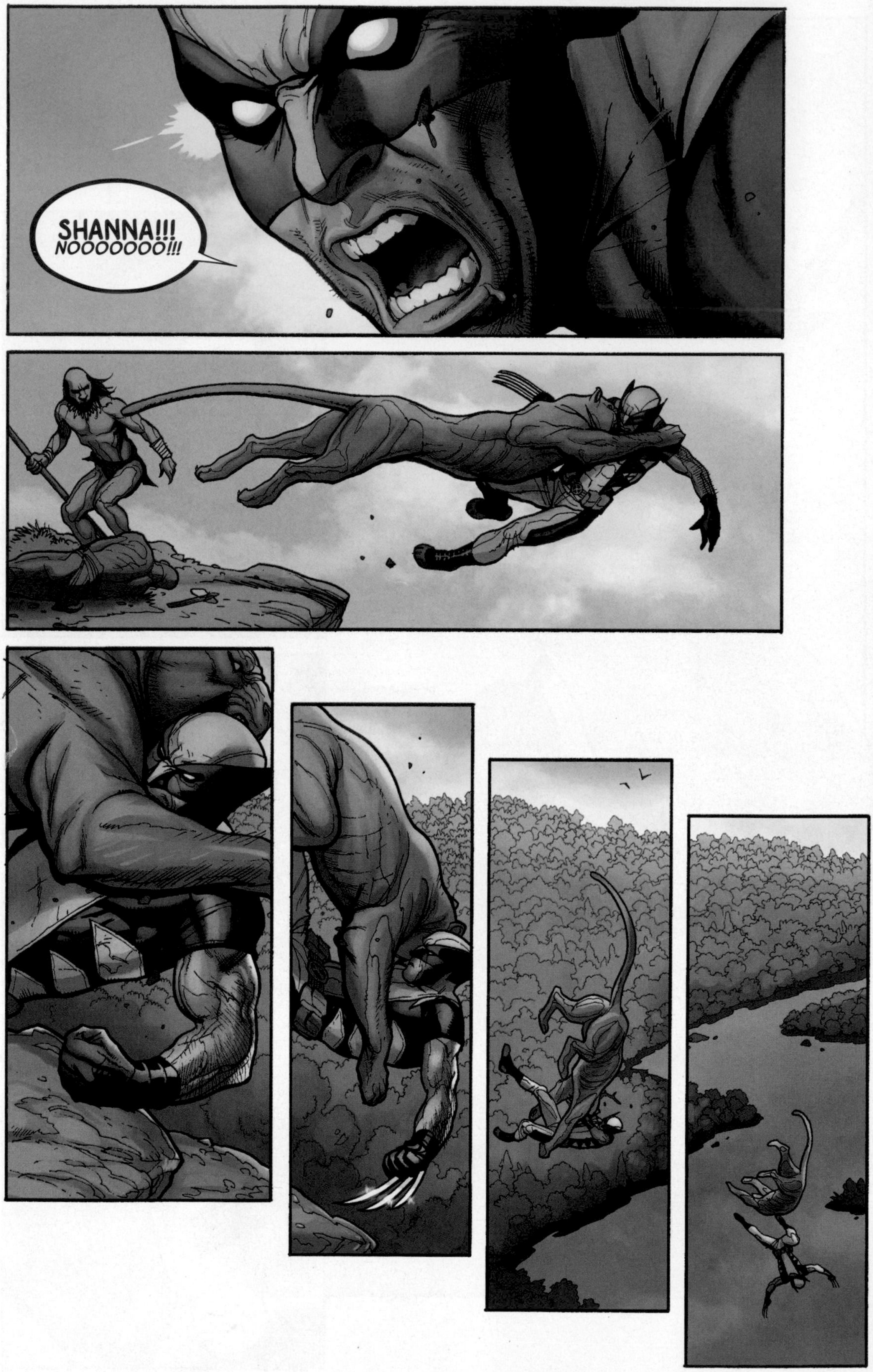
SHANNA!!! NOOOOOOO!!!

AW DAMN. I WAS RIGHT. IT'S SHANNA. SHE'S BLEEDING OUT. CALVIN, I NEED A FULL DIAGNOSIS.

HER INFERIOR VENA CAVA IS LACERATED. HER BLOOD PRESSURE IS DROPPING AND HER ORGANS ARE SHUTTING DOWN. MORTALITY 100% IF UNTREATED IN THE NEXT FIVE MINUTES.

CHIEF, SAVE HER. USE YOUR POTION ON HER NOW.

BUT SHE'S THE ENEMY, MY GOD.

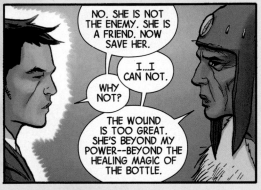

NO. SHE IS NOT THE ENEMY. SHE IS A FRIEND. NOW SAVE HER.

I...I CAN NOT.

WHY NOT?

THE WOUND IS TOO GREAT. SHE'S BEYOND MY POWER--BEYOND THE HEALING MAGIC OF THE BOTTLE.

PERHAPS...

PERHAPS WHAT?

THERE IS AN ANCIENT RITUAL. IT'S DANGEROUS...

DO IT!

YES, MY GOD.

QUICKLY. GATHER THE GIRL. THERE'S NO TIME TO WASTE.

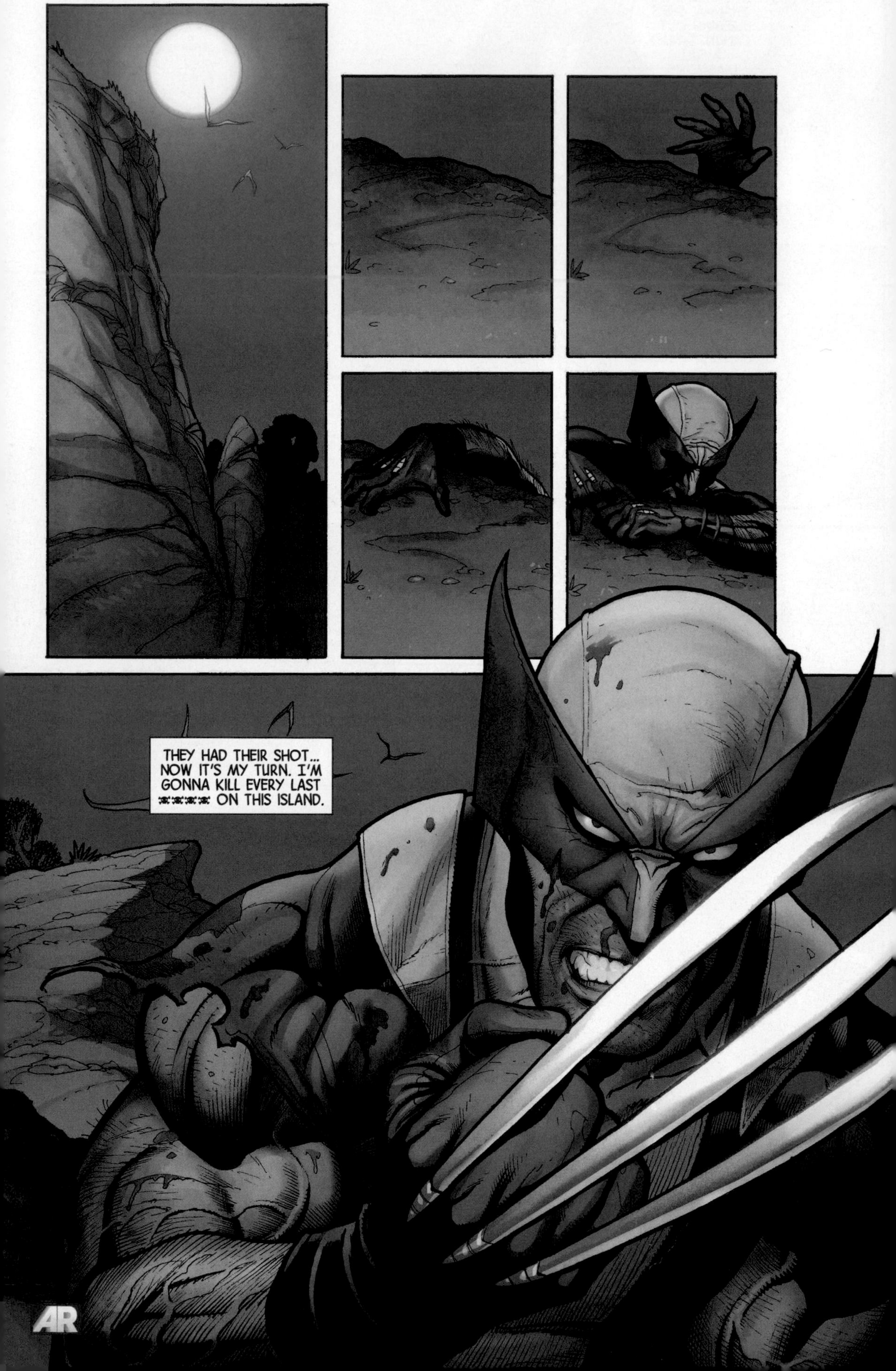
THEY HAD THEIR SHOT... NOW IT'S MY TURN. I'M GONNA KILL EVERY LAST ON THIS ISLAND.

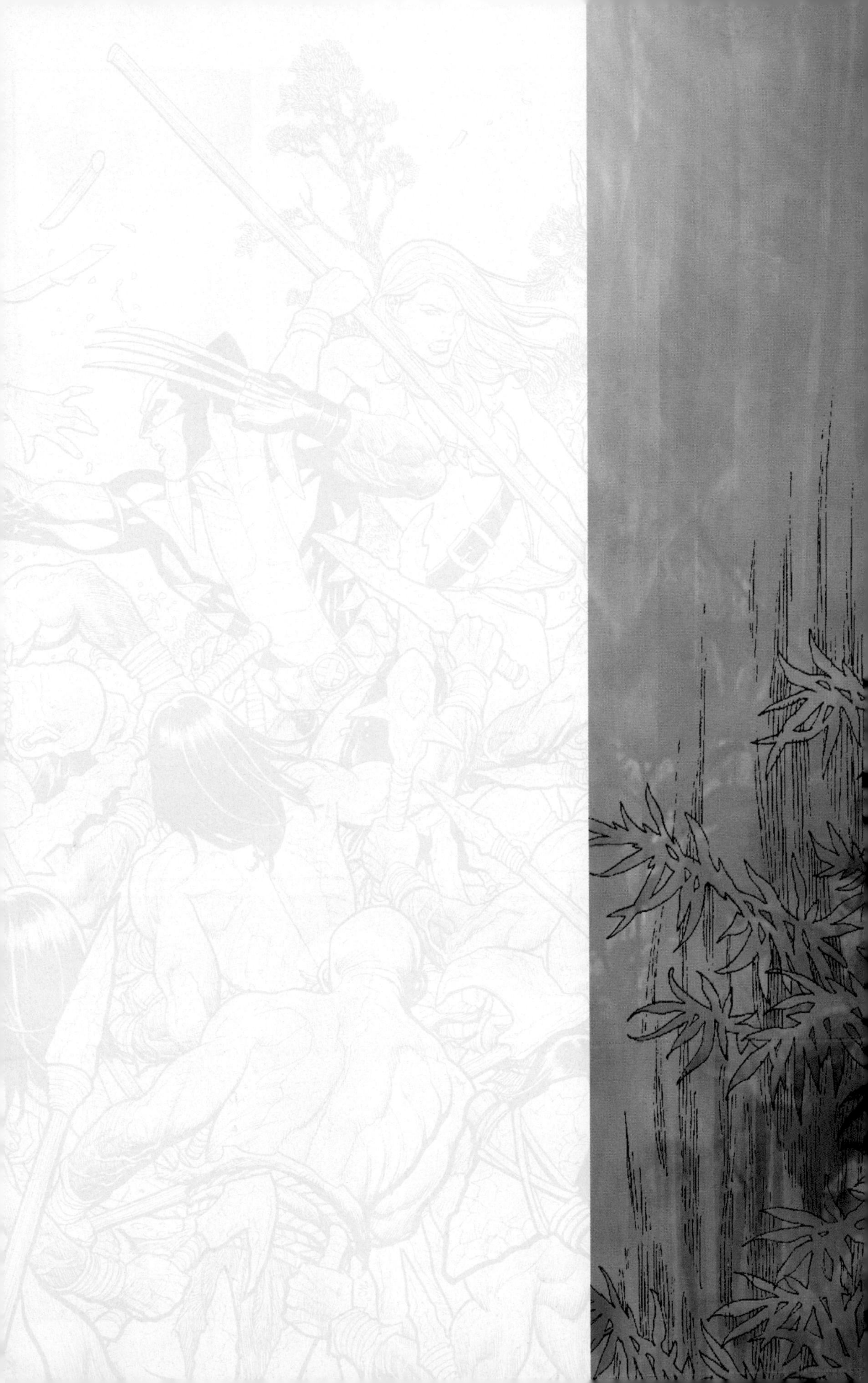

4

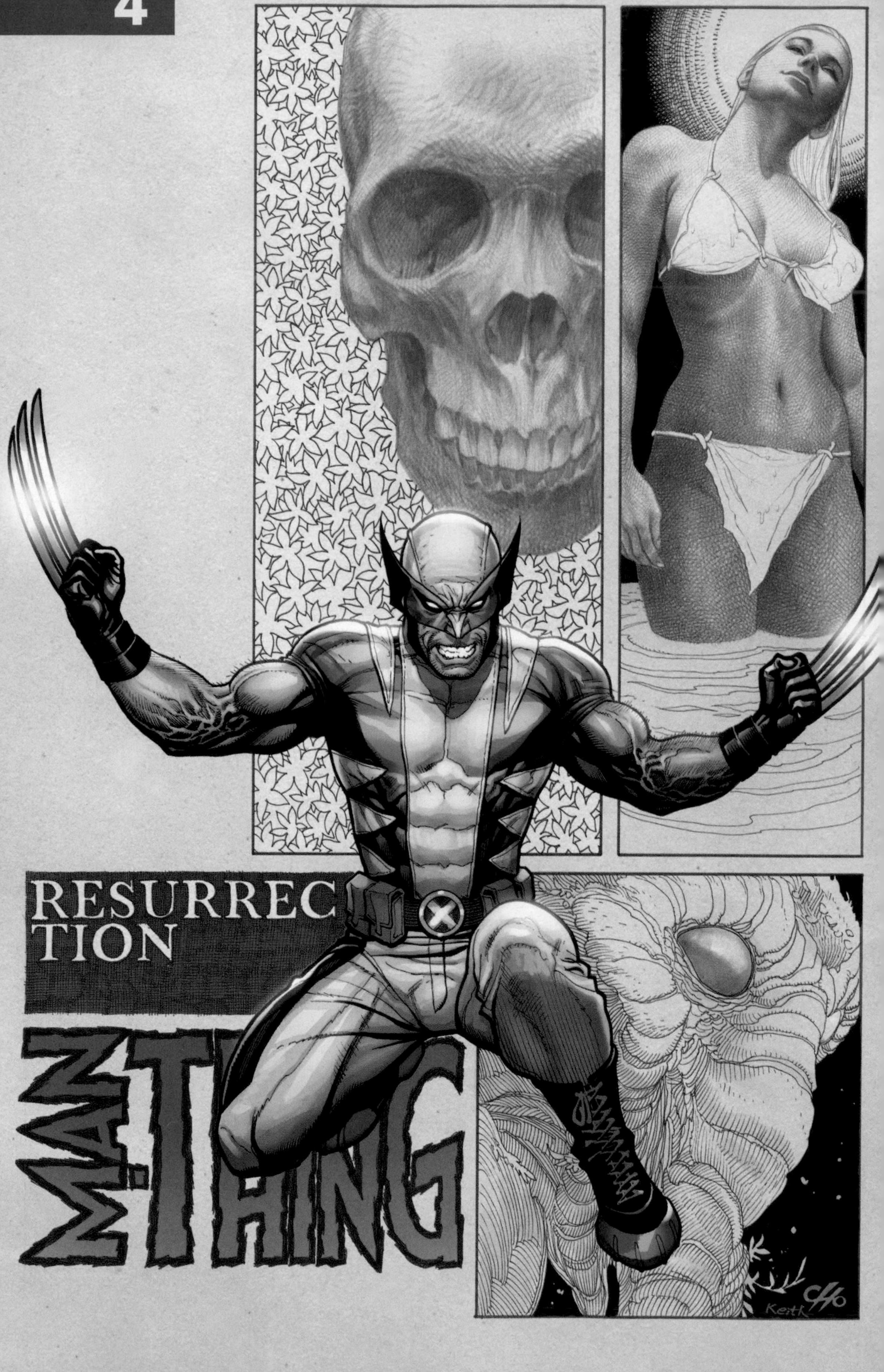
RESURRECTION
MAN-THING

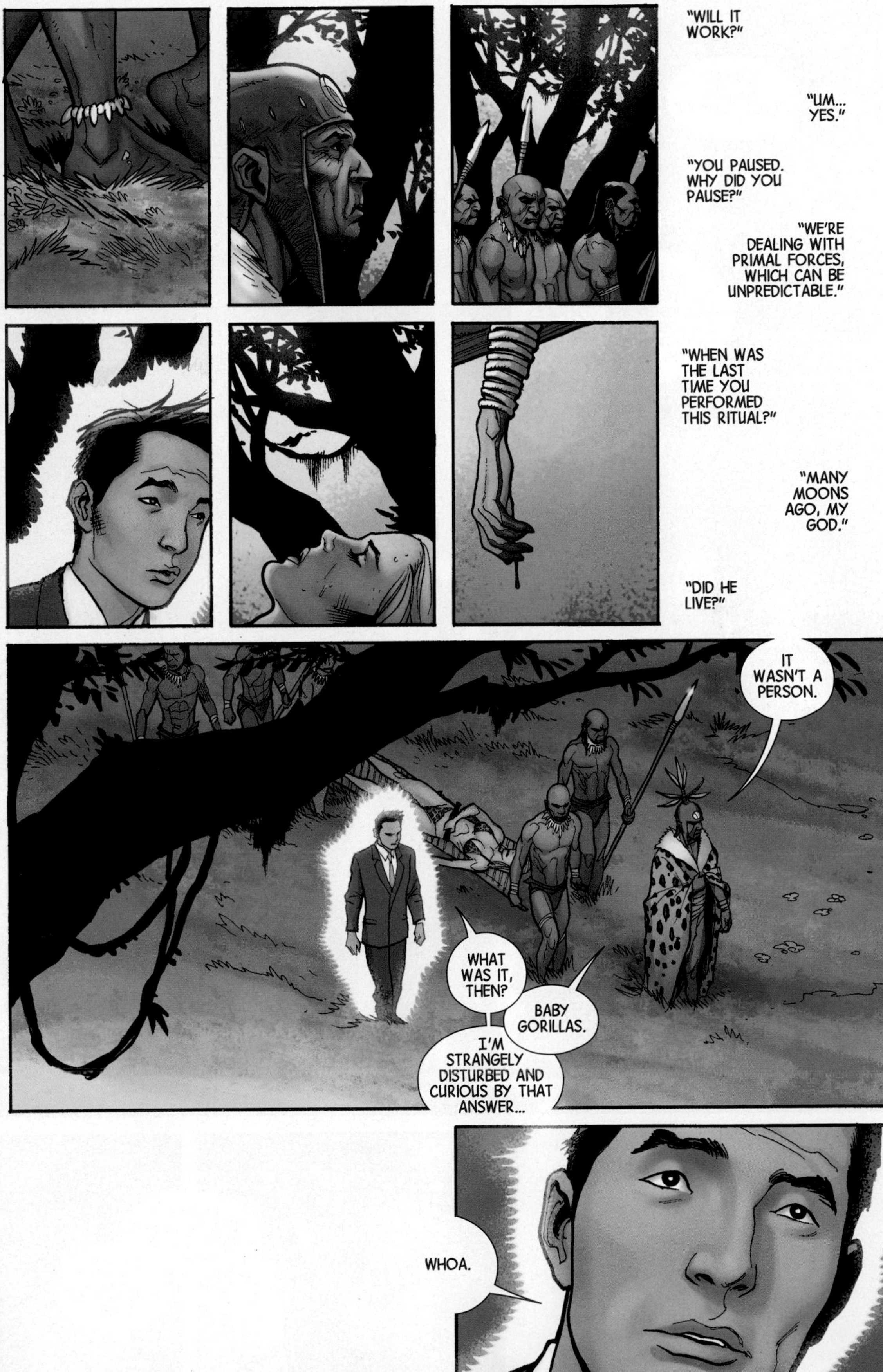
"WILL IT WORK?"
"UM... YES."
"YOU PAUSED. WHY DID YOU PAUSE?"
"WE'RE DEALING WITH PRIMAL FORCES, WHICH CAN BE UNPREDICTABLE."
"WHEN WAS THE LAST TIME YOU PERFORMED THIS RITUAL?"
"MANY MOONS AGO, MY GOD."
"DID HE LIVE?"
IT WASN'T A PERSON.
WHAT WAS IT, THEN?
BABY GORILLAS.
I'M STRANGELY DISTURBED AND CURIOUS BY THAT ANSWER...
WHOA.

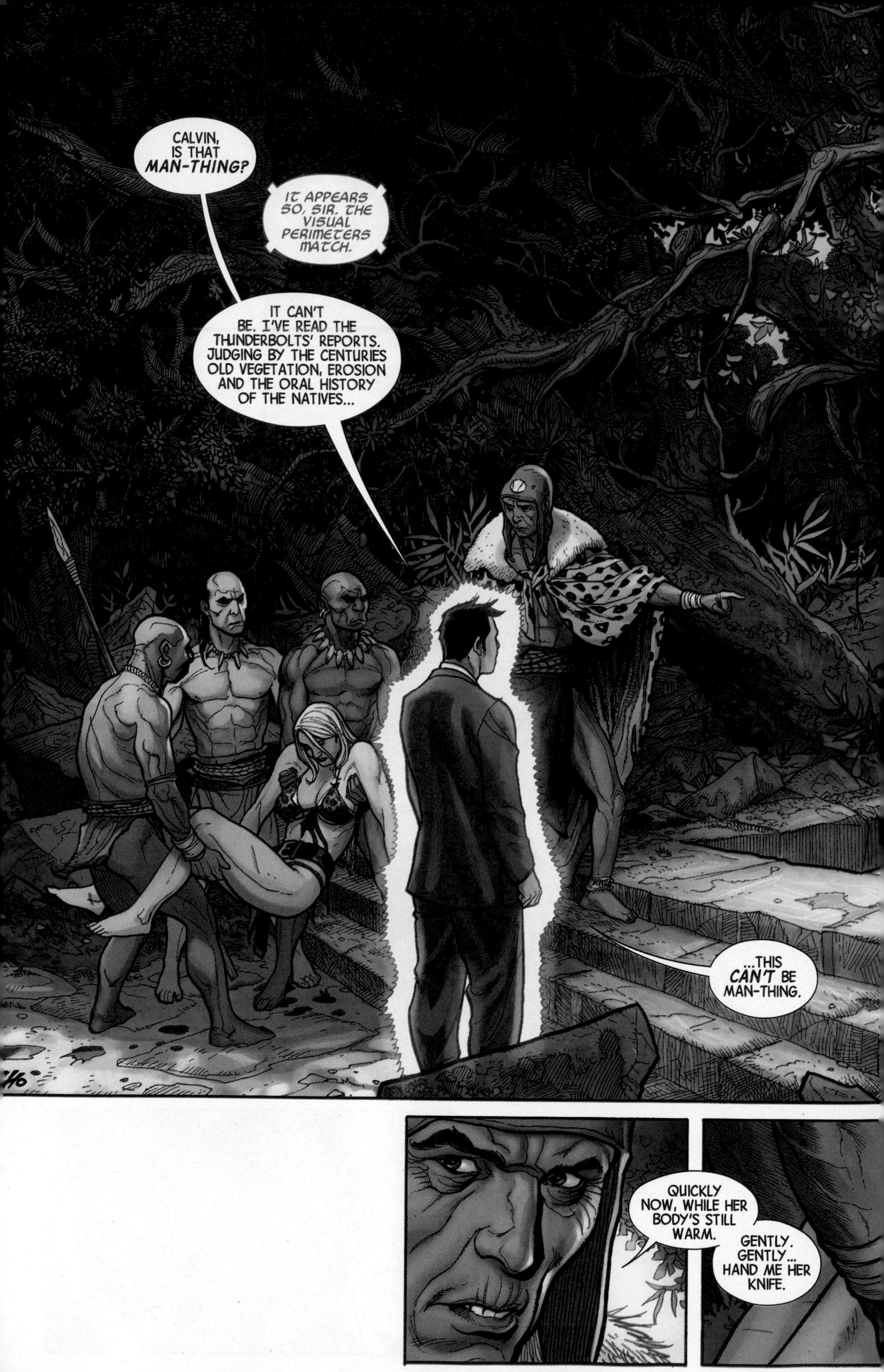
CALVIN, IS THAT MAN-THING?
IT APPEARS SO, SIR. THE VISUAL PERIMETERS MATCH.
IT CAN'T BE. I'VE READ THE THUNDERBOLTS' REPORTS. JUDGING BY THE CENTURIES OLD VEGETATION, EROSION AND THE ORAL HISTORY OF THE NATIVES...
...THIS CAN'T BE MAN-THING.
QUICKLY NOW, WHILE HER BODY'S STILL WARM.
GENTLY. GENTLY... HAND ME HER KNIFE.

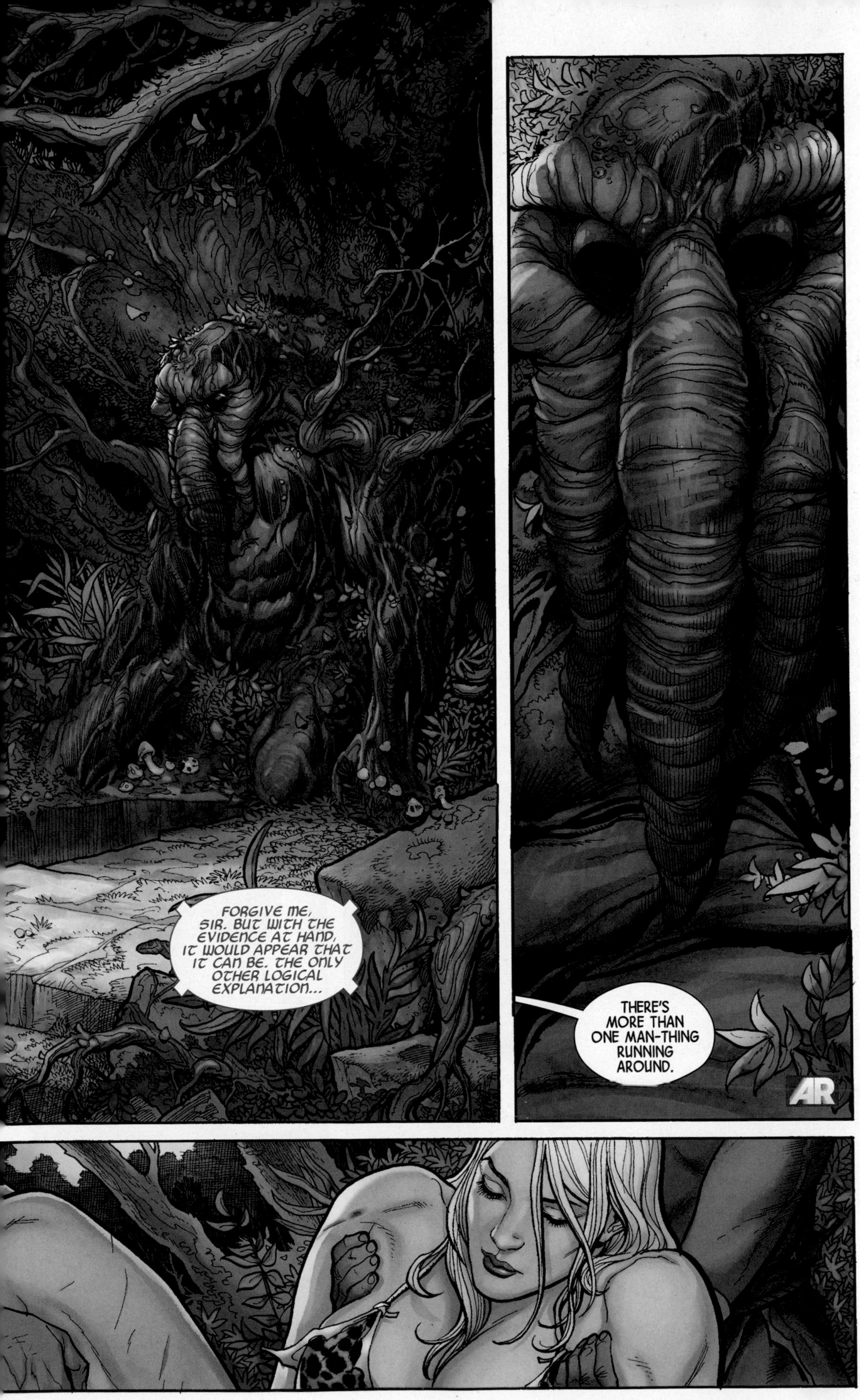
FORGIVE ME, SIR. BUT WITH THE EVIDENCE AT HAND, IT WOULD APPEAR THAT IT CAN BE. THE ONLY OTHER LOGICAL EXPLANATION...
THERE'S MORE THAN ONE MAN-THING RUNNING AROUND.

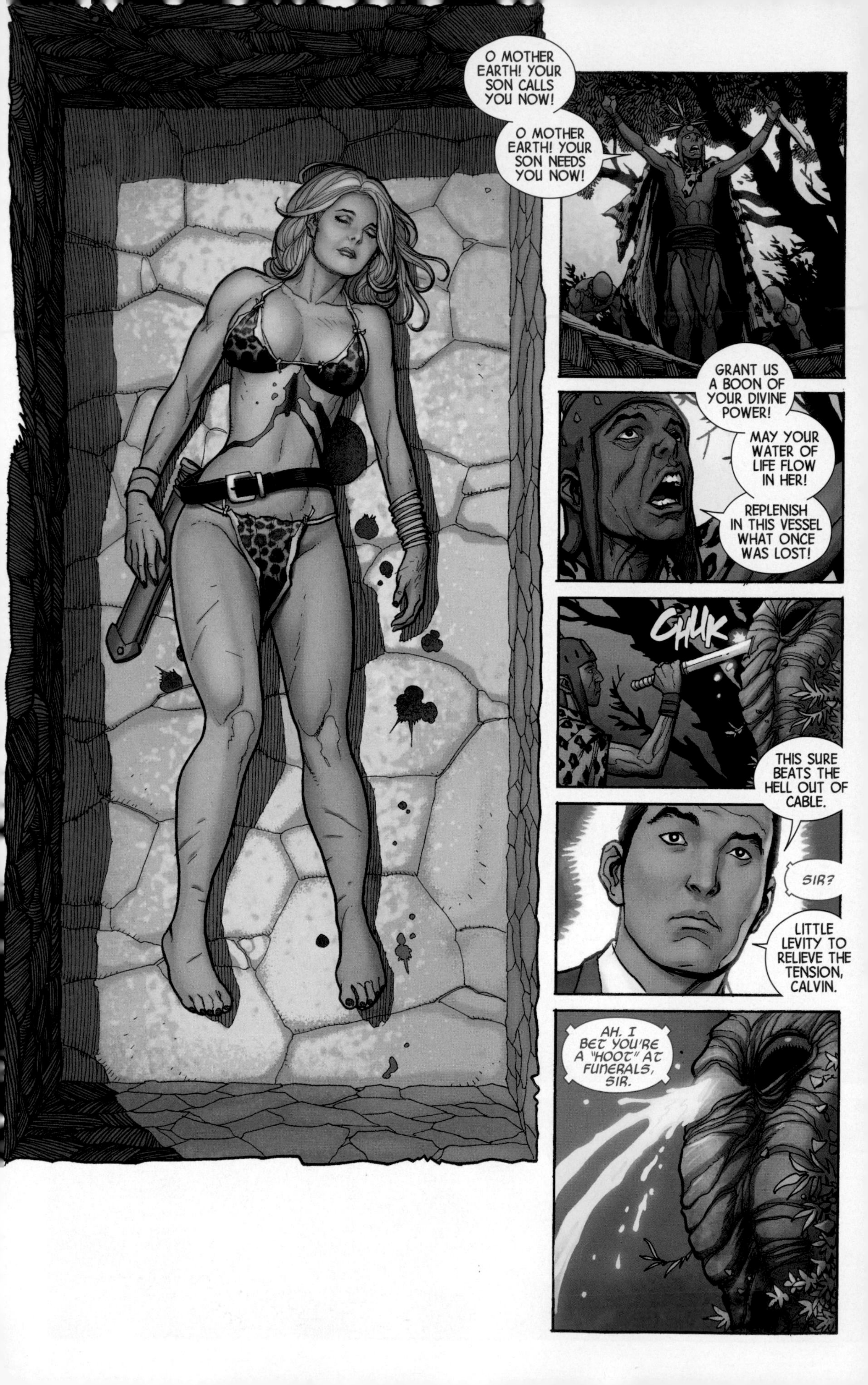
O MOTHER EARTH! YOUR SON CALLS YOU NOW!
O MOTHER EARTH! YOUR SON NEEDS YOU NOW!
GRANT US A BOON OF YOUR DIVINE POWER!
MAY YOUR WATER OF LIFE FLOW IN HER!
REPLENISH IN THIS VESSEL WHAT ONCE WAS LOST!
CHUK
THIS SURE BEATS THE HELL OUT OF CABLE.
SIR?
LITTLE LEVITY TO RELIEVE THE TENSION, CALVIN.
AH. I BET YOU'RE A "HOOT" AT FUNERALS, SIR.

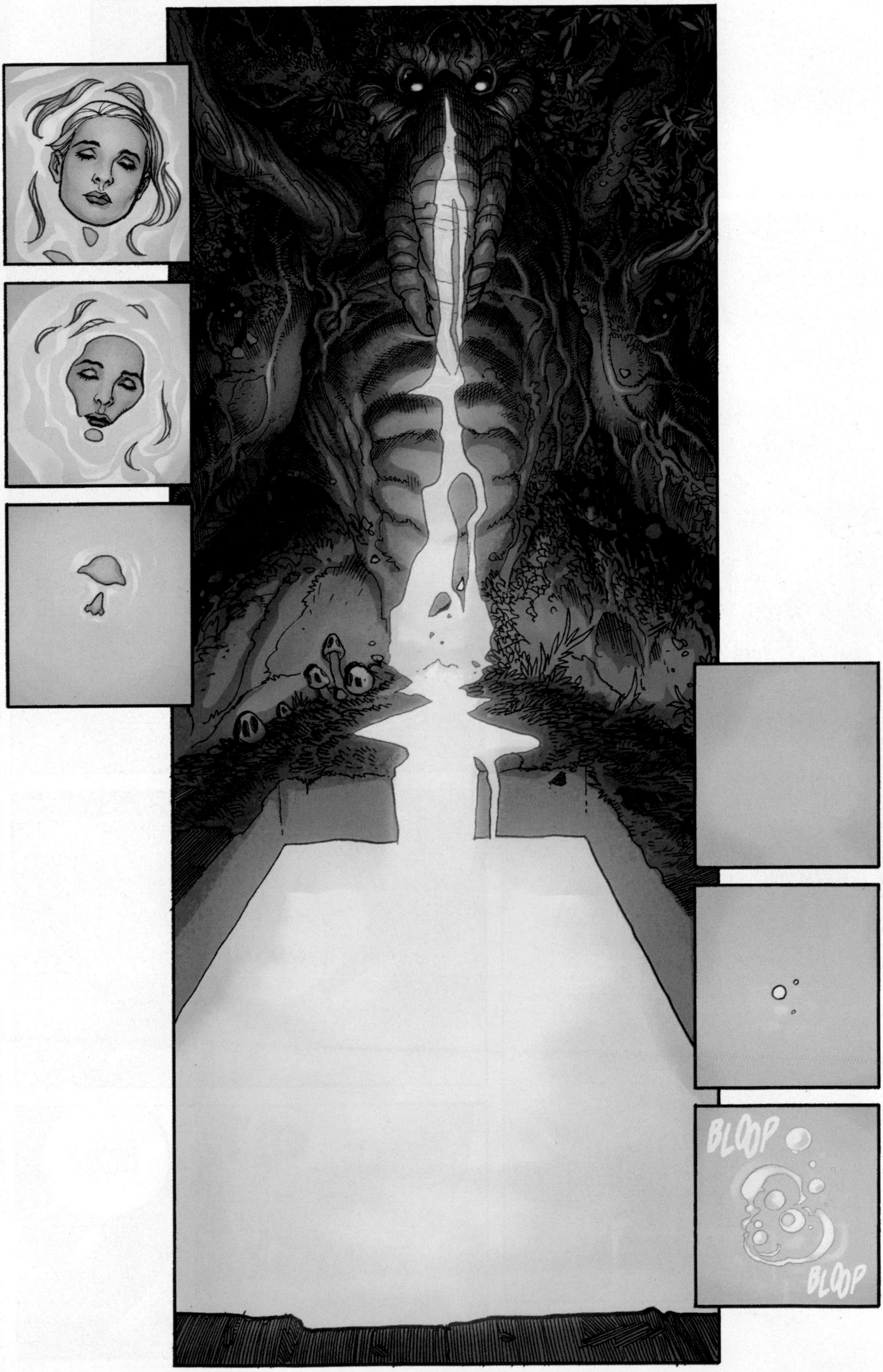
BLOOP
BLOOP

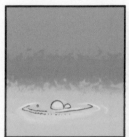

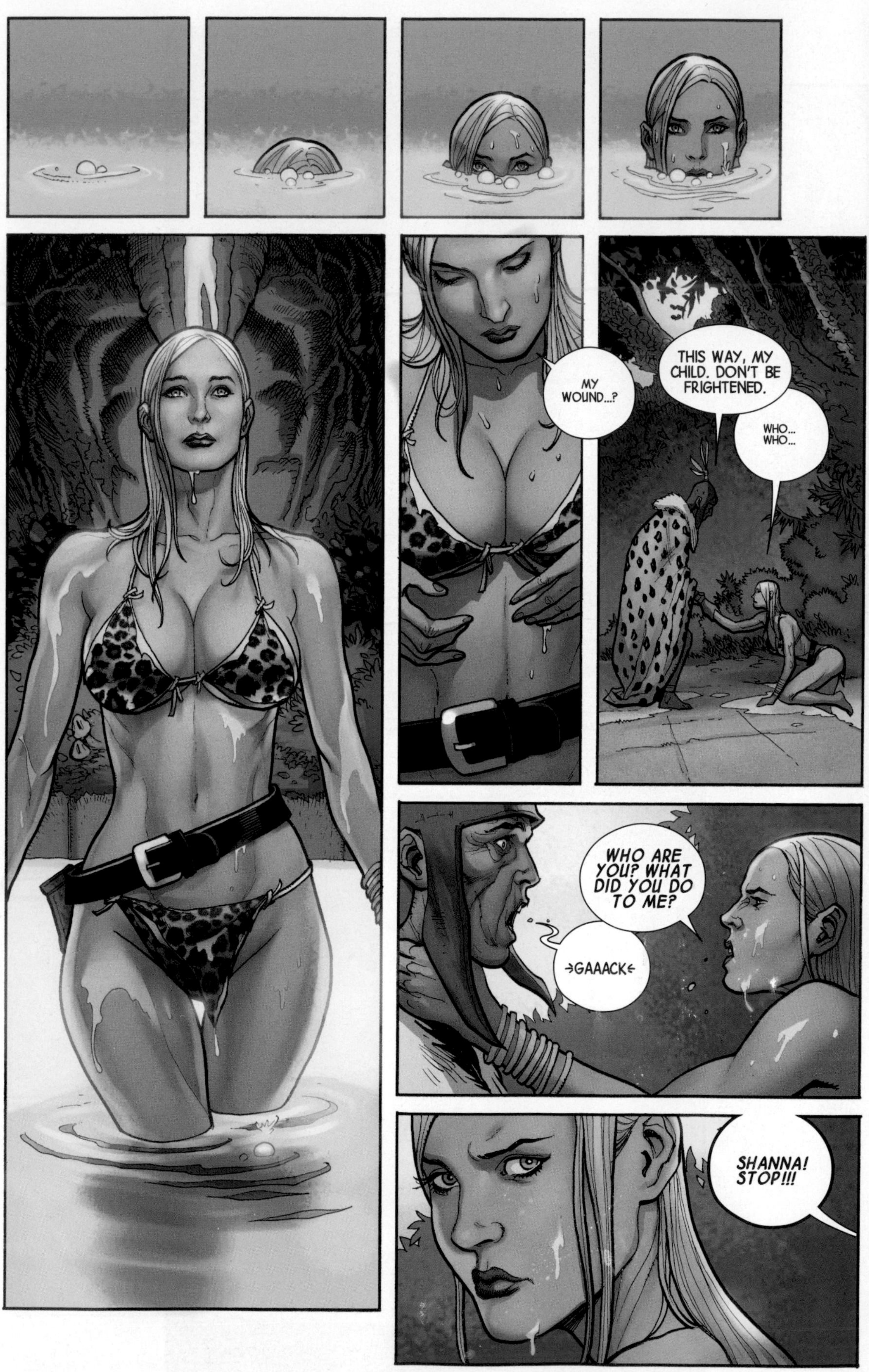
MY WOUND...?
THIS WAY, MY CHILD. DON'T BE FRIGHTENED.
WHO... WHO...
WHO ARE YOU? WHAT DID YOU DO TO ME?
GAAACK
SHANNA! STOP!!!

PLEASE DON'T KILL THE MAN WHO JUST SAVED YOU. BAD KARMA.

NOW LISTEN CAREFULLY. I NEED YOU TO FOCUS AND ANSWER ME HONESTLY-- DO YOU KNOW WHO WON THE SUPER BOWL?

WHAT?

IT WAS WORTH A SHOT.

WHO ARE YOU AND WHAT DID YOU DO TO ME?

I'M AMADEUS CHO, FREELANCER.

FREELANCER OF WHAT?

SCIENCE.

BACK UP. WHAT EXACTLY DID YOU GUYS DO TO ME? AND WHERE'S WOLVERINE?

→COUGH← YOU DIED AND WE RESURRECTED YOU, MY CHILD.

WHAT?

HOW DO YOU FEEL? ARE YOU IN ANY PAIN?

NO. NO... I FEEL FINE. I FEEL...GREAT, ACTUALLY.

WAIT. DID YOU SAY THAT I DIED?!

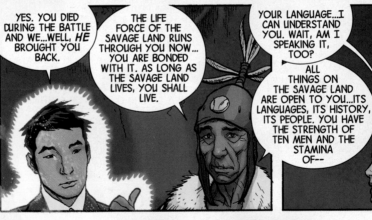

YES. YOU DIED DURING THE BATTLE AND WE...WELL, HE BROUGHT YOU BACK.

THE LIFE FORCE OF THE SAVAGE LAND RUNS THROUGH YOU NOW... YOU ARE BONDED WITH IT. AS LONG AS THE SAVAGE LAND LIVES, YOU SHALL LIVE.

YOUR LANGUAGE...I CAN UNDERSTAND YOU. WAIT, AM I SPEAKING IT, TOO?

ALL THINGS ON THE SAVAGE LAND ARE OPEN TO YOU...ITS LANGUAGES, ITS HISTORY, ITS PEOPLE. YOU HAVE THE STRENGTH OF TEN MEN AND THE STAMINA OF--

SHE CAN READ THE BROCHURE LATER, CHIEF. I KNOW HOW I GOT HERE, BUT HOW DID YOU GET HERE? I FOUND A PIECE OF TORN S.H.I.E.L.D. UNIFORM IN THE JUNGLE... WERE YOU HERE WITH THEM?

YES. I WAS THEIR GUIDE. WE WERE SURVEYING THIS REGION. WHEN WE GOT TOO CLOSE TO THE ISLAND, OUR SHIP...

RIGHT, RIGHT. AND HOW HIGH WAS YOUR SHIP BEFORE YOUR MAG-LEVS FAILED?

WE WERE-- HOW DID YOU KNOW OUR MAG-LEVS FAILED?

I KNOW ABOUT THE DAMPENING FIELD.

WE WERE AT OBSERVATION HEIGHT. UNDER 800 FEET. WHAT DOES THIS HAVE TO DO WITH ANYTHING? AND CAN SOMEONE TELL ME, WHERE IS WOLVERINE?!

CHIEF, HOW LONG DOES IT TAKE TO WALK THE PERIMETER OF THE ISLAND?

FOUR DAYS, O HOLY ONE.

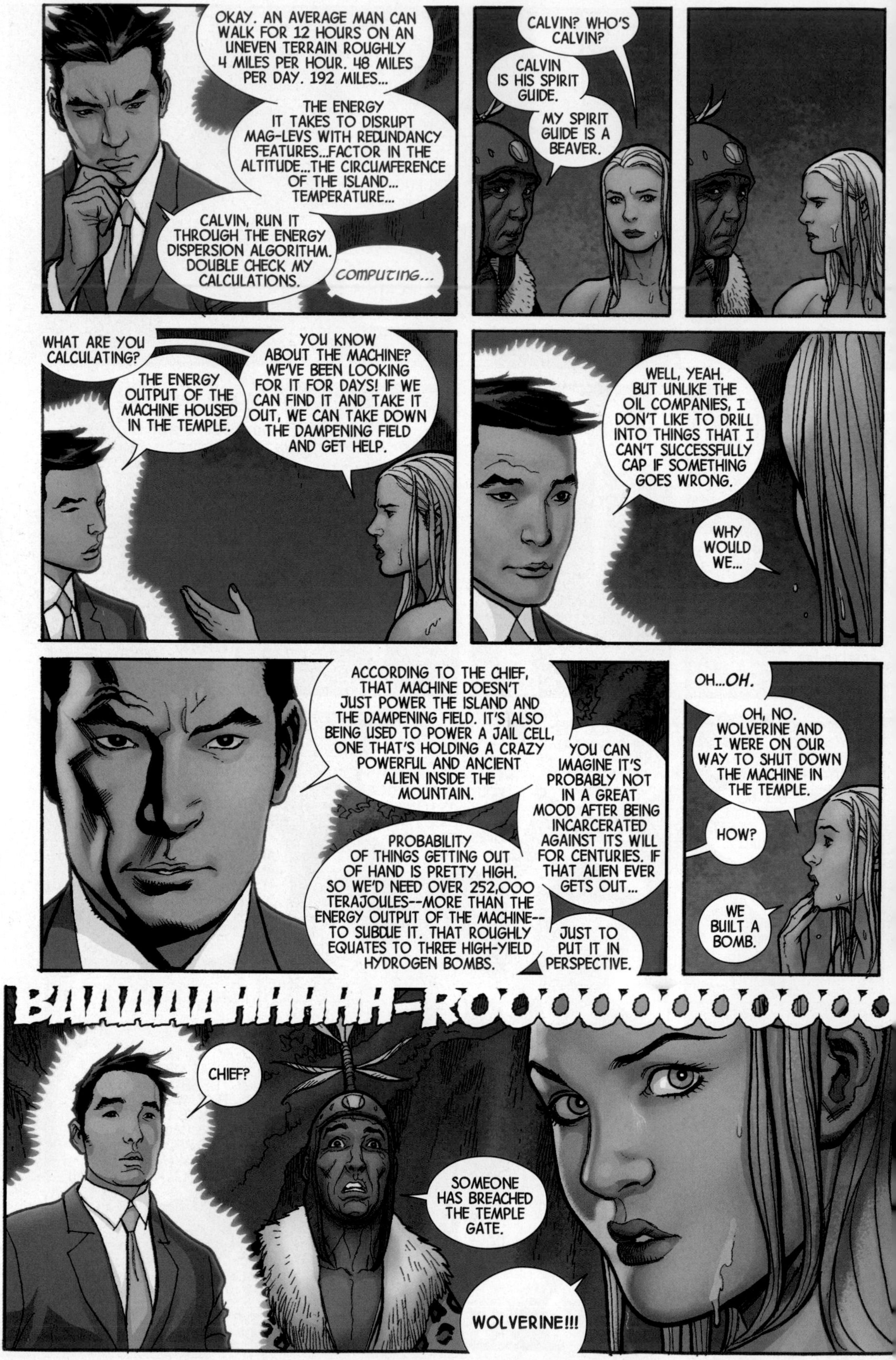
OKAY. AN AVERAGE MAN CAN WALK FOR 12 HOURS ON AN UNEVEN TERRAIN ROUGHLY 4 MILES PER HOUR. 48 MILES PER DAY. 192 MILES...
THE ENERGY IT TAKES TO DISRUPT MAG-LEVS WITH REDUNDANCY FEATURES...FACTOR IN THE ALTITUDE...THE CIRCUMFERENCE OF THE ISLAND... TEMPERATURE...
CALVIN, RUN IT THROUGH THE ENERGY DISPERSION ALGORITHM. DOUBLE CHECK MY CALCULATIONS.
COMPUTING...
CALVIN? WHO'S CALVIN?
CALVIN IS HIS SPIRIT GUIDE.
MY SPIRIT GUIDE IS A BEAVER.
WHAT ARE YOU CALCULATING?
THE ENERGY OUTPUT OF THE MACHINE HOUSED IN THE TEMPLE.
YOU KNOW ABOUT THE MACHINE? WE'VE BEEN LOOKING FOR IT FOR DAYS! IF WE CAN FIND IT AND TAKE IT OUT, WE CAN TAKE DOWN THE DAMPENING FIELD AND GET HELP.
WELL, YEAH. BUT UNLIKE THE OIL COMPANIES, I DON'T LIKE TO DRILL INTO THINGS THAT I CAN'T SUCCESSFULLY CAP IF SOMETHING GOES WRONG.
WHY WOULD WE...
ACCORDING TO THE CHIEF, THAT MACHINE DOESN'T JUST POWER THE ISLAND AND THE DAMPENING FIELD. IT'S ALSO BEING USED TO POWER A JAIL CELL, ONE THAT'S HOLDING A CRAZY POWERFUL AND ANCIENT ALIEN INSIDE THE MOUNTAIN.
YOU CAN IMAGINE IT'S PROBABLY NOT IN A GREAT MOOD AFTER BEING INCARCERATED AGAINST ITS WILL FOR CENTURIES. IF THAT ALIEN EVER GETS OUT...
PROBABILITY OF THINGS GETTING OUT OF HAND IS PRETTY HIGH. SO WE'D NEED OVER 252,000 TERAJOULES--MORE THAN THE ENERGY OUTPUT OF THE MACHINE--TO SUBDUE IT. THAT ROUGHLY EQUATES TO THREE HIGH-YIELD HYDROGEN BOMBS.
JUST TO PUT IT IN PERSPECTIVE.
OH...OH.
OH, NO. WOLVERINE AND I WERE ON OUR WAY TO SHUT DOWN THE MACHINE IN THE TEMPLE.
HOW?
WE BUILT A BOMB.
BWWWWHHHHH-ROOOOOOOOOOOO
CHIEF?
SOMEONE HAS BREACHED THE TEMPLE GATE.
WOLVERINE!!!

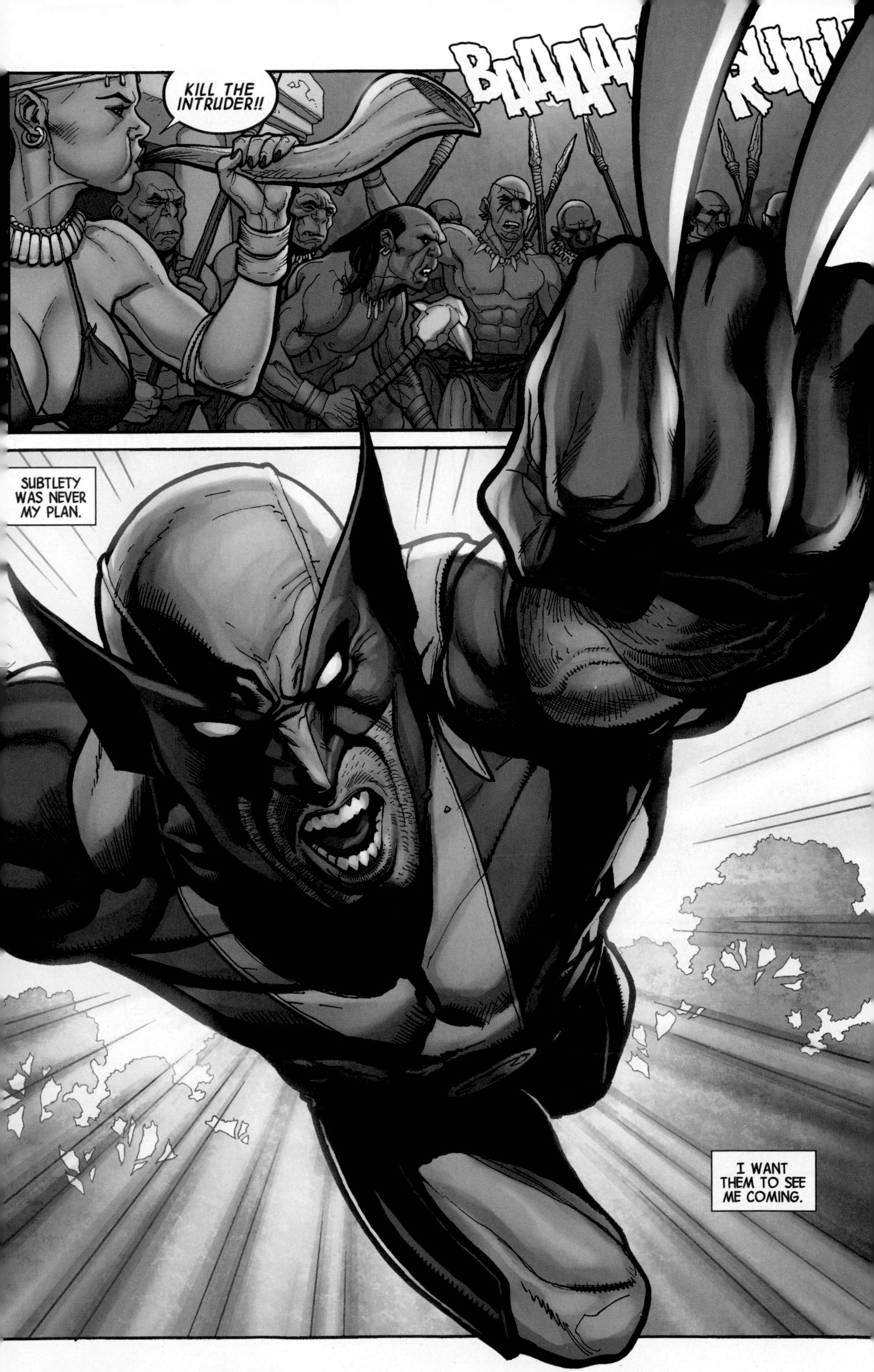
KILL THE INTRUDER!!
SUBTLETY WAS NEVER MY PLAN.
I WANT THEM TO SEE ME COMING.

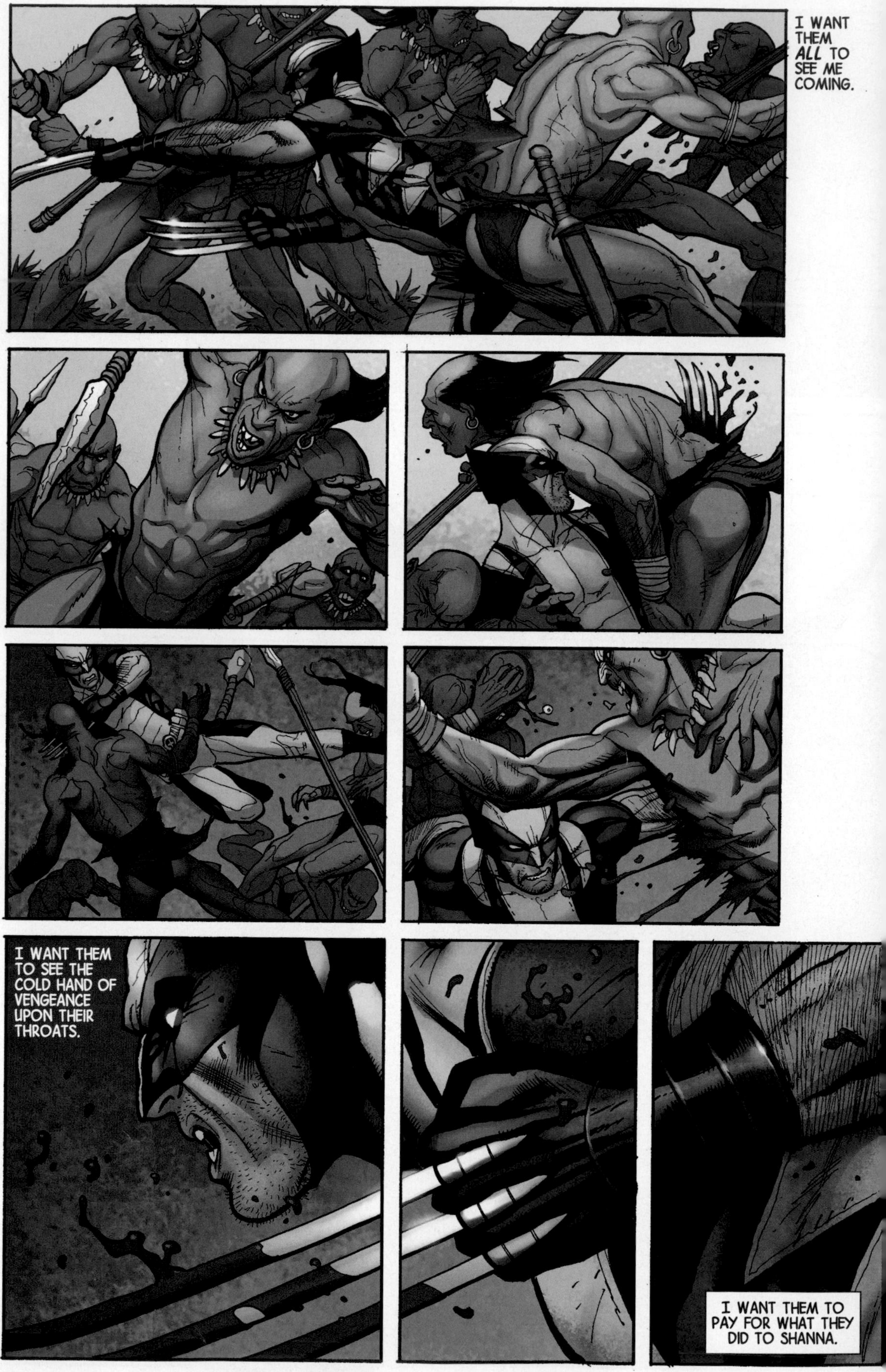
I WANT THEM ALL TO SEE ME COMING.
I WANT THEM TO SEE THE COLD HAND OF VENGEANCE UPON THEIR THROATS.
I WANT THEM TO PAY FOR WHAT THEY DID TO SHANNA.

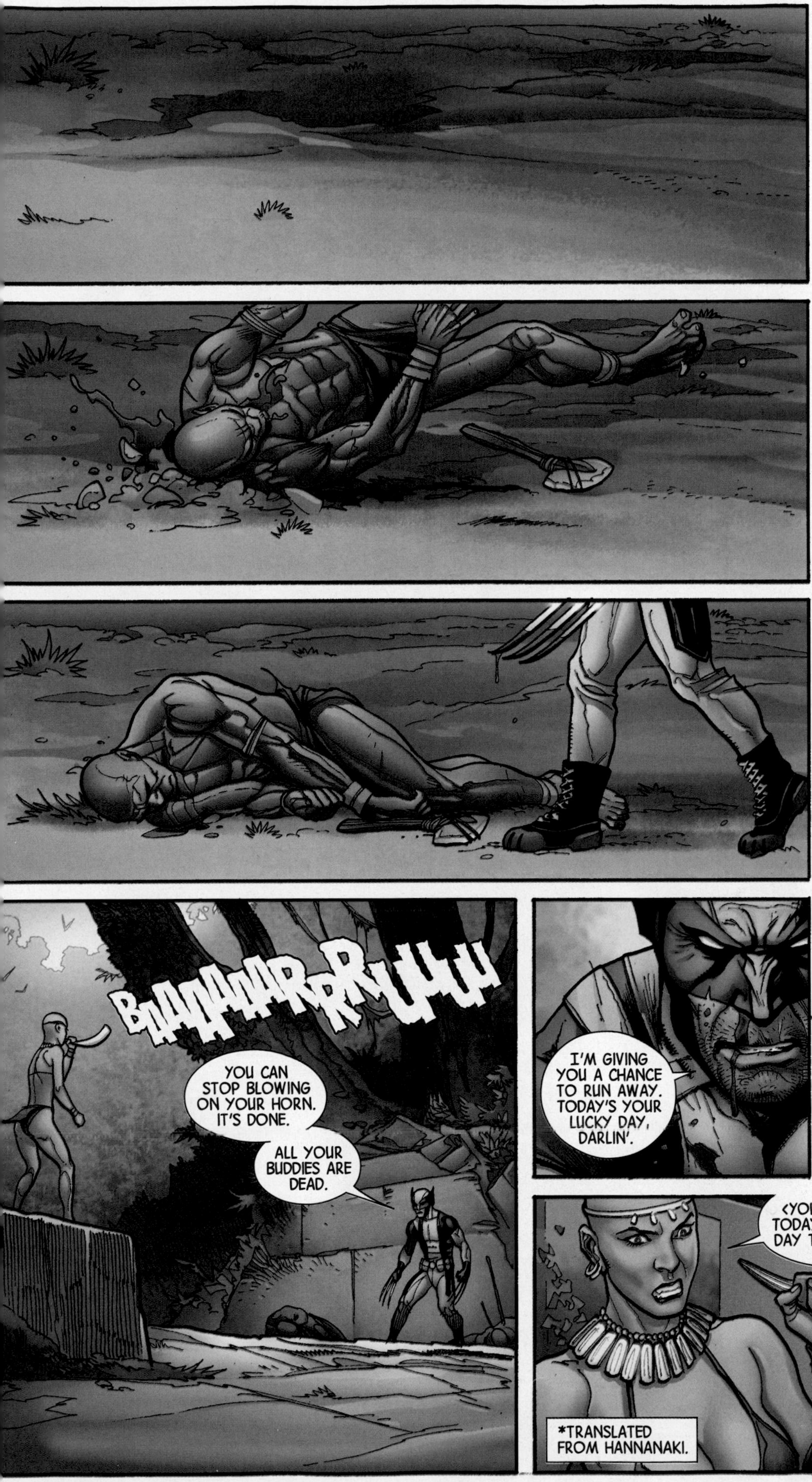
BWAAAARRRUUU
YOU CAN STOP BLOWING ON YOUR HORN. IT'S DONE.
ALL YOUR BUDDIES ARE DEAD.
I'M GIVING YOU A CHANCE TO RUN AWAY. TODAY'S YOUR LUCKY DAY, DARLIN'.
‹YOU FOOL. TODAY'S YOUR DAY TO DIE.›*
*TRANSLATED FROM HANNANAKI.

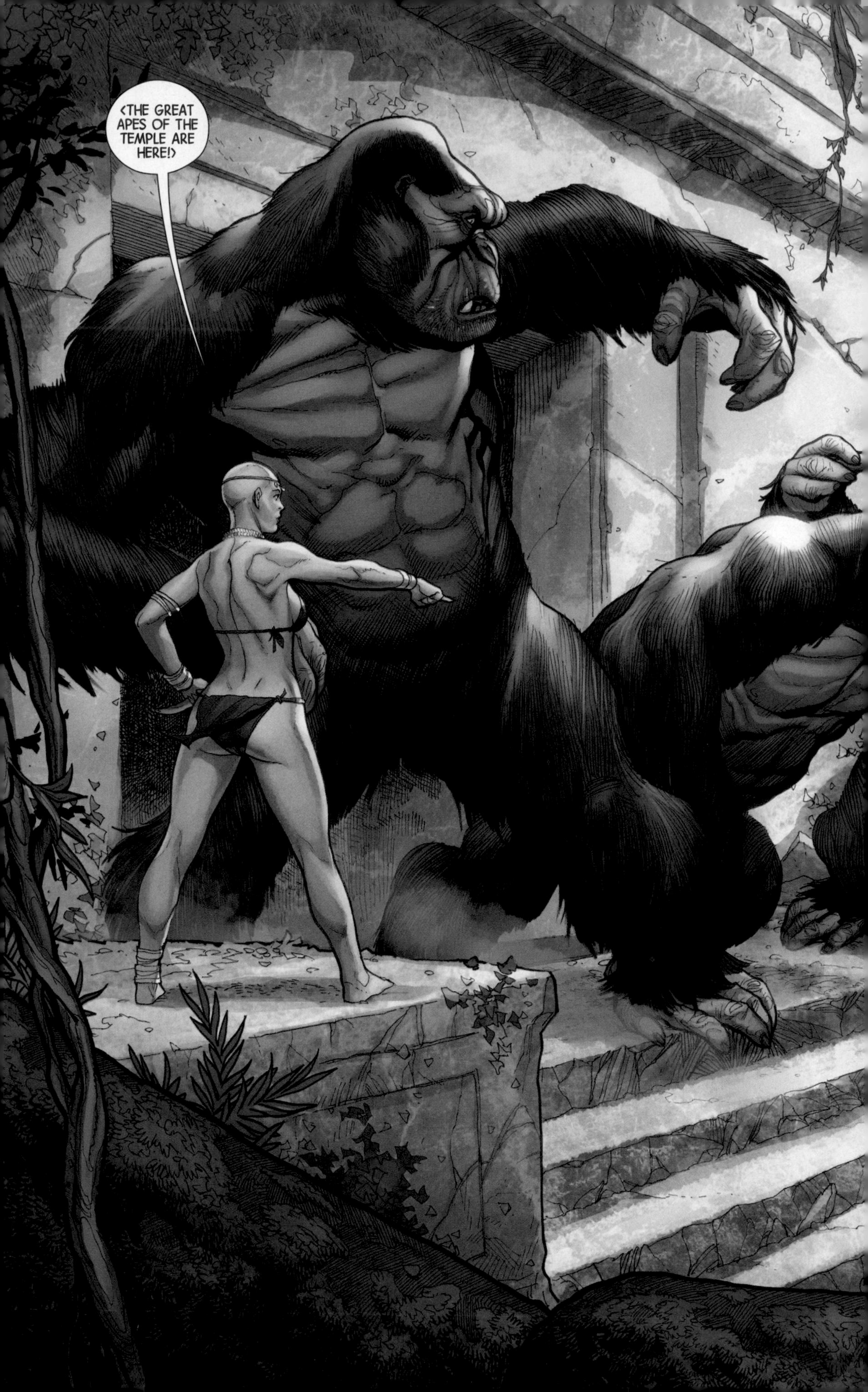
‹THE GREAT APES OF THE TEMPLE ARE HERE!›

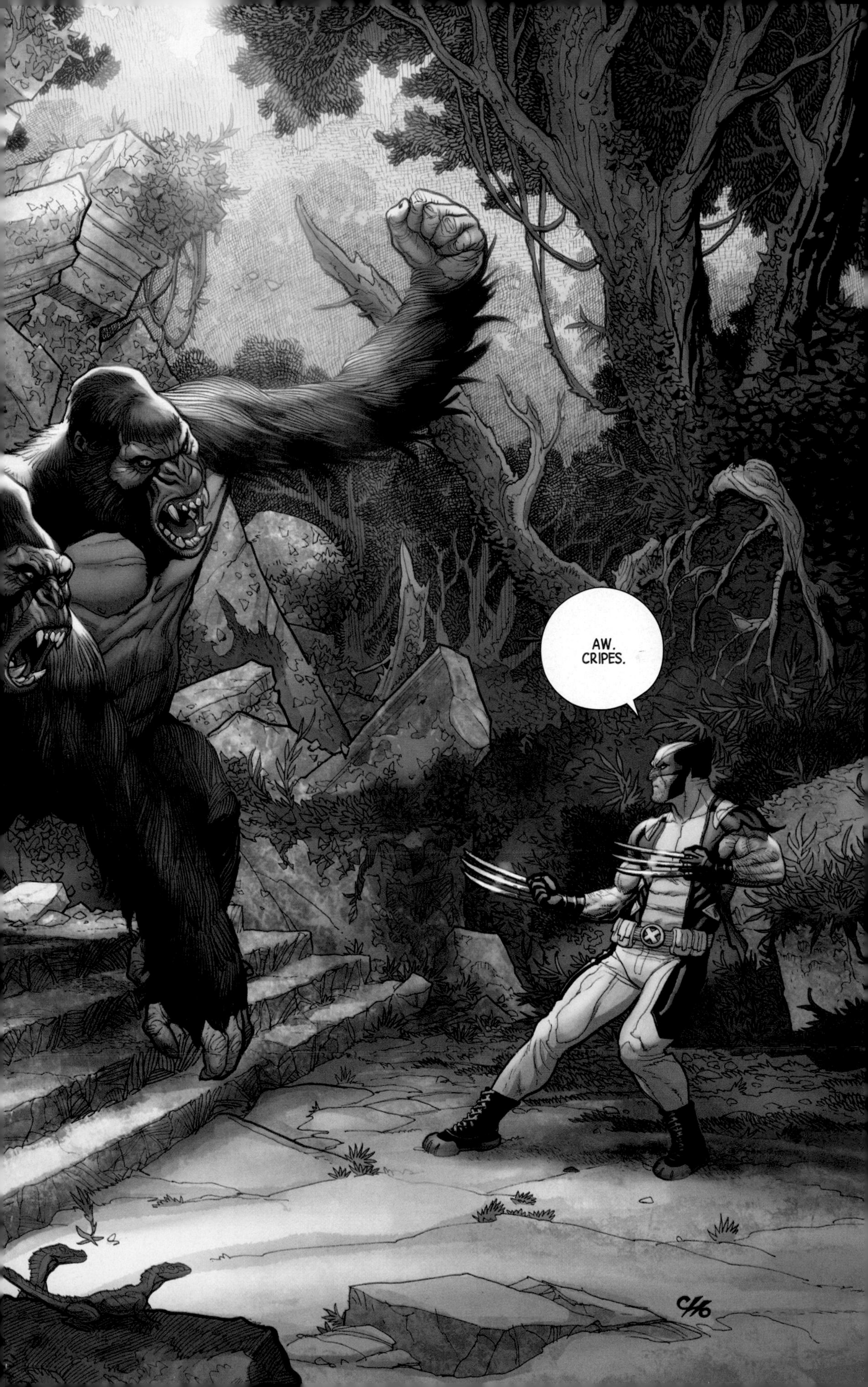
AW. CRIPES.
CHO

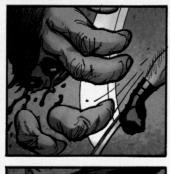

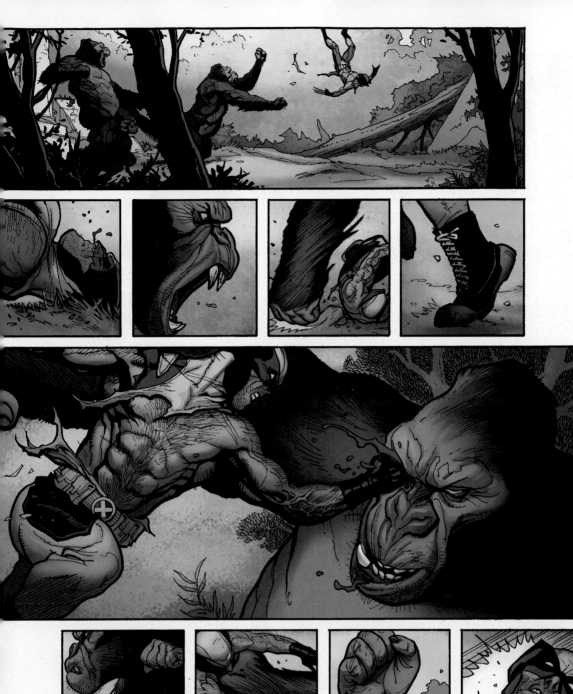

DISLOCATED RIGHT SHOULDER.

RUPTURED EARDRUM.

BOTH KNEES HYPEREXTENDED.

LACERATED SPINAL TENDONS.

TWISTED HIPS.

TORN RIGHT HAMSTRING.

I SHOULDN'T BE BREATHING...LET ALONE STANDING.

THE TEMPLE IS TWENTY YARDS AWAY. MIGHT AS WELL BE TWENTY MILES.

I THINK OF SHANNA. AND I KEEP GOING.

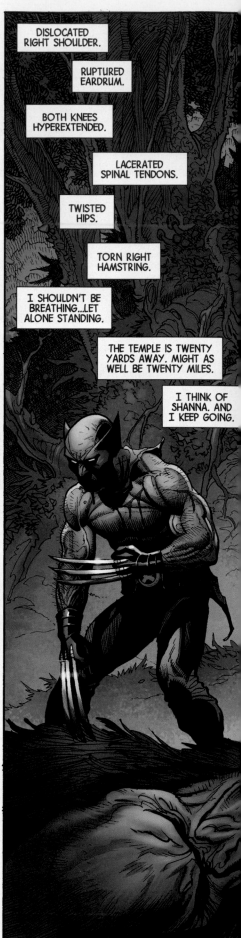

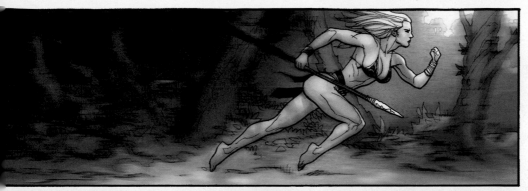

TIME TO GO HOME.

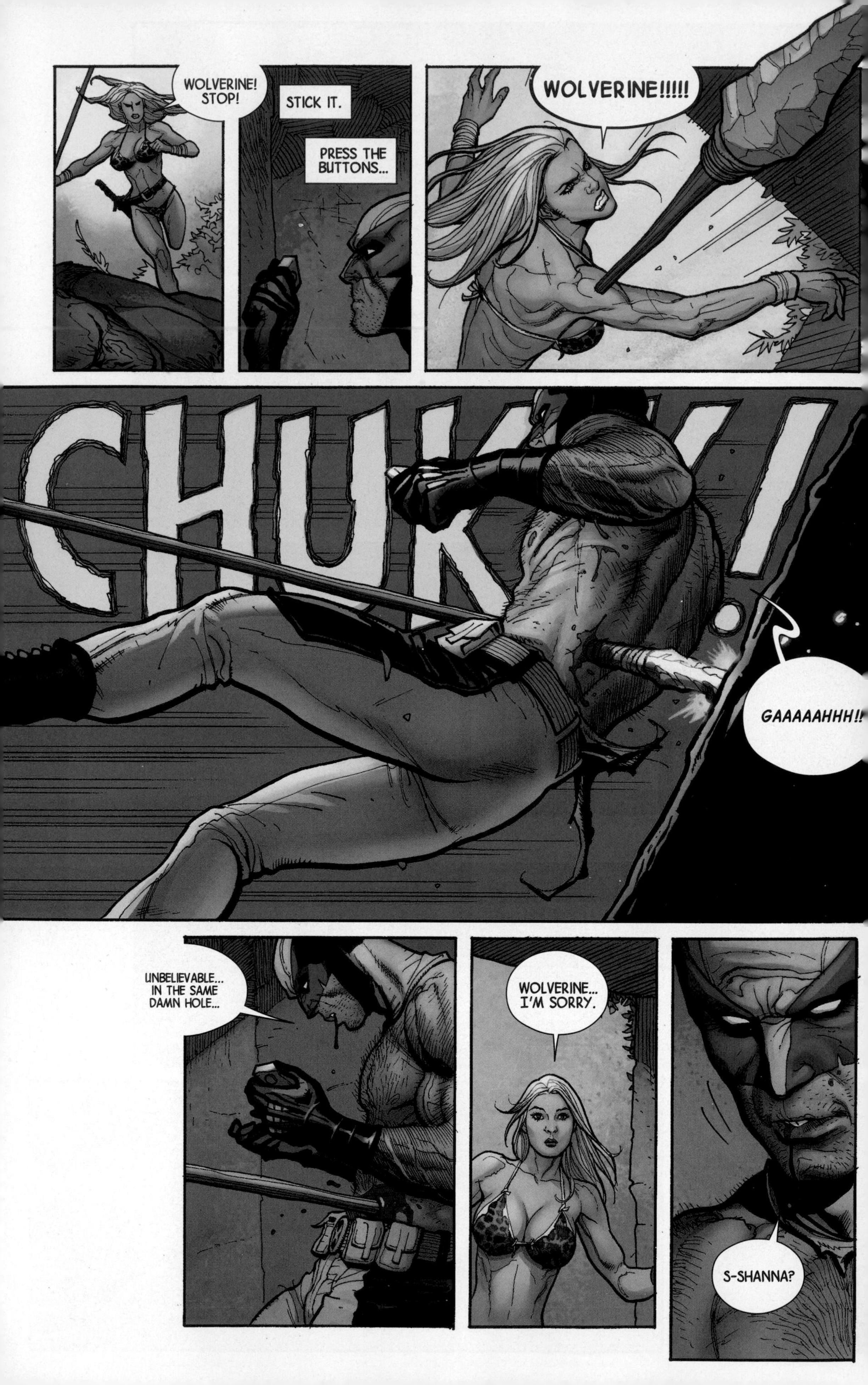
WOLVERINE! STOP!
STICK IT.
PRESS THE BUTTONS...
WOLVERINE!!!!!
CHUK!!
GAAAAAHHH!!
UNBELIEVABLE... IN THE SAME DAMN HOLE...
WOLVERINE... I'M SORRY.
S-SHANNA?

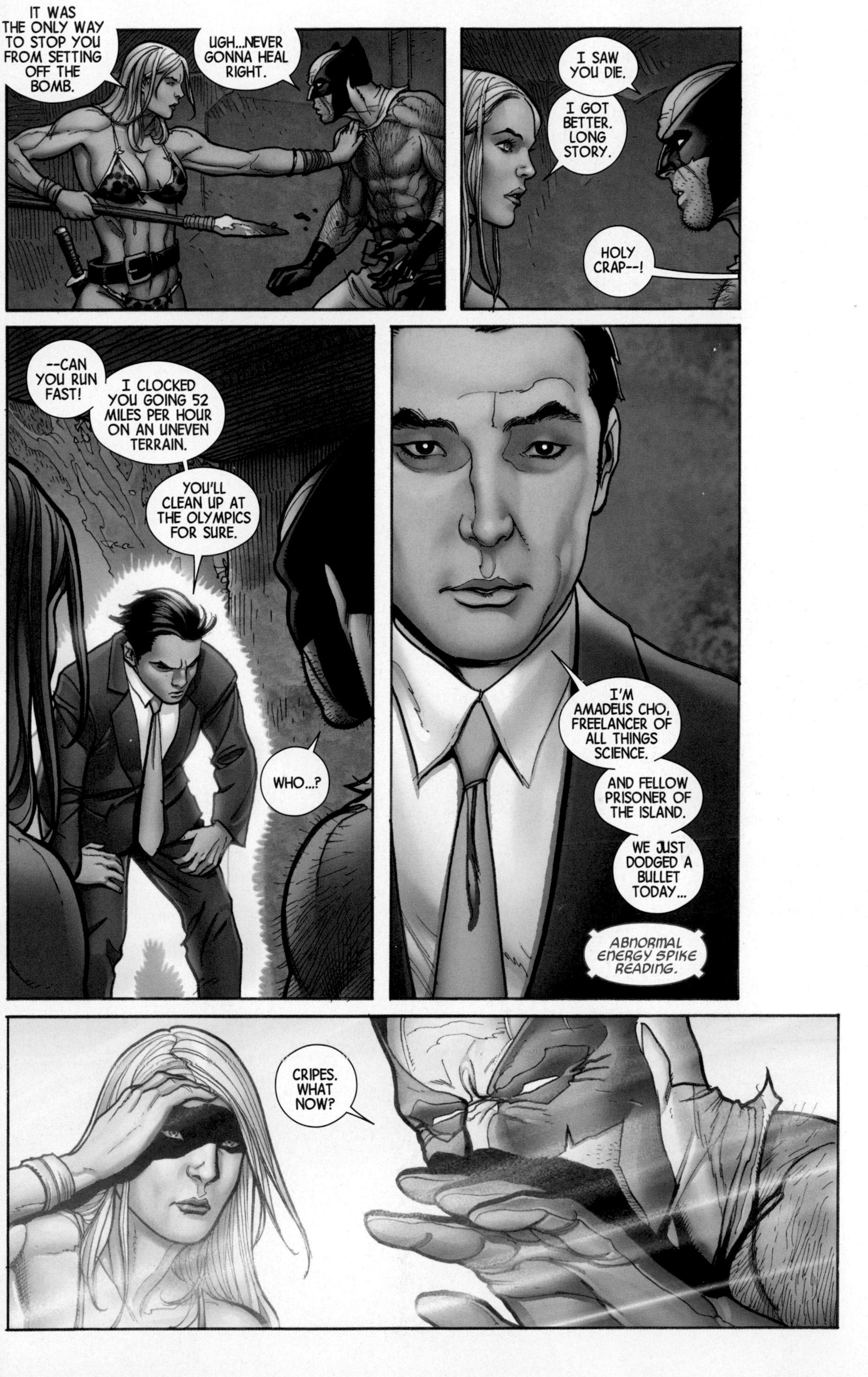
IT WAS THE ONLY WAY TO STOP YOU FROM SETTING OFF THE BOMB.
UGH...NEVER GONNA HEAL RIGHT.
I SAW YOU DIE.
I GOT BETTER. LONG STORY.
HOLY CRAP--!
--CAN YOU RUN FAST!
I CLOCKED YOU GOING 52 MILES PER HOUR ON AN UNEVEN TERRAIN.
YOU'LL CLEAN UP AT THE OLYMPICS FOR SURE.
WHO...?
I'M AMADEUS CHO, FREELANCER OF ALL THINGS SCIENCE.
AND FELLOW PRISONER OF THE ISLAND.
WE JUST DODGED A BULLET TODAY...
ABNORMAL ENERGY SPIKE READING.
CRIPES. WHAT NOW?

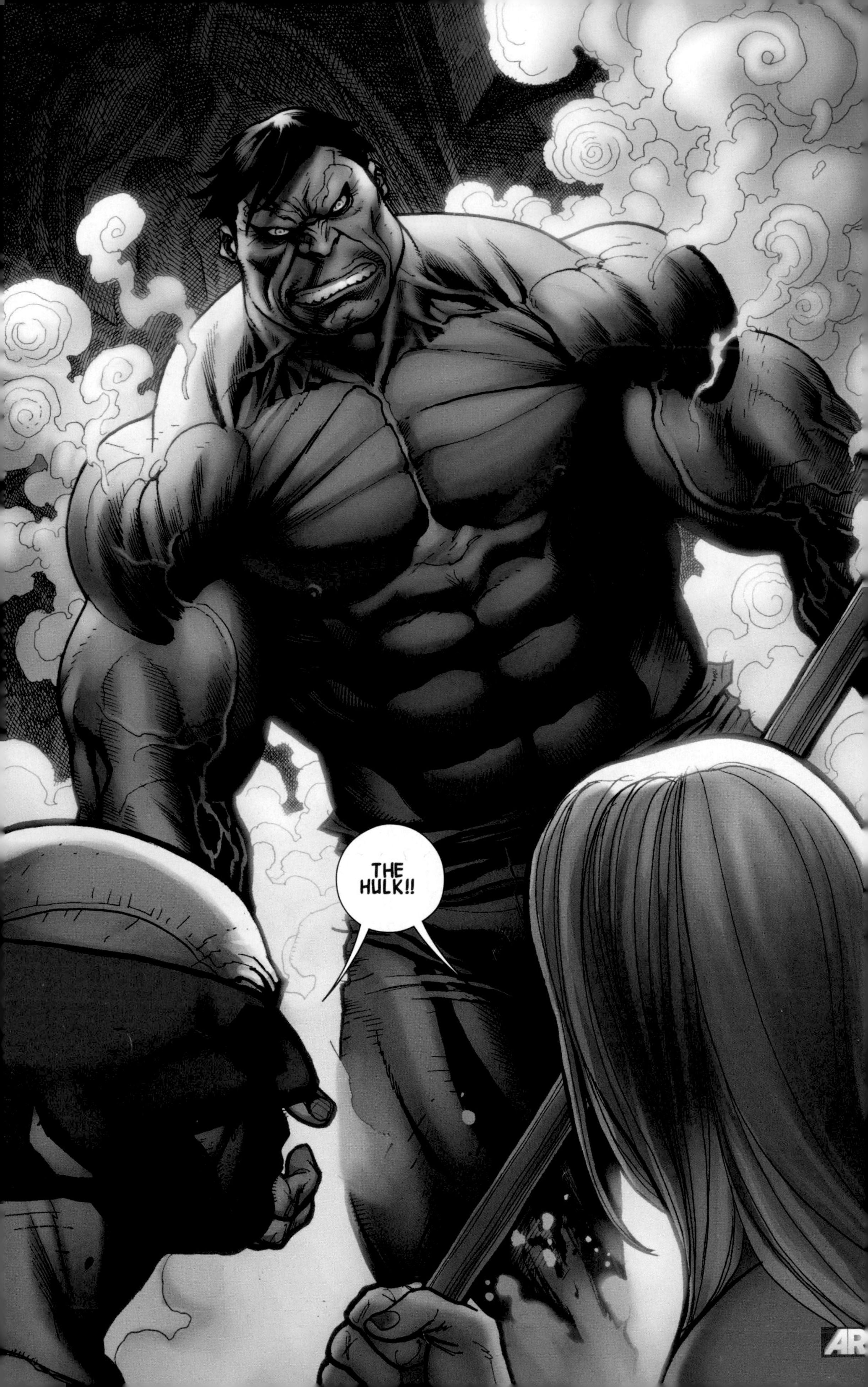
THE HULK!!

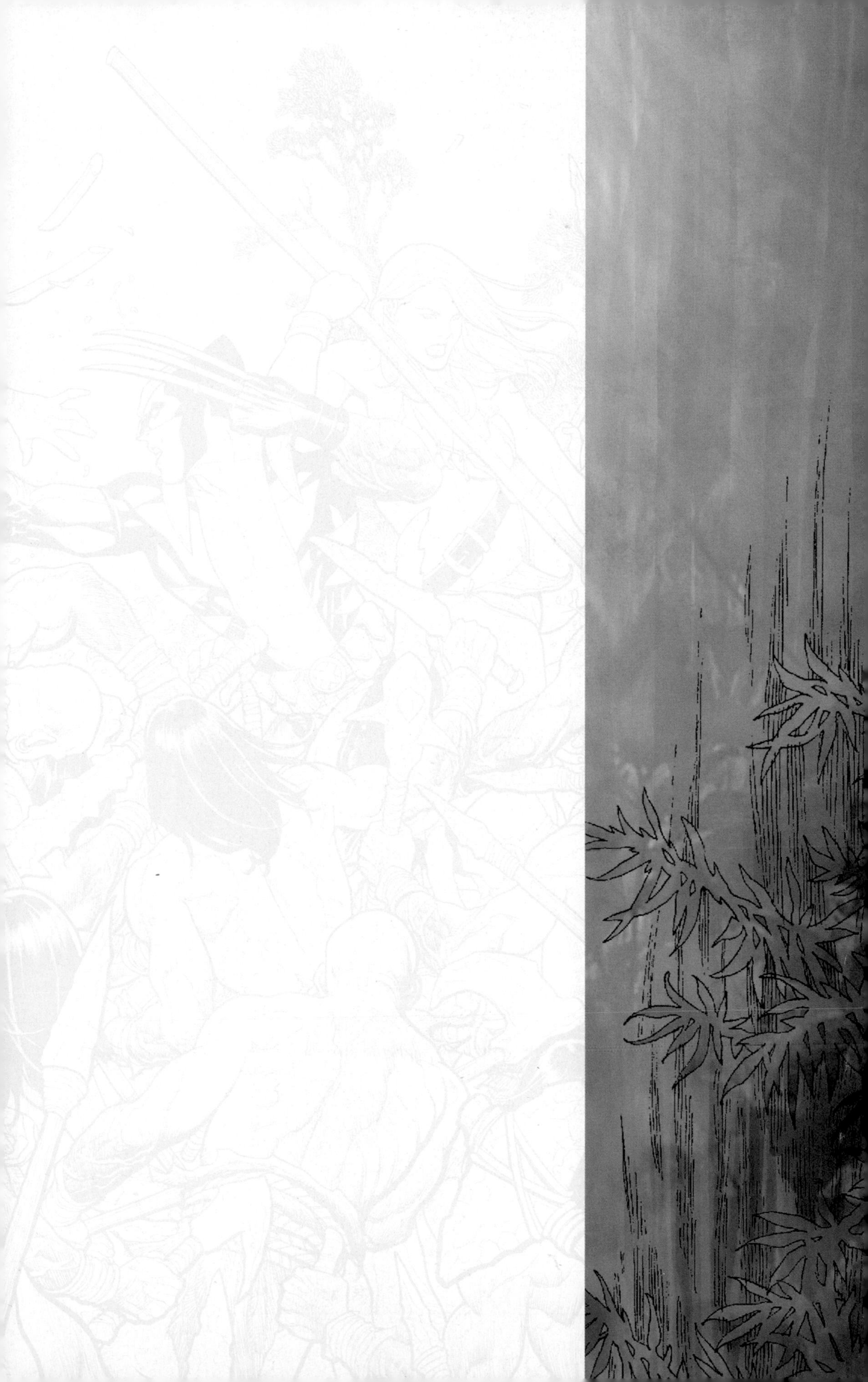

5

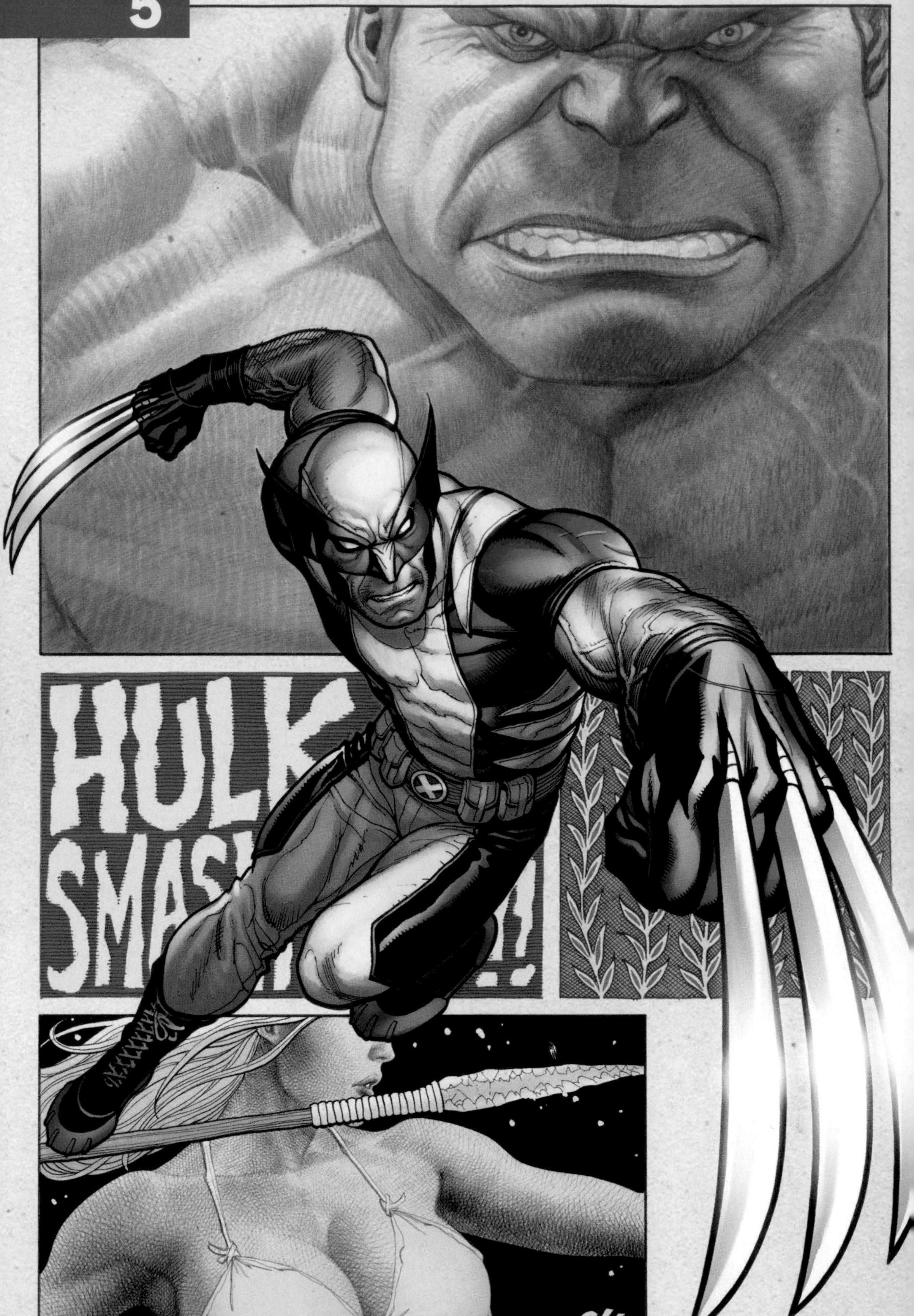
HULK
Keith CHO

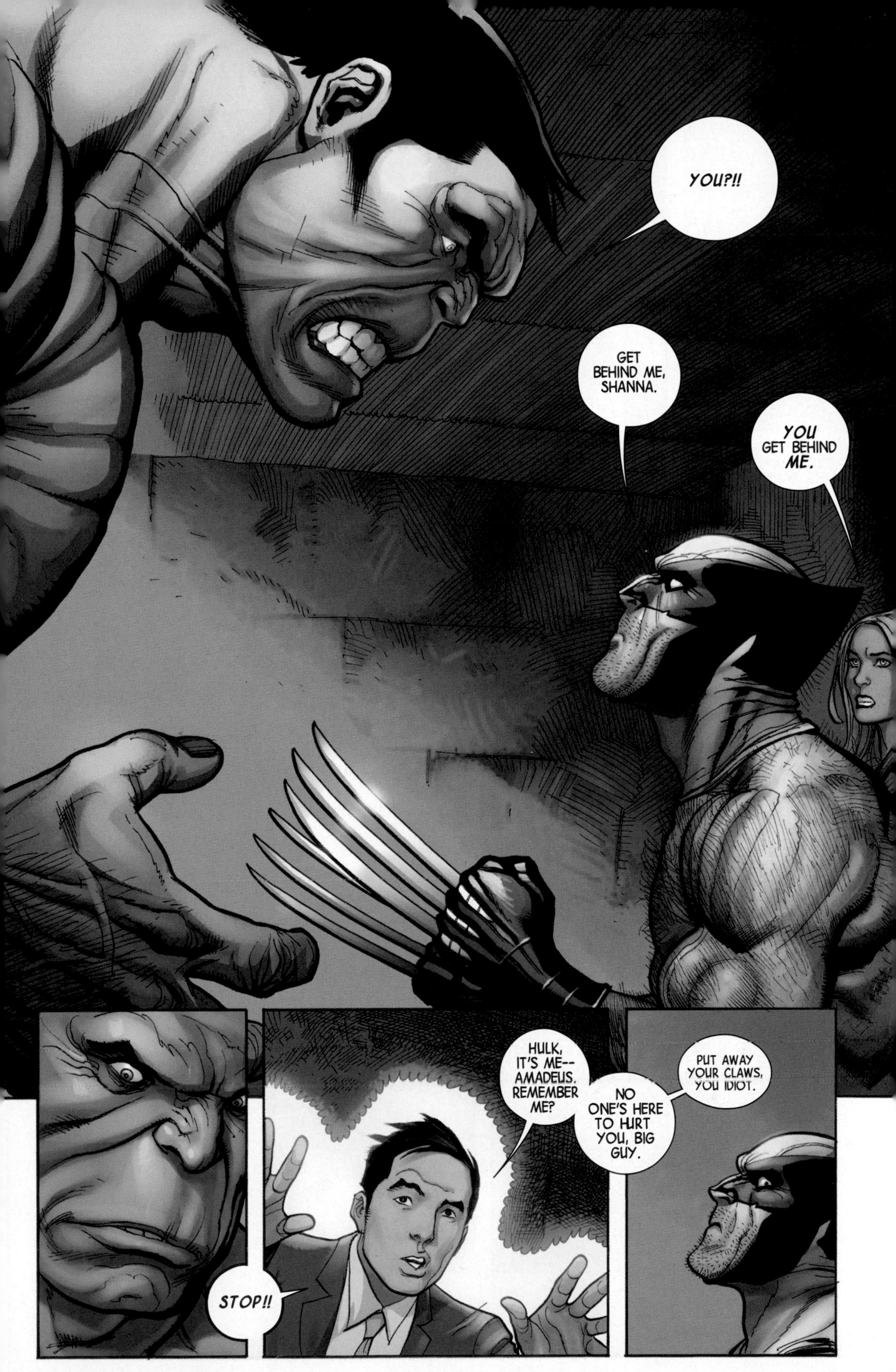

YOU?!!
GET BEHIND ME, SHANNA.
YOU GET BEHIND ME.
STOP!!
HULK, IT'S ME-- AMADEUS. REMEMBER ME?
NO ONE'S HERE TO HURT YOU, BIG GUY.
PUT AWAY YOUR CLAWS, YOU IDIOT.

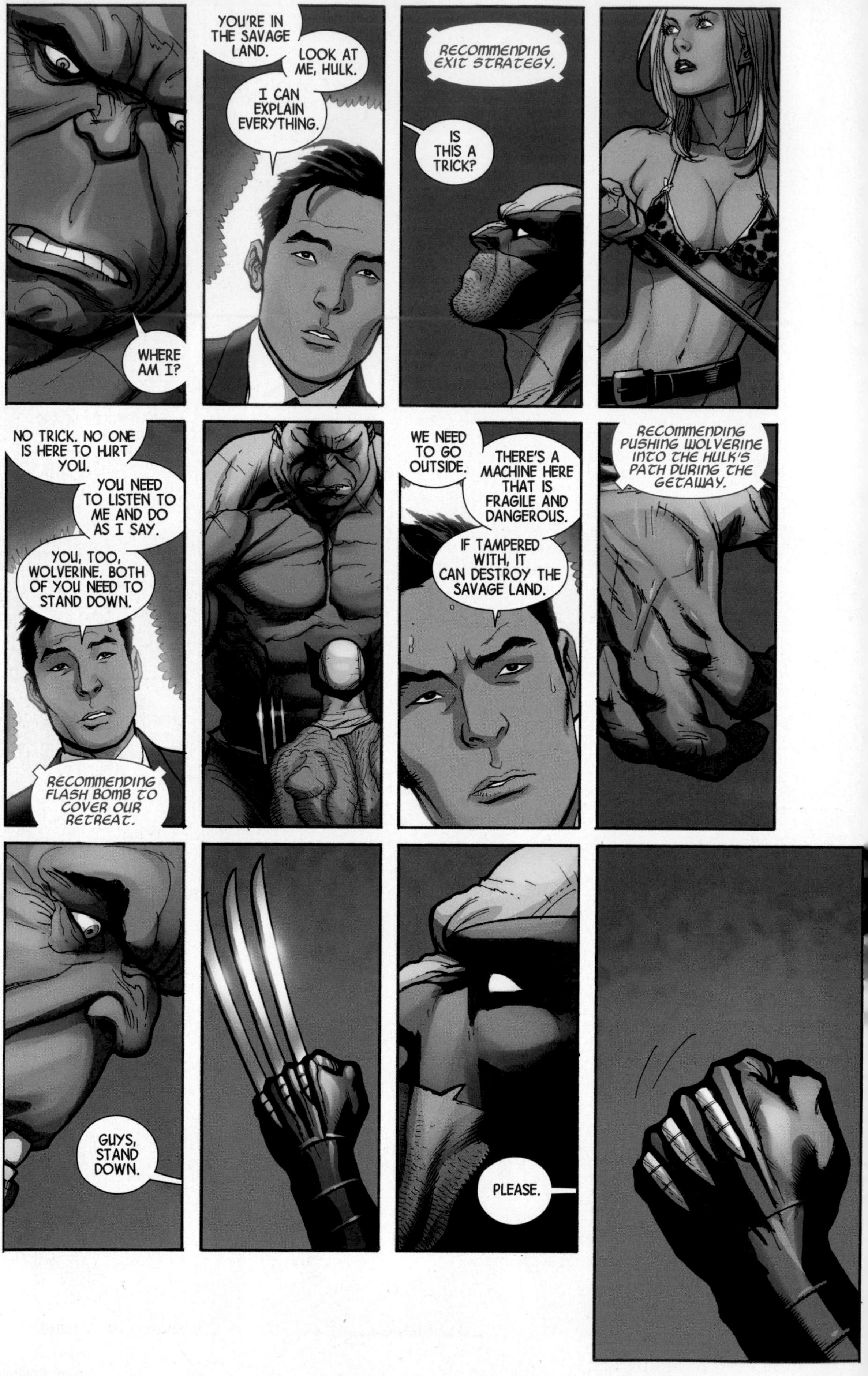
WHERE AM I?
YOU'RE IN THE SAVAGE LAND.
LOOK AT ME, HULK.
I CAN EXPLAIN EVERYTHING.
RECOMMENDING EXIT STRATEGY.
IS THIS A TRICK?
NO TRICK. NO ONE IS HERE TO HURT YOU.
YOU NEED TO LISTEN TO ME AND DO AS I SAY.
YOU, TOO, WOLVERINE. BOTH OF YOU NEED TO STAND DOWN.
RECOMMENDING FLASH BOMB TO COVER OUR RETREAT.
WE NEED TO GO OUTSIDE.
THERE'S A MACHINE HERE THAT IS FRAGILE AND DANGEROUS.
IF TAMPERED WITH, IT CAN DESTROY THE SAVAGE LAND.
RECOMMENDING PUSHING WOLVERINE INTO THE HULK'S PATH DURING THE GETAWAY.
GUYS, STAND DOWN.
PLEASE.

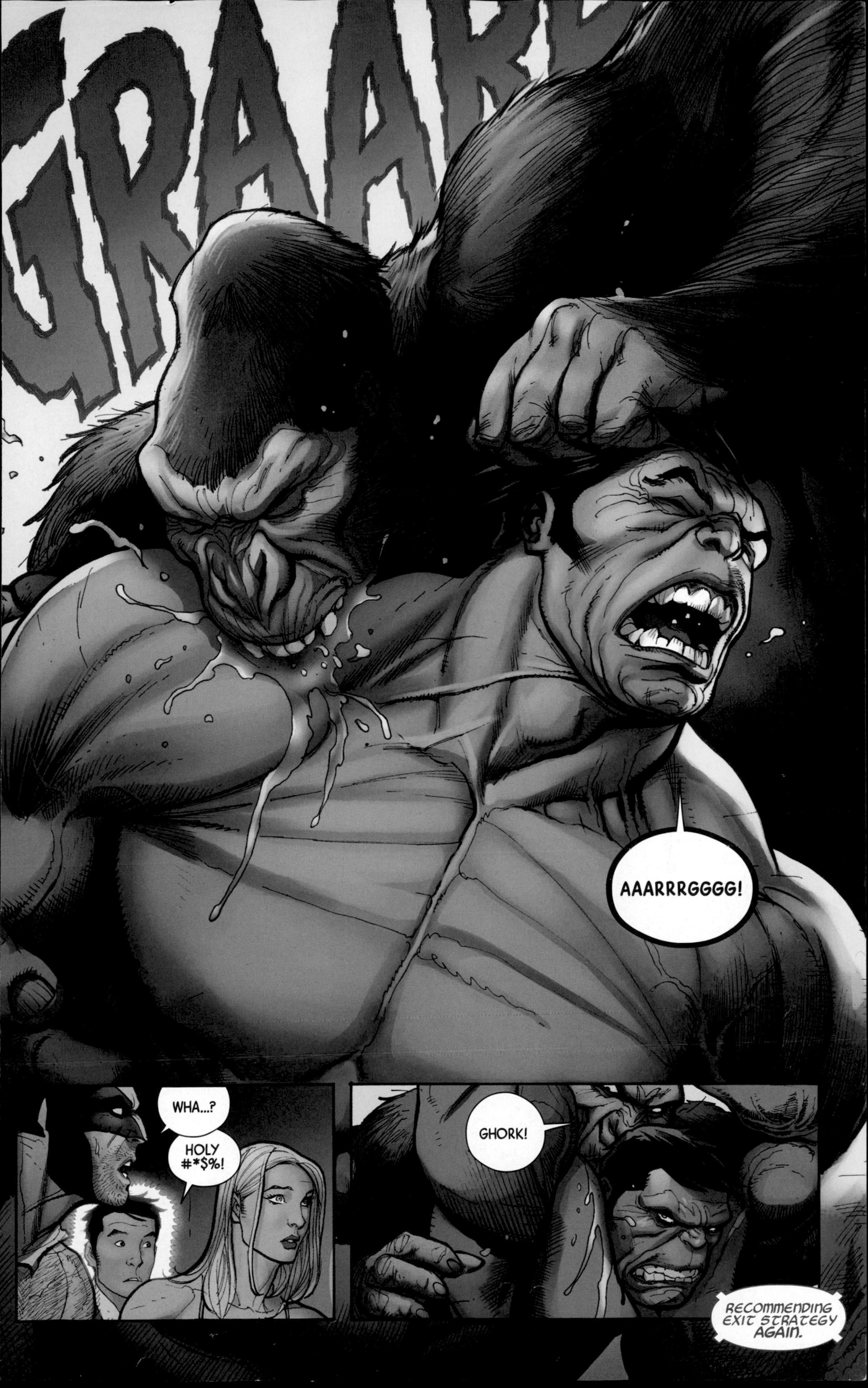
GRAAR
AAARRRGGGG!
WHA...?
HOLY #*$%!
GHORK!
RECOMMENDING EXIT STRATEGY AGAIN.

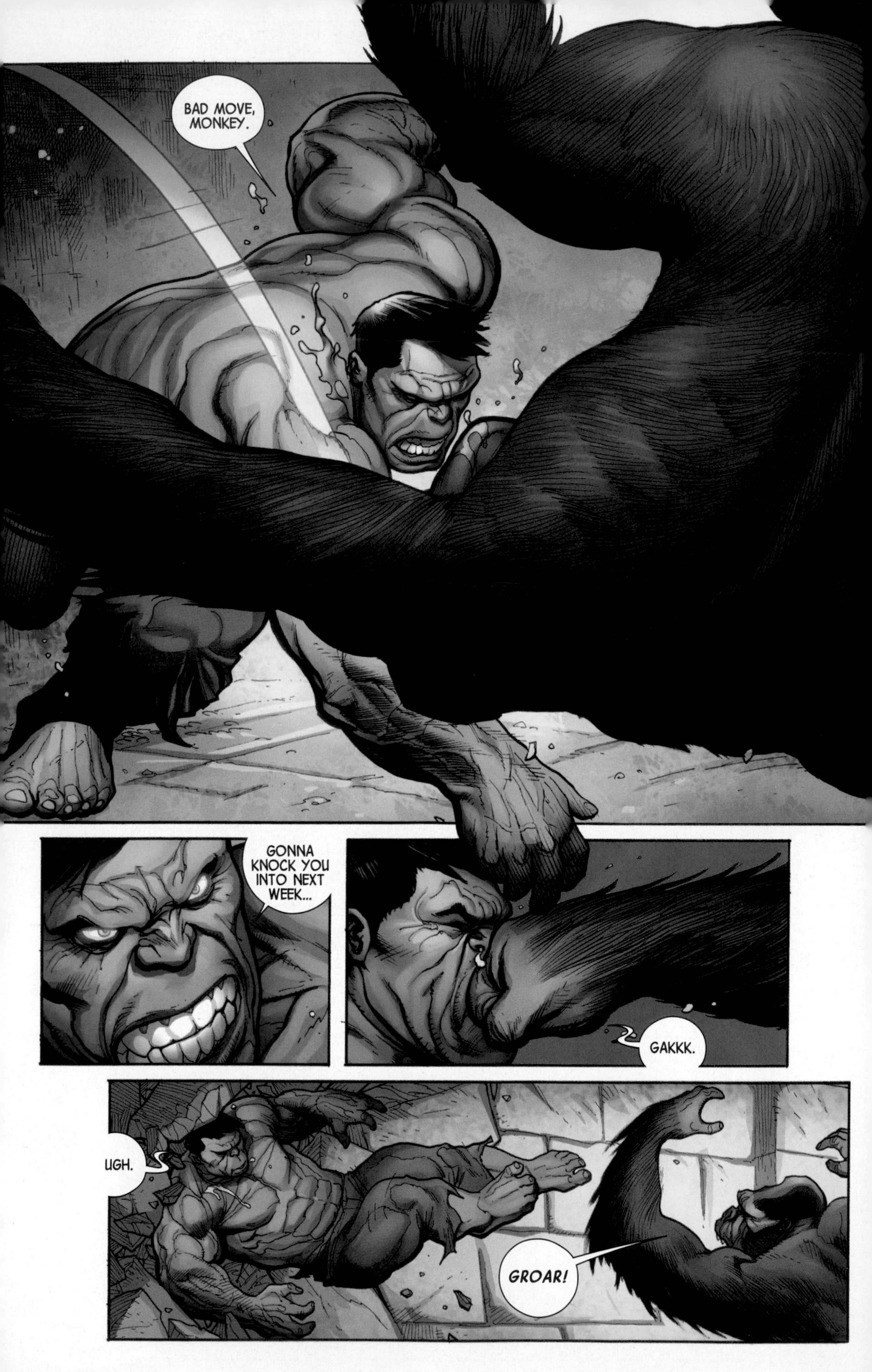
BAD MOVE, MONKEY.
GONNA KNOCK YOU INTO NEXT WEEK...
GAKKK.
UGH.
GROAR!

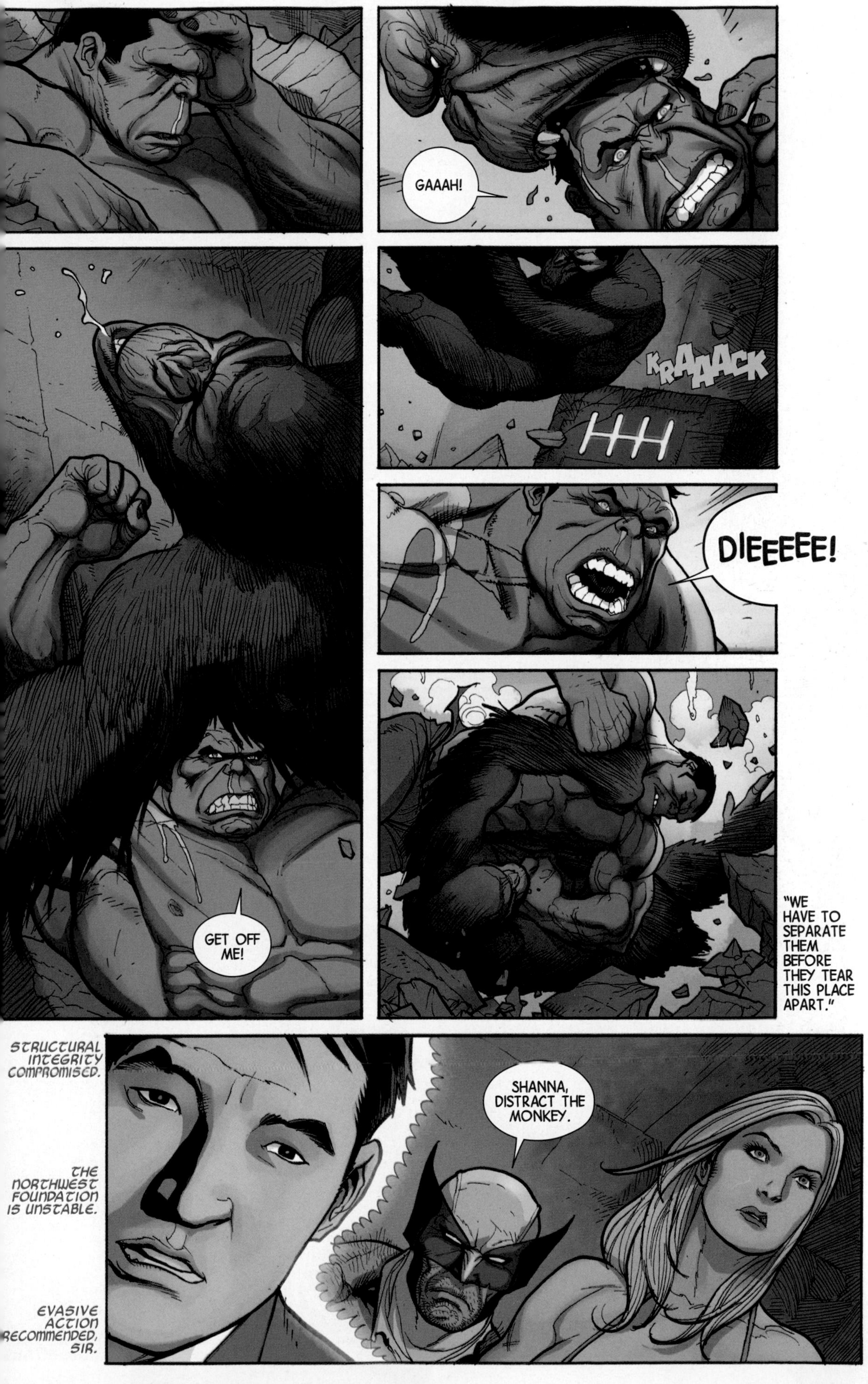
GAAAH!
KRAAACK
DIEEEEE!
GET OFF ME!
"WE HAVE TO SEPARATE THEM BEFORE THEY TEAR THIS PLACE APART."
STRUCTURAL INTEGRITY COMPROMISED.
SHANNA, DISTRACT THE MONKEY.
THE NORTHWEST FOUNDATION IS UNSTABLE.
EVASIVE ACTION RECOMMENDED, SIR.

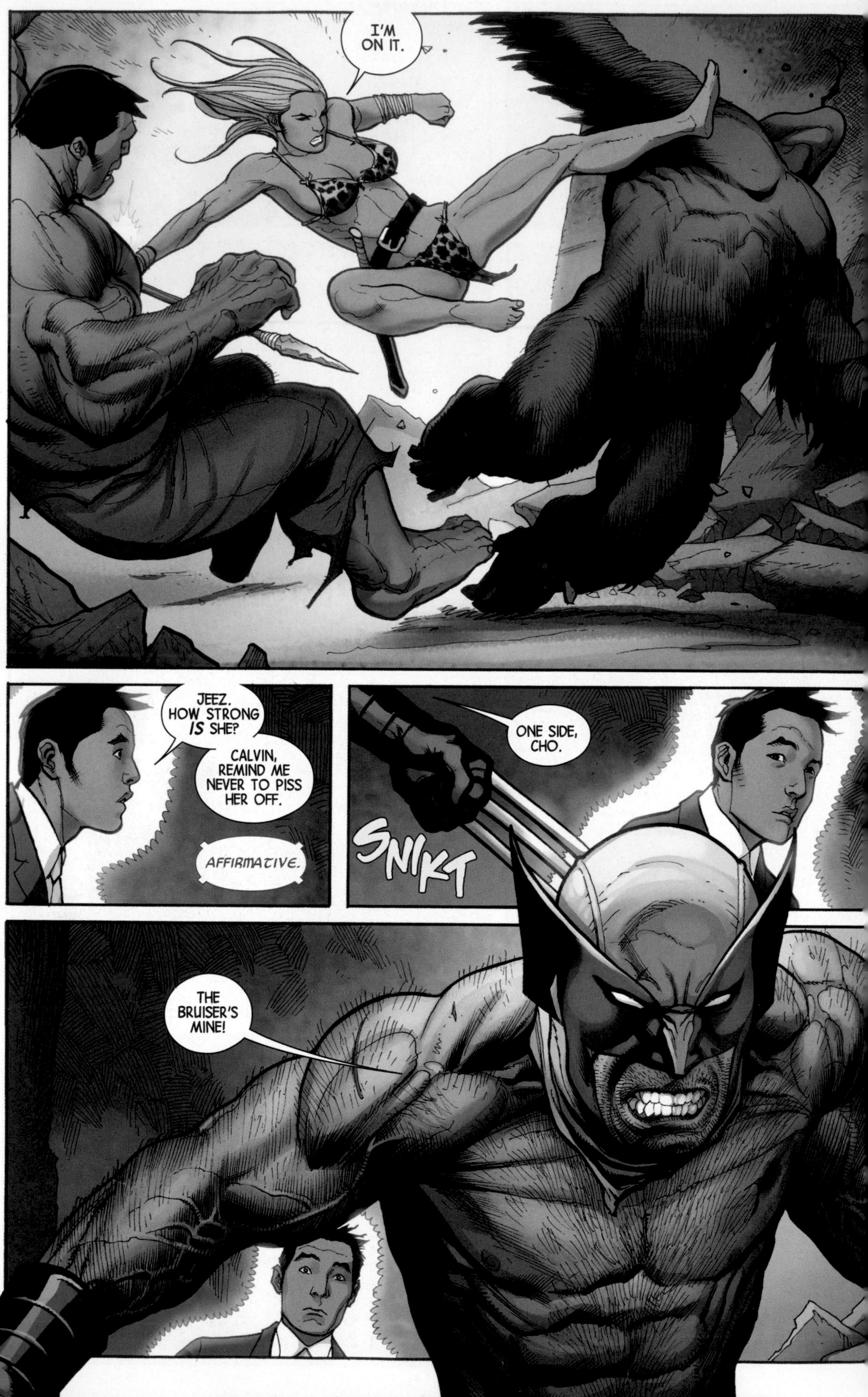
I'M ON IT.
JEEZ. HOW STRONG IS SHE?
CALVIN, REMIND ME NEVER TO PISS HER OFF.
AFFIRMATIVE.
ONE SIDE, CHO.
SNIKT
THE BRUISER'S MINE!

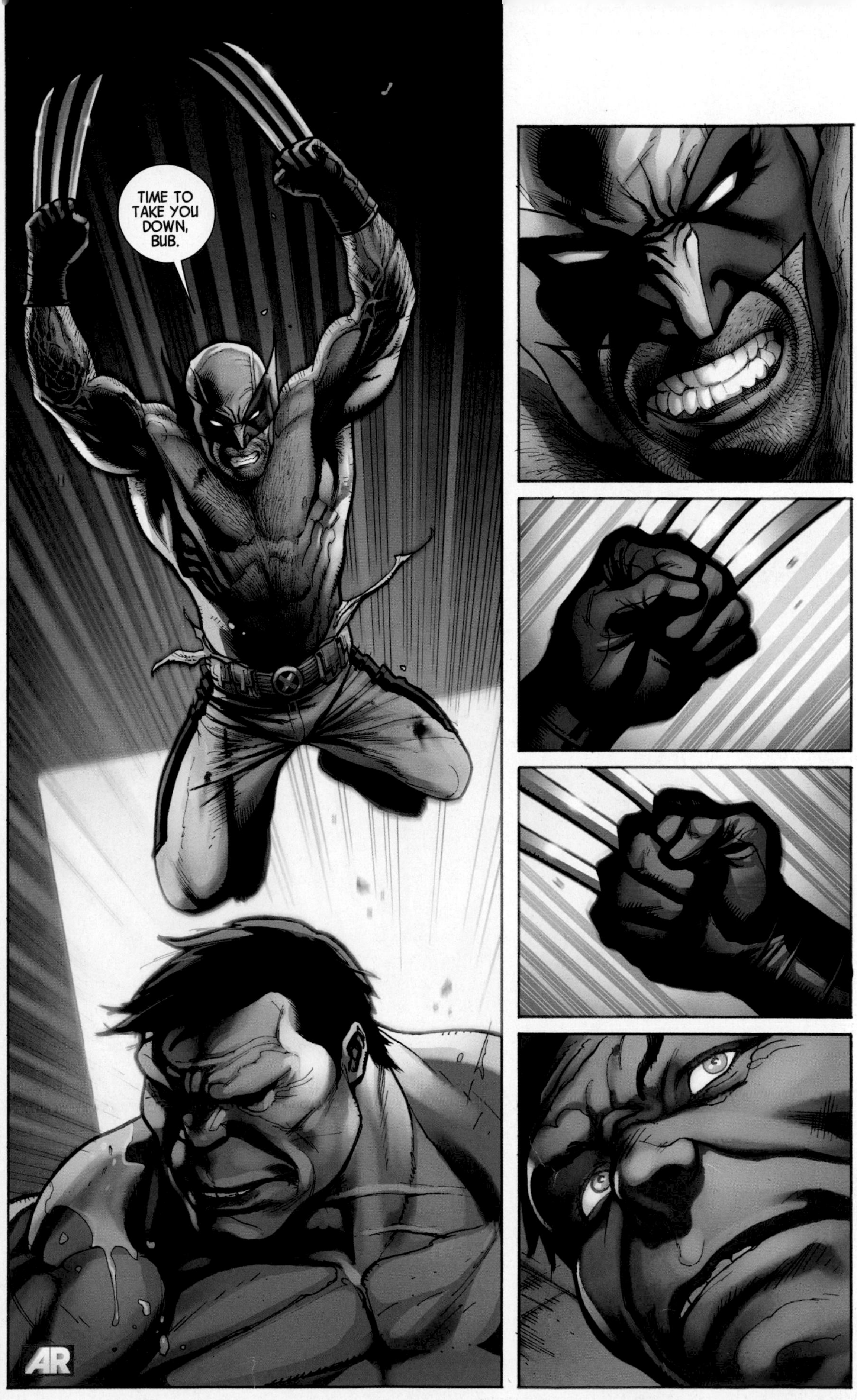
TIME TO TAKE YOU DOWN, BUB.
AR

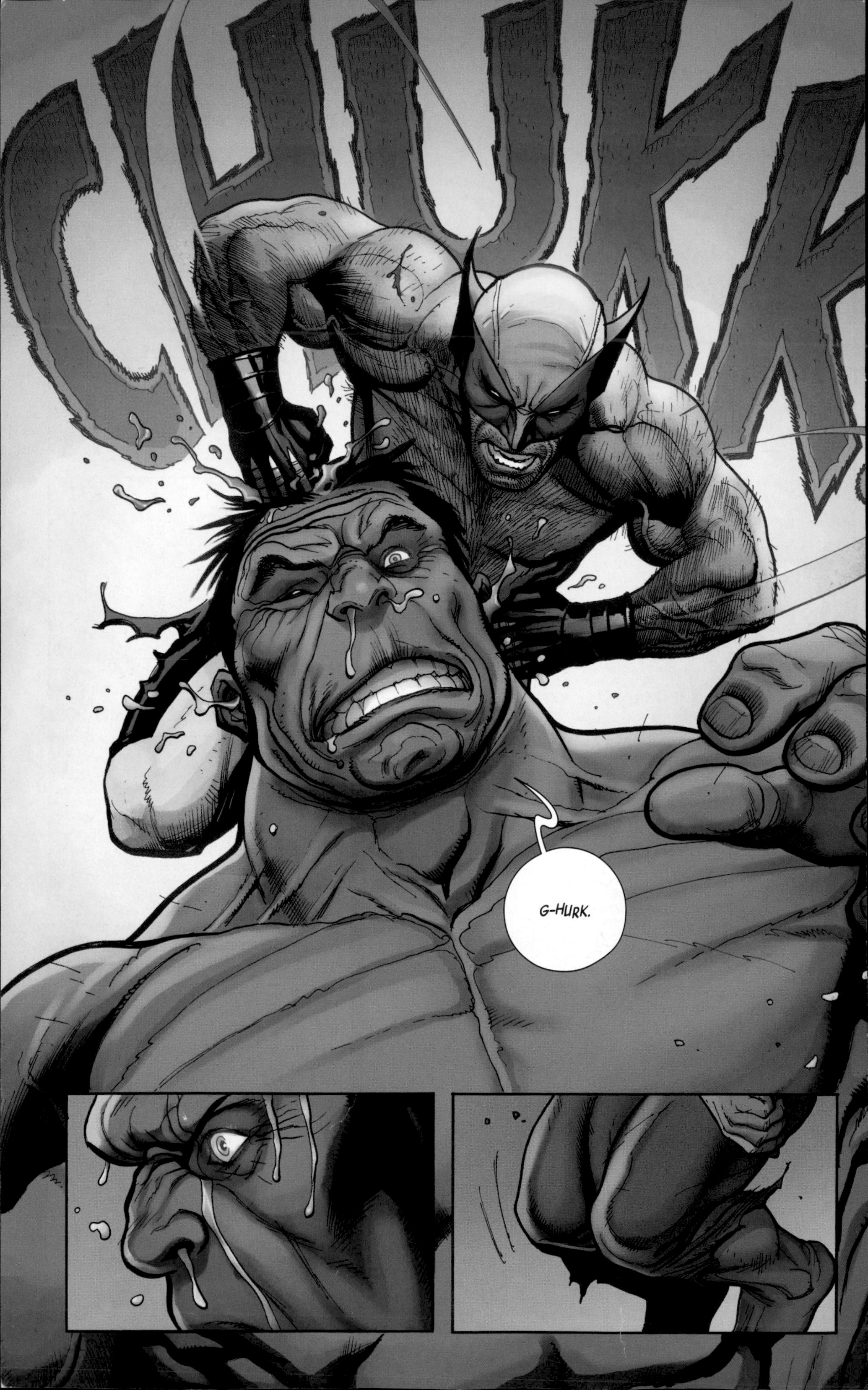
G-HURK.

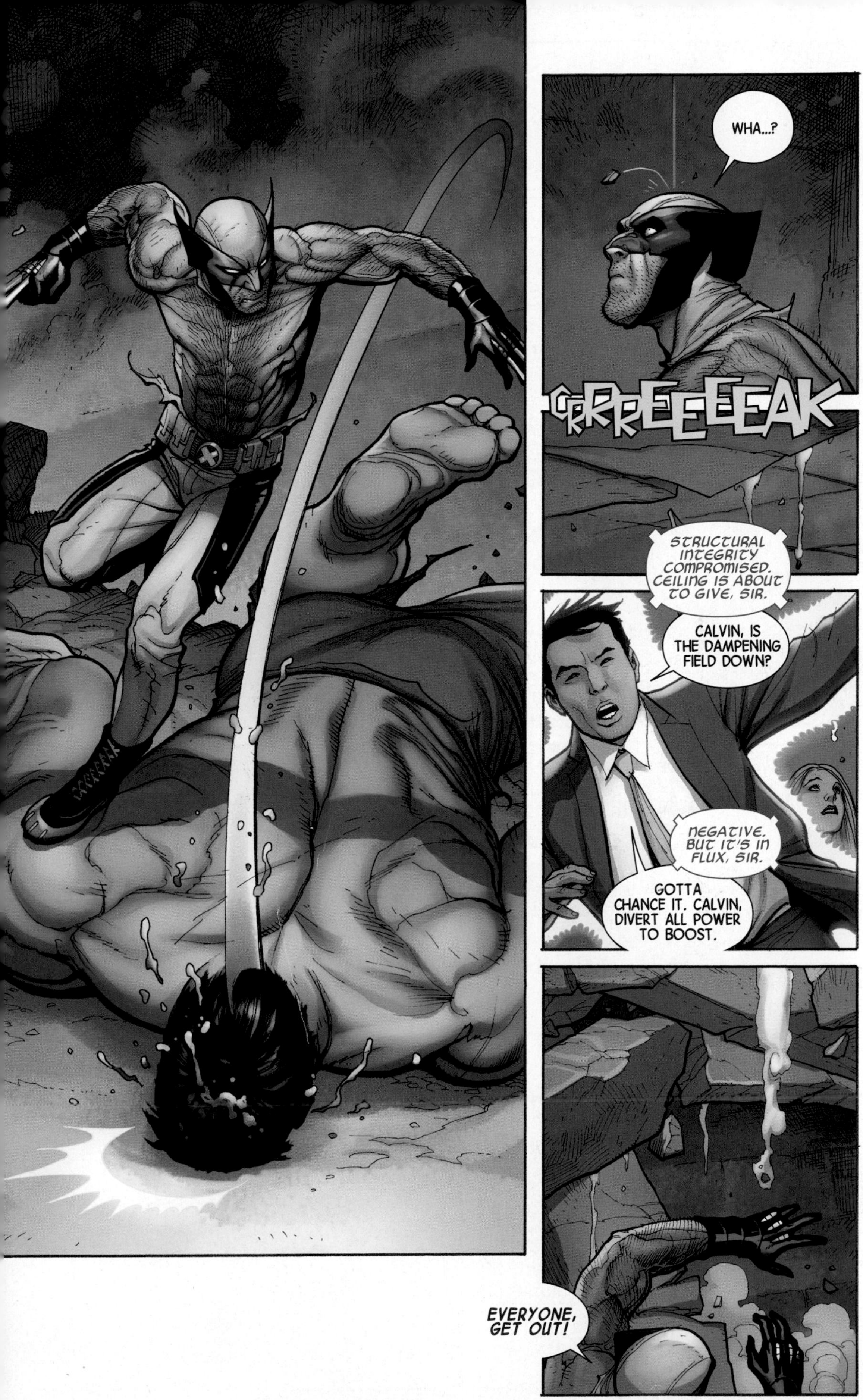
WHA...?
CRRRREEEEEAK
STRUCTURAL INTEGRITY COMPROMISED. CEILING IS ABOUT TO GIVE, SIR.
CALVIN, IS THE DAMPENING FIELD DOWN?
NEGATIVE. BUT IT'S IN FLUX, SIR.
GOTTA CHANCE IT. CALVIN, DIVERT ALL POWER TO BOOST.
EVERYONE, GET OUT!

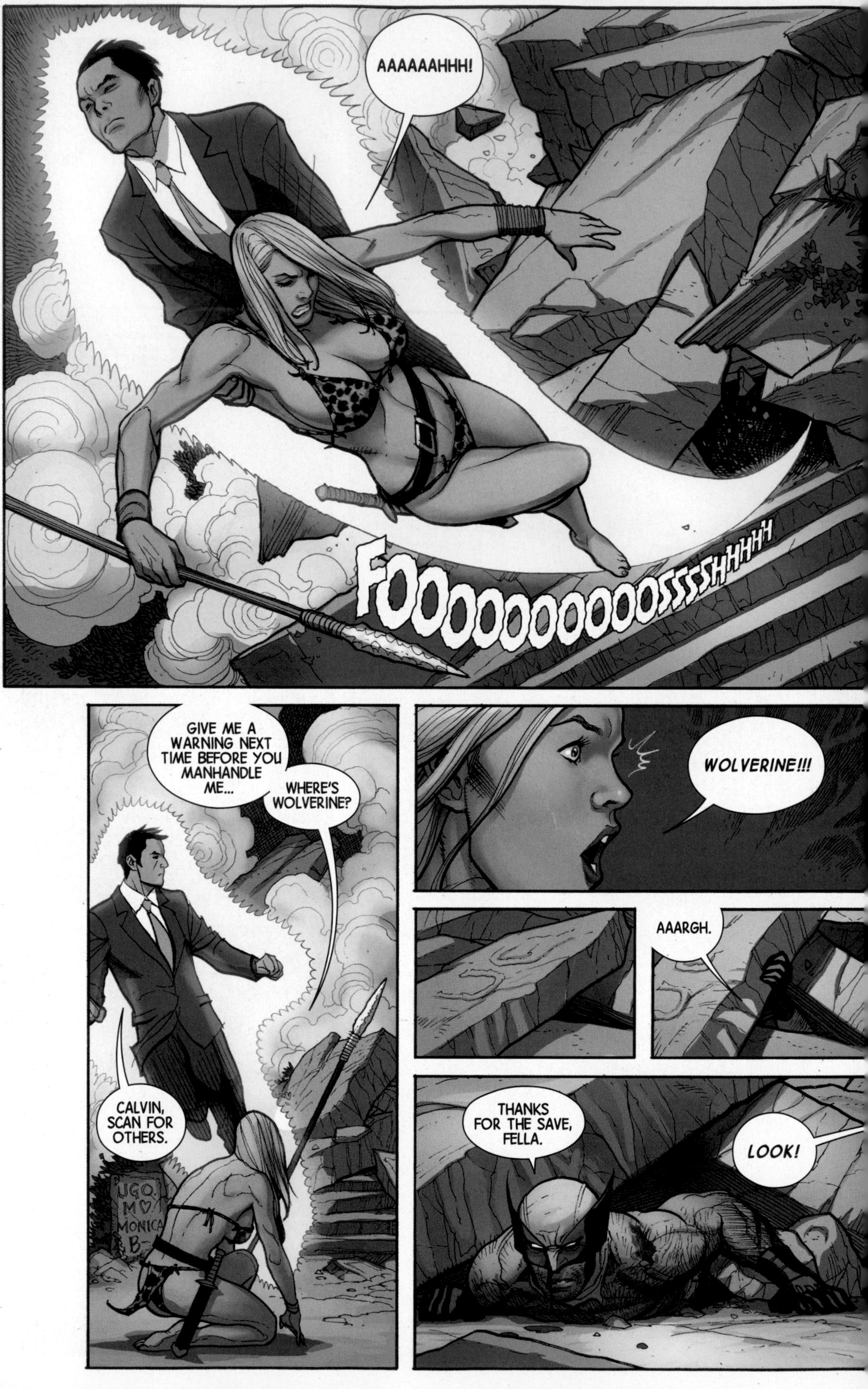
AAAAAAHHH!
FOOOOOOOOOOOSSSSSHHHHH
GIVE ME A WARNING NEXT TIME BEFORE YOU MANHANDLE ME...
WHERE'S WOLVERINE?
CALVIN, SCAN FOR OTHERS.
UGO M♡ MONICA B.
WOLVERINE!!!
AAARGH.
THANKS FOR THE SAVE, FELLA.
LOOK!

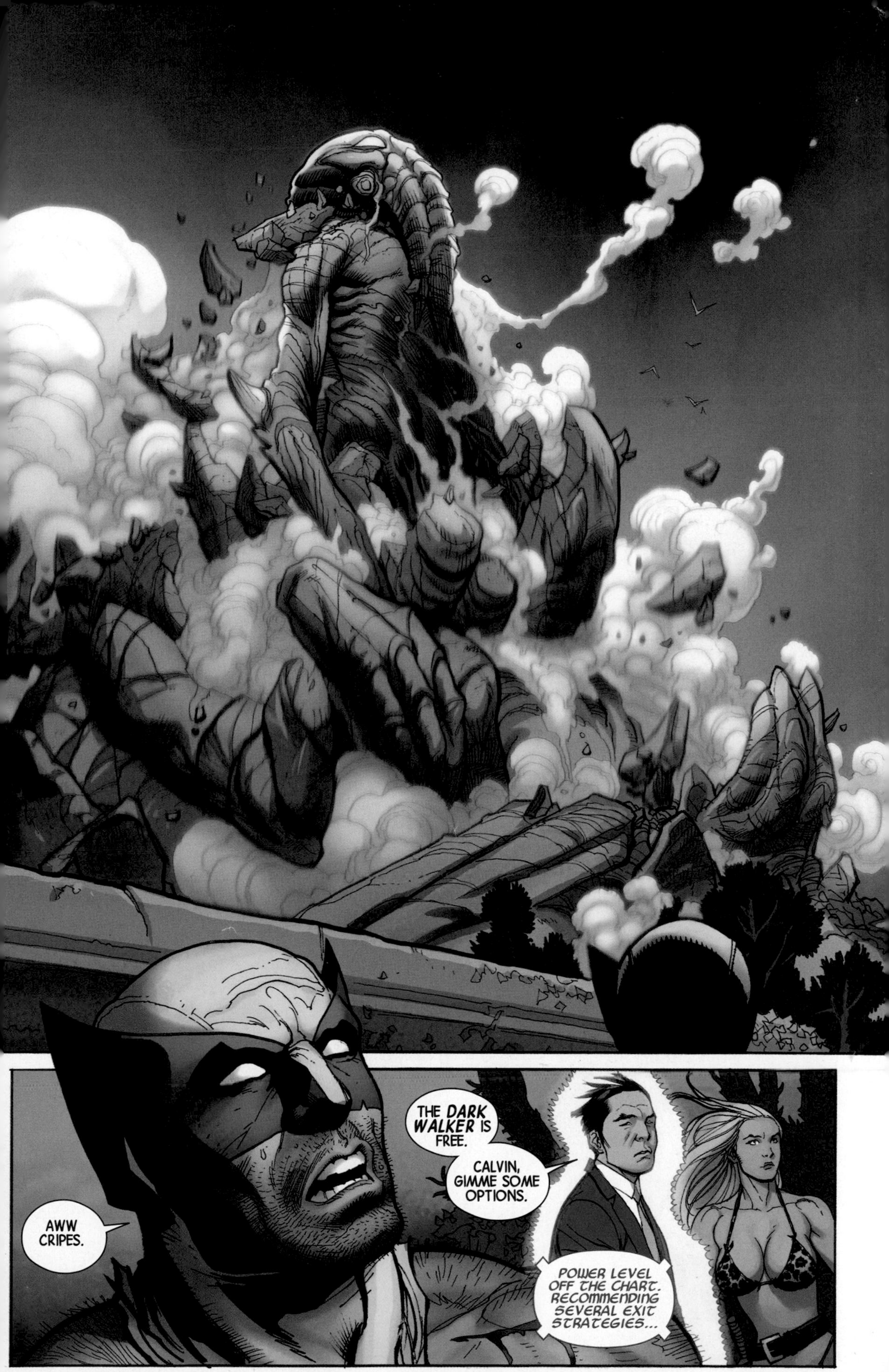
THE DARK WALKER IS FREE.
CALVIN, GIMME SOME OPTIONS.
AWW CRIPES.
POWER LEVEL OFF THE CHART. RECOMMENDING SEVERAL EXIT STRATEGIES...

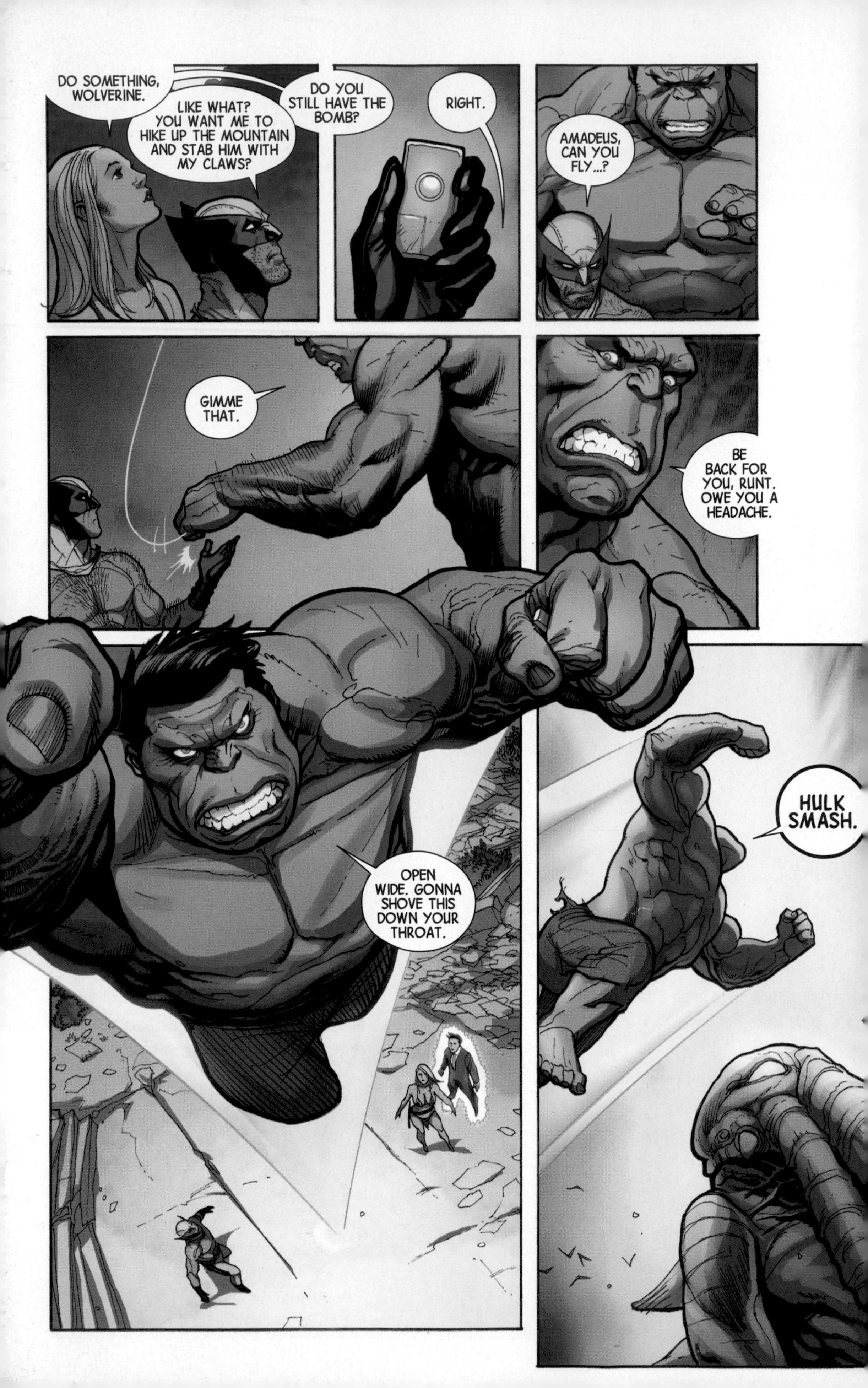
DO SOMETHING, WOLVERINE.
LIKE WHAT? YOU WANT ME TO HIKE UP THE MOUNTAIN AND STAB HIM WITH MY CLAWS?
DO YOU STILL HAVE THE BOMB?
RIGHT.
AMADEUS, CAN YOU FLY...?
GIMME THAT.
BE BACK FOR YOU, RUNT. OWE YOU A HEADACHE.
OPEN WIDE. GONNA SHOVE THIS DOWN YOUR THROAT.
HULK SMASH.

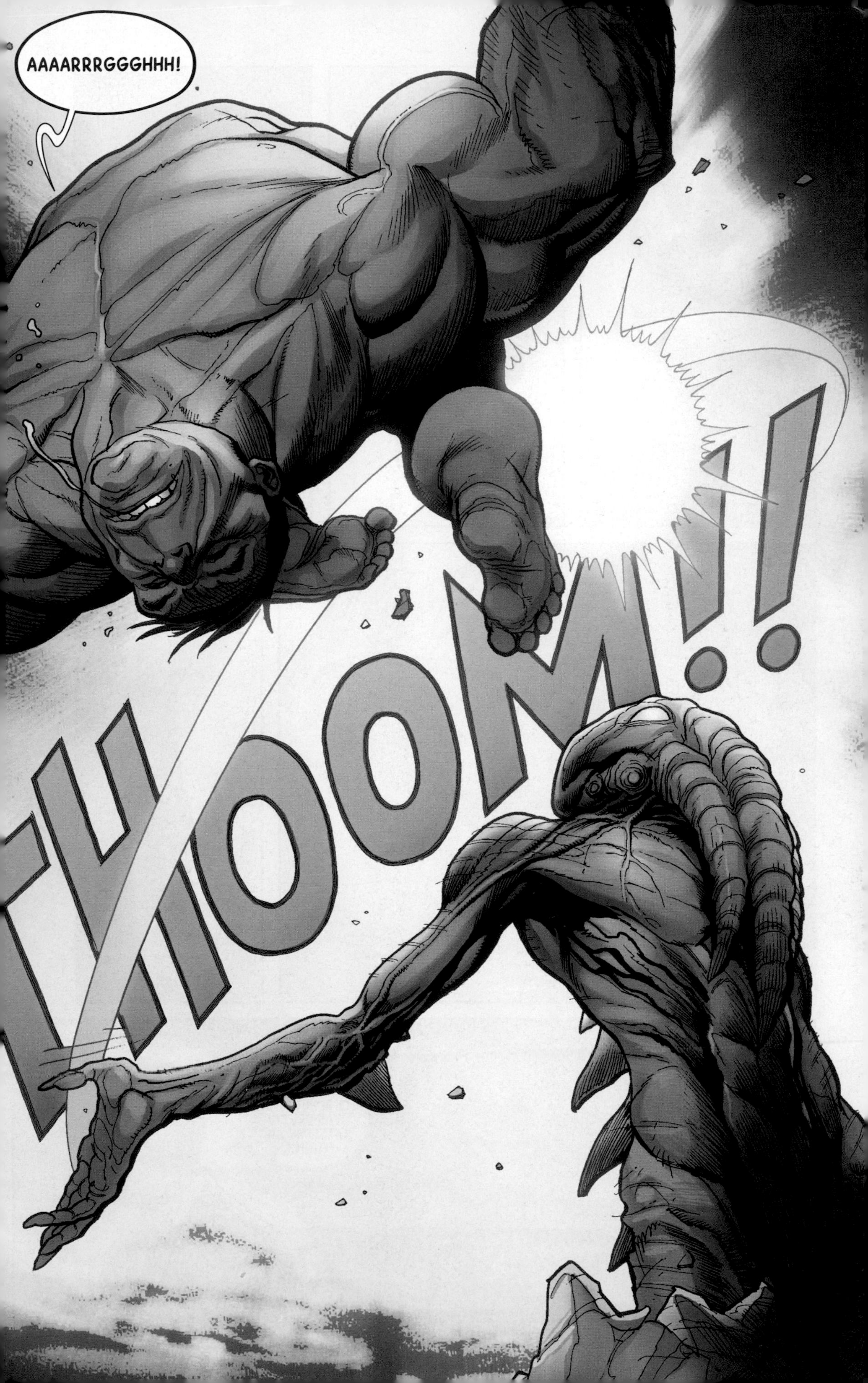
AAAARRRGGGHHH!
THOOOM!!

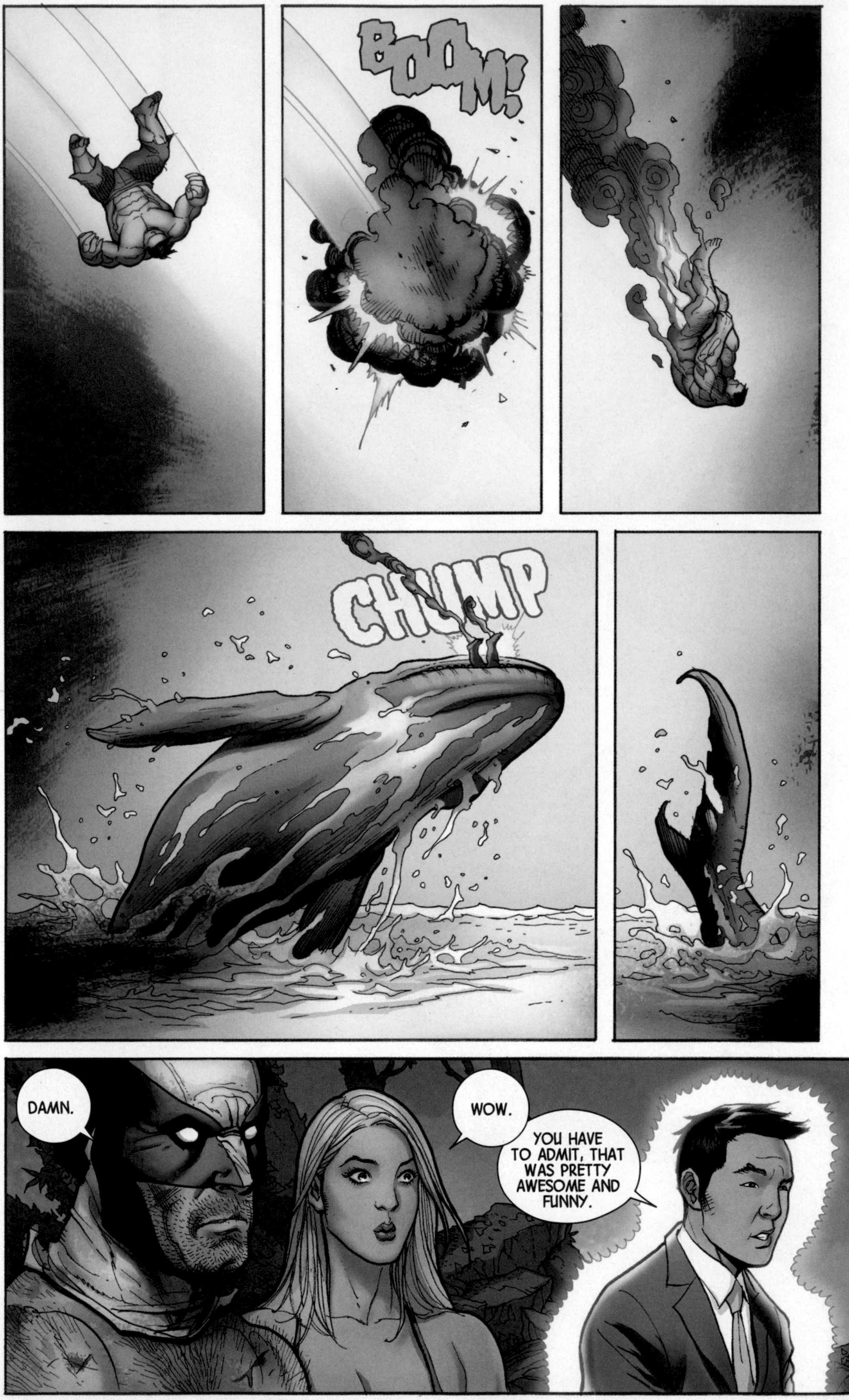
BOOM!
CHUMP
DAMN.
WOW.
YOU HAVE TO ADMIT, THAT WAS PRETTY AWESOME AND FUNNY.

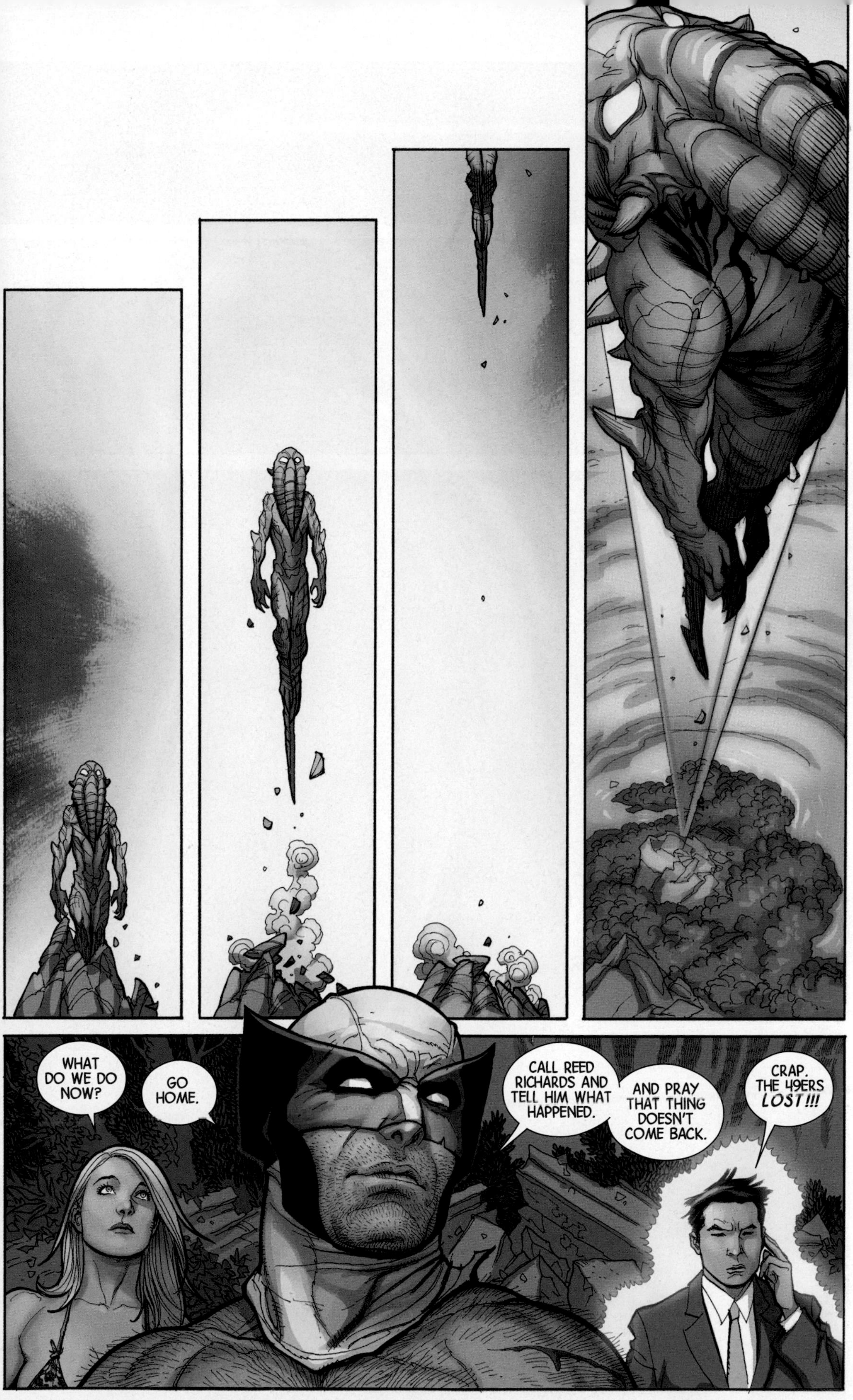
WHAT DO WE DO NOW?
GO HOME.
CALL REED RICHARDS AND TELL HIM WHAT HAPPENED.
AND PRAY THAT THING DOESN'T COME BACK.
CRAP. THE 49ERS LOST!!!

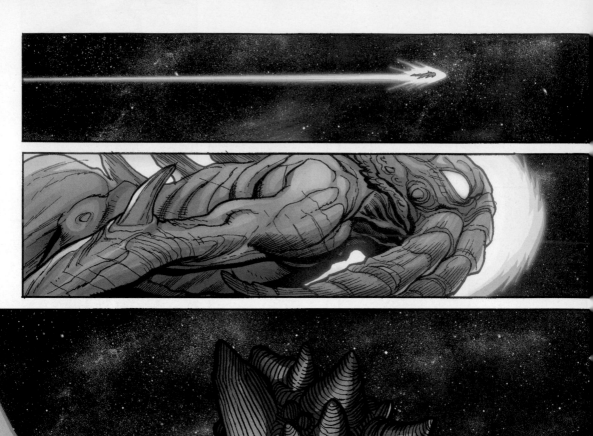

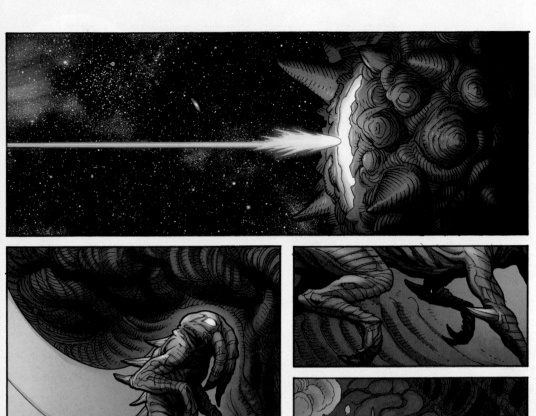

MASTER VISHER-RAKK...

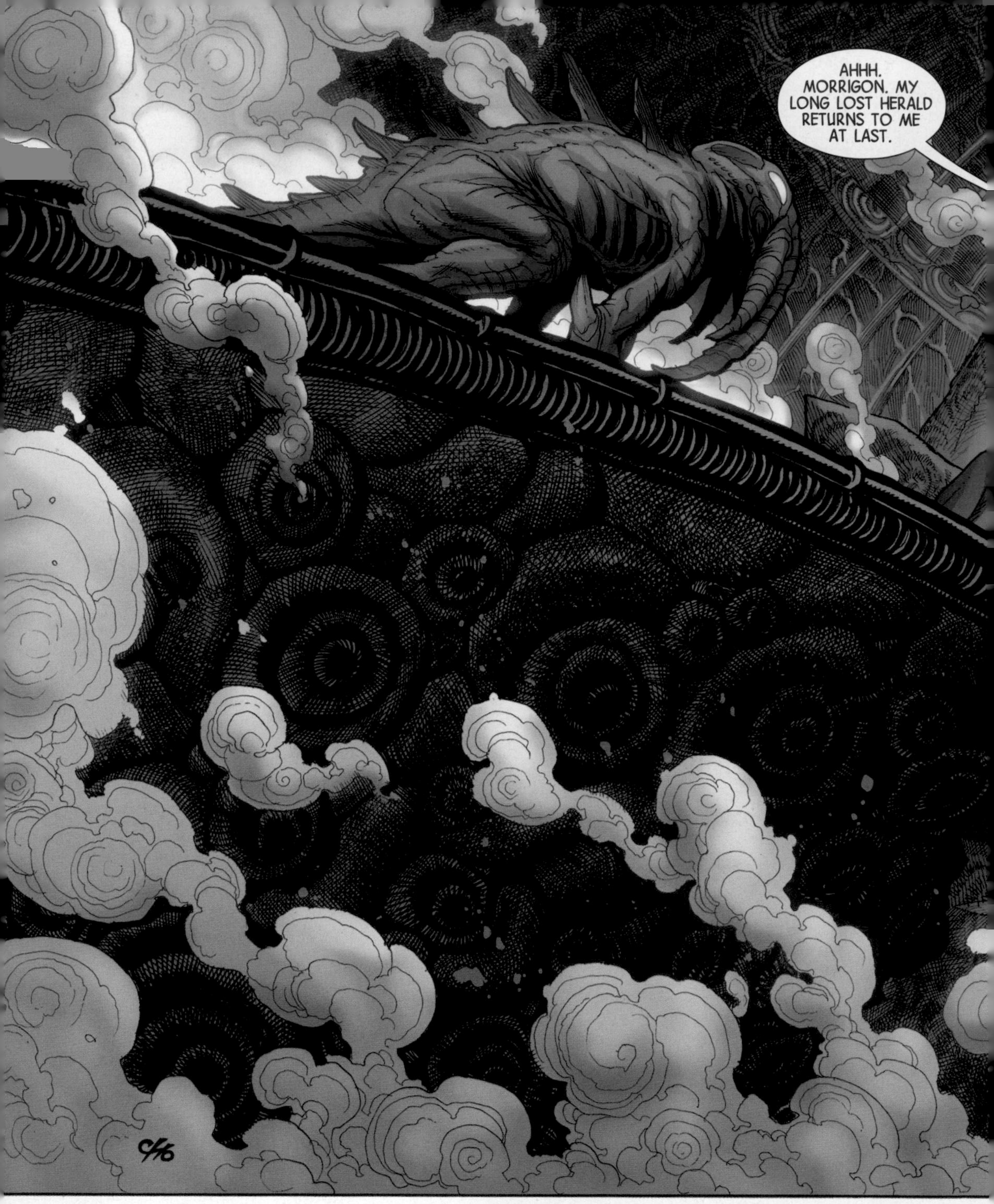
AHHH. MORRIGON. MY LONG LOST HERALD RETURNS TO ME AT LAST.
C/HO

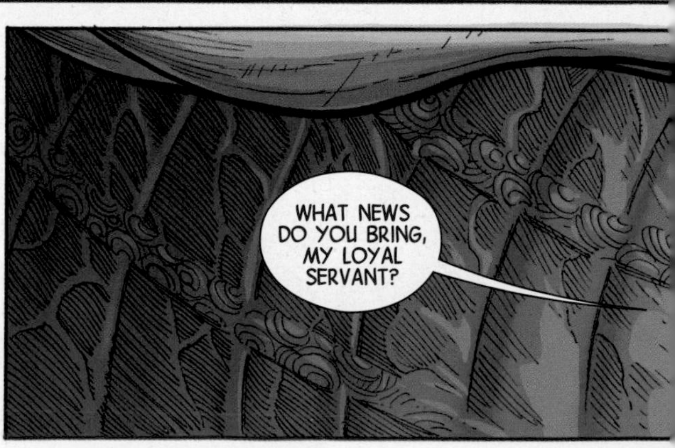
WHAT NEWS DO YOU BRING, MY LOYAL SERVANT?

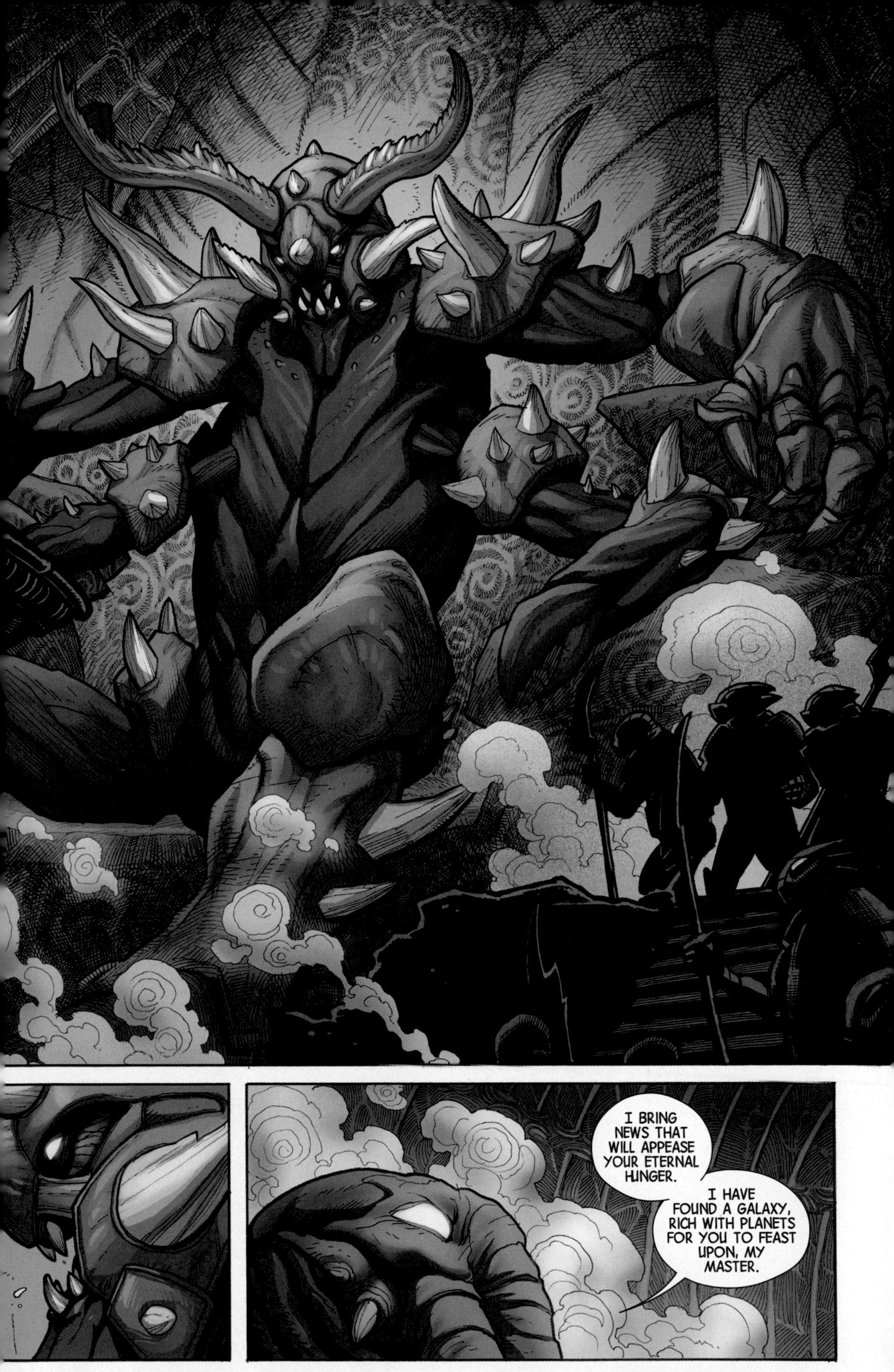
I BRING NEWS THAT WILL APPEASE YOUR ETERNAL HUNGER.
I HAVE FOUND A GALAXY, RICH WITH PLANETS FOR YOU TO FEAST UPON, MY MASTER.

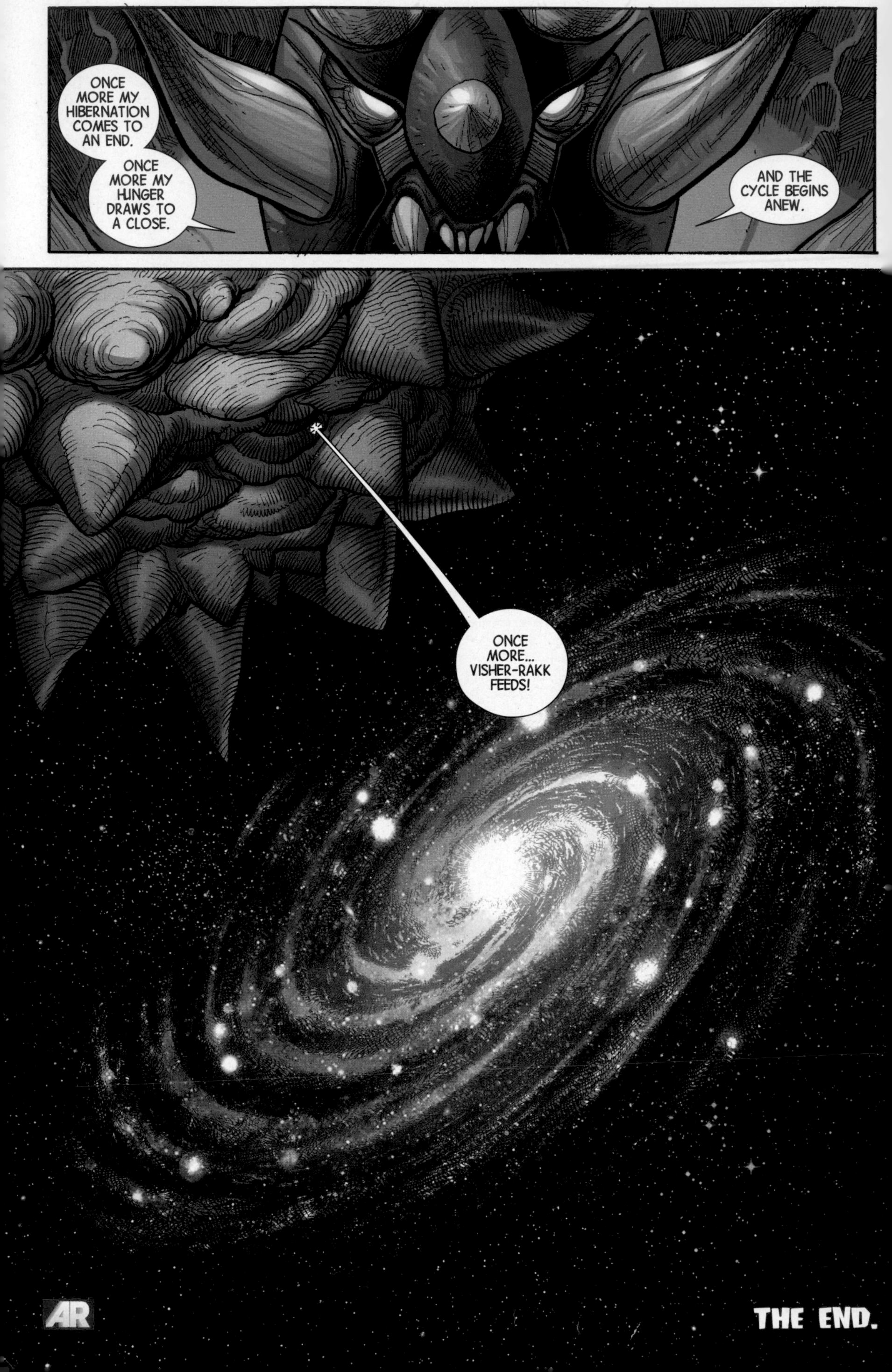
ONCE MORE MY HIBERNATION COMES TO AN END.
ONCE MORE MY HUNGER DRAWS TO A CLOSE.
AND THE CYCLE BEGINS ANEW.
ONCE MORE... VISHER-RAKK FEEDS!
THE END.

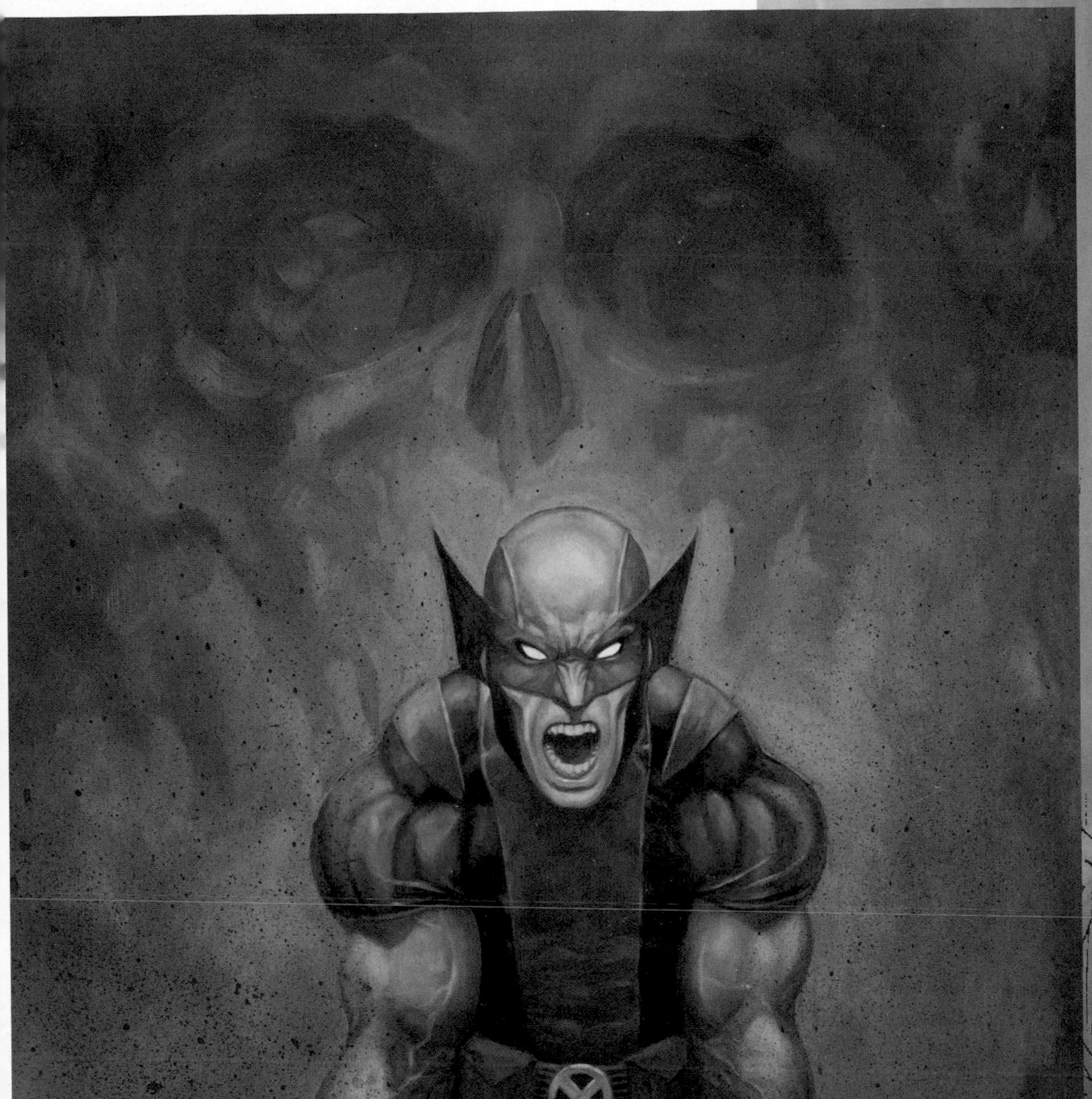

VARIANT BY FRANK CHO

1

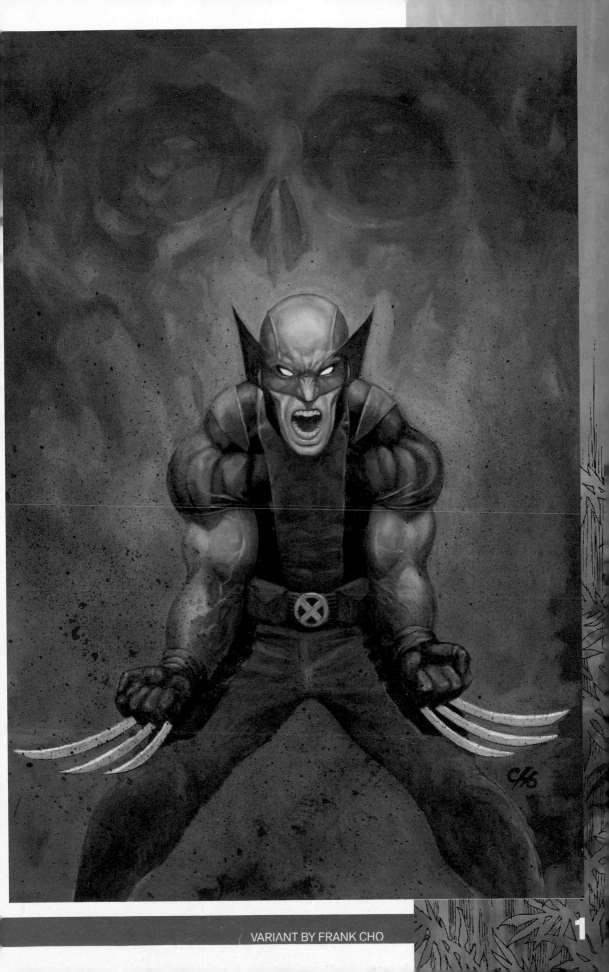

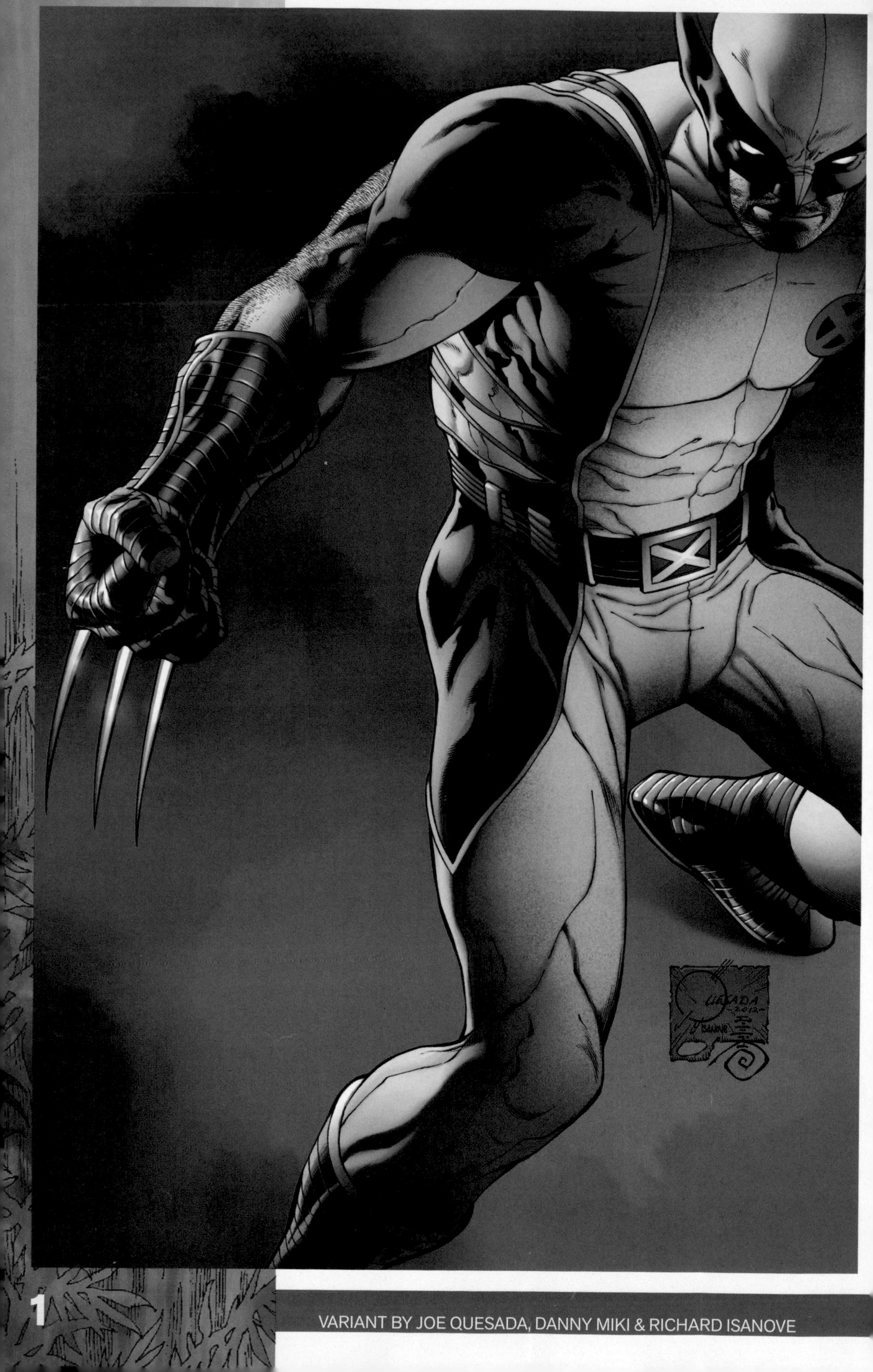

1

VARIANT BY JOE QUESADA, DANNY MIKI & RICHARD ISANOVE

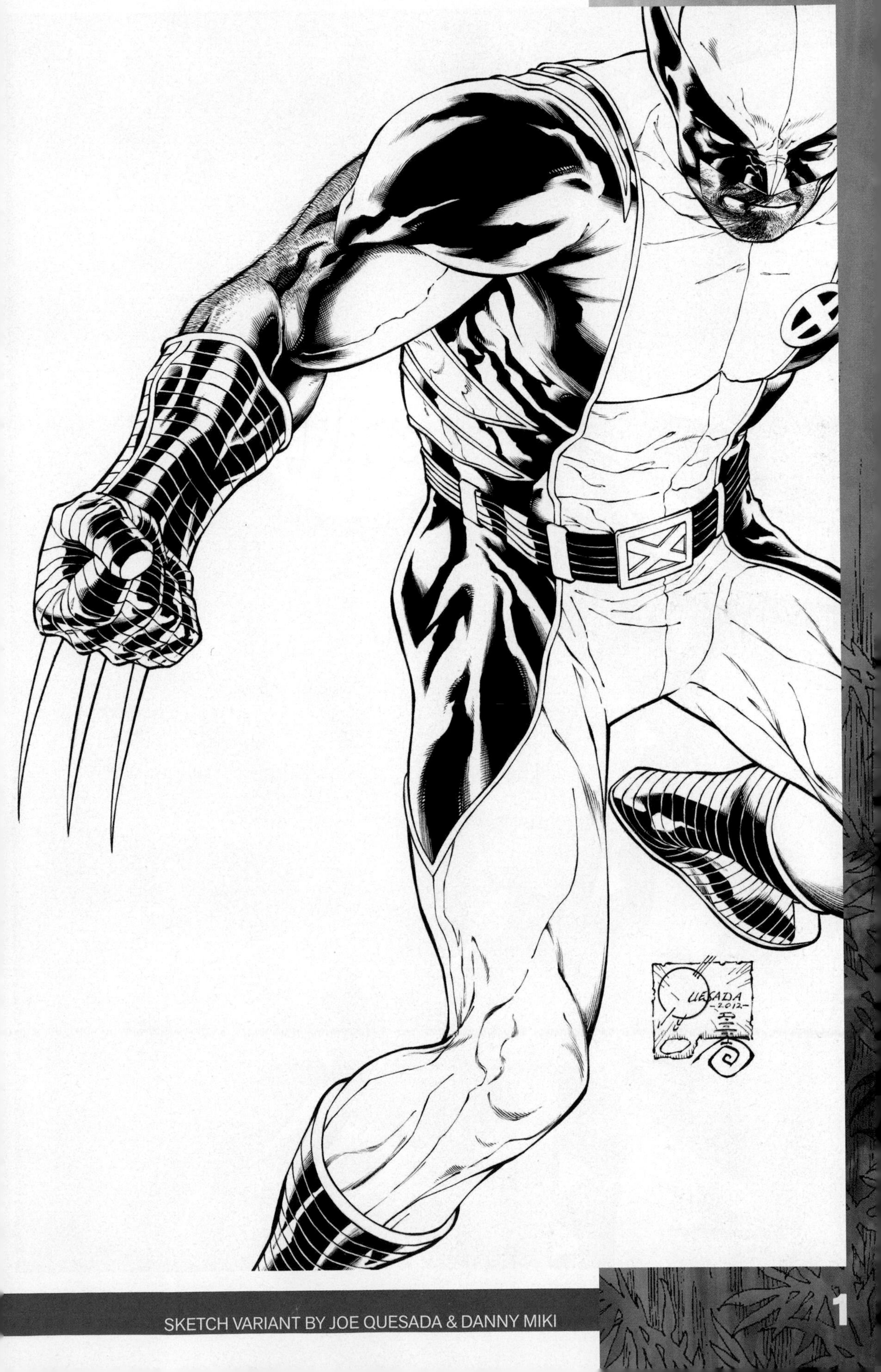
QUESADA
2012

SKETCH VARIANT BY JOE QUESADA & DANNY MIKI

1

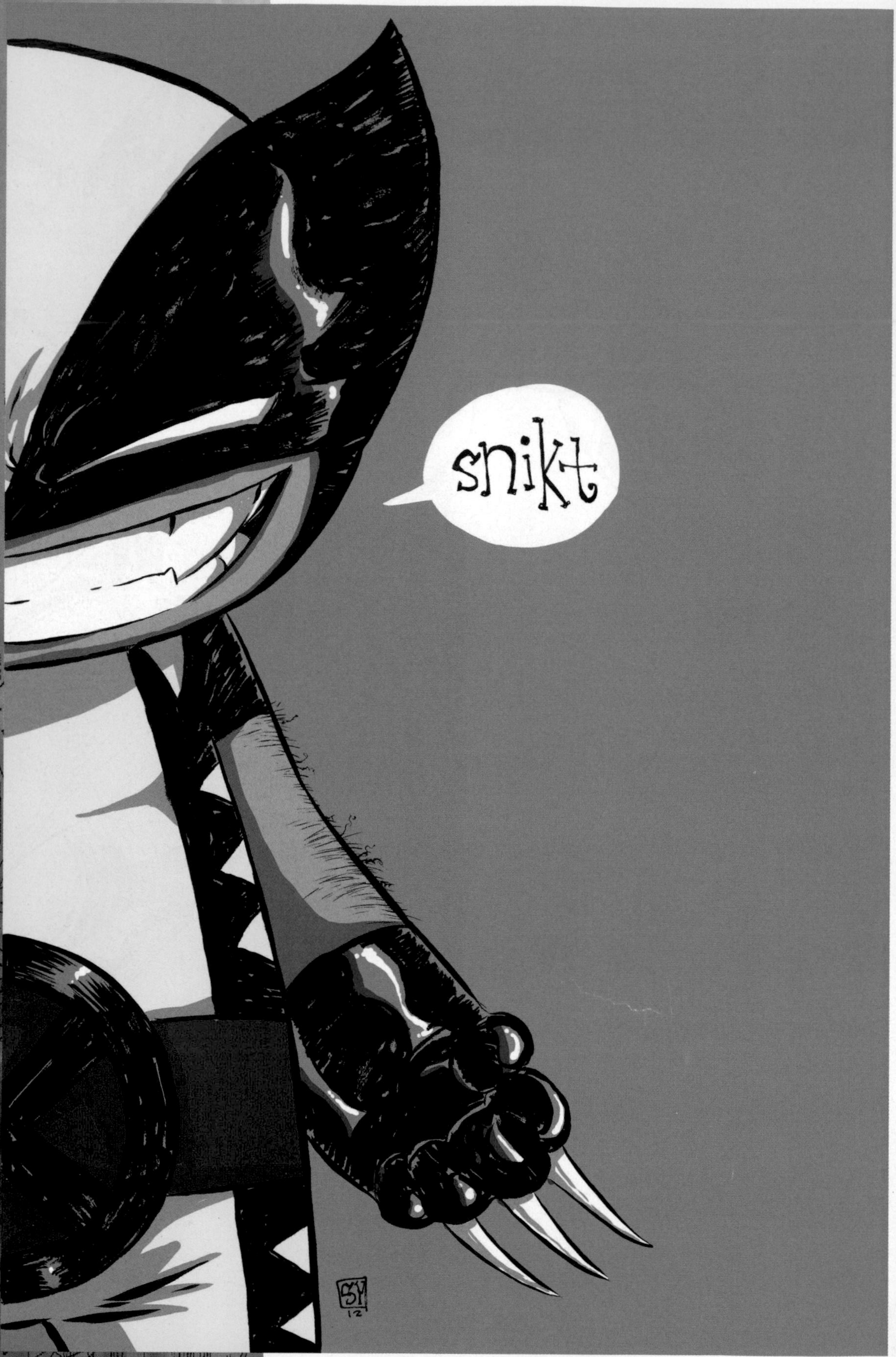
snikt

VARIANT BY SKOTTIE YOUNG

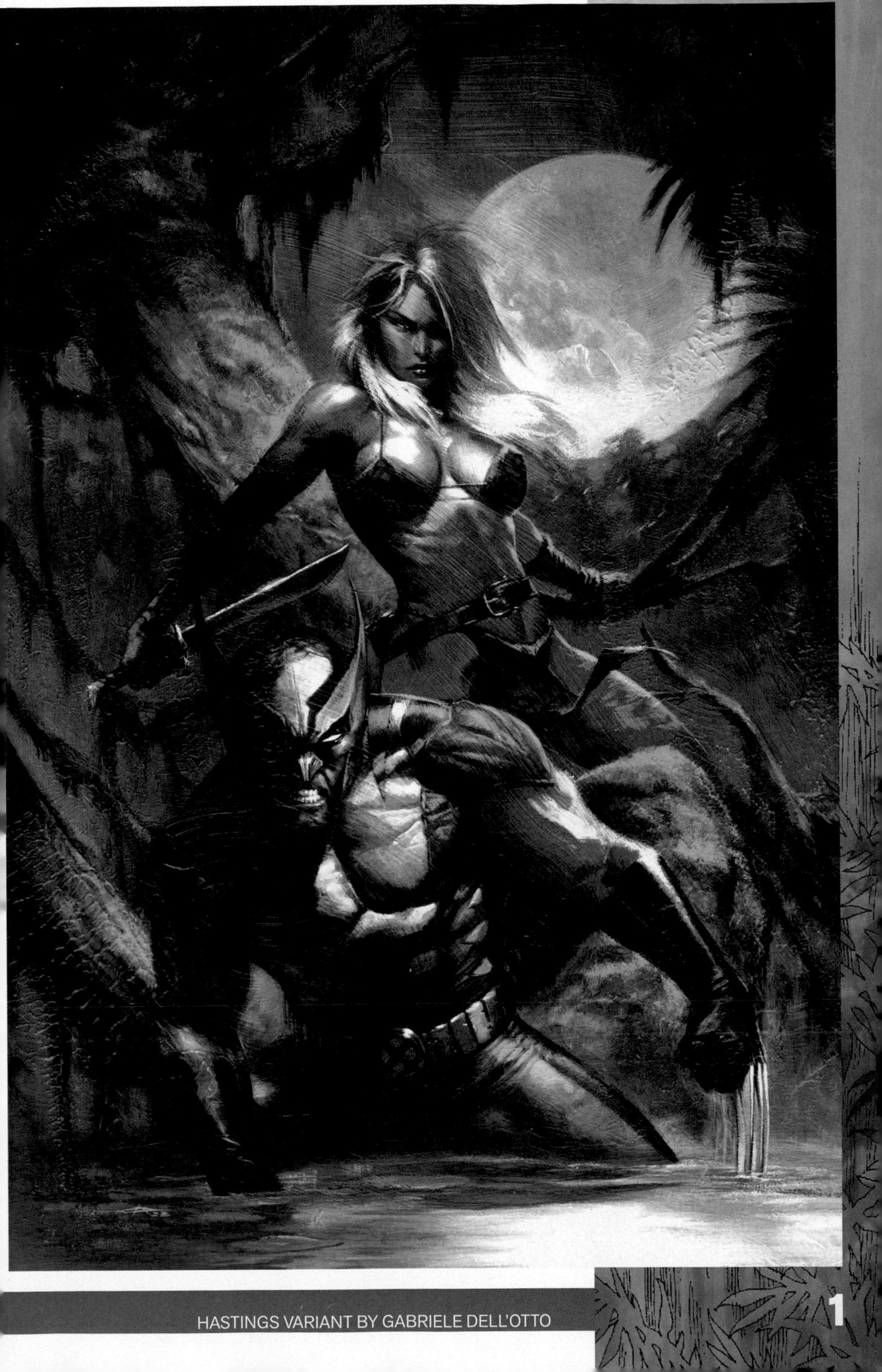

HASTINGS VARIANT BY GABRIELE DELL'OTTO

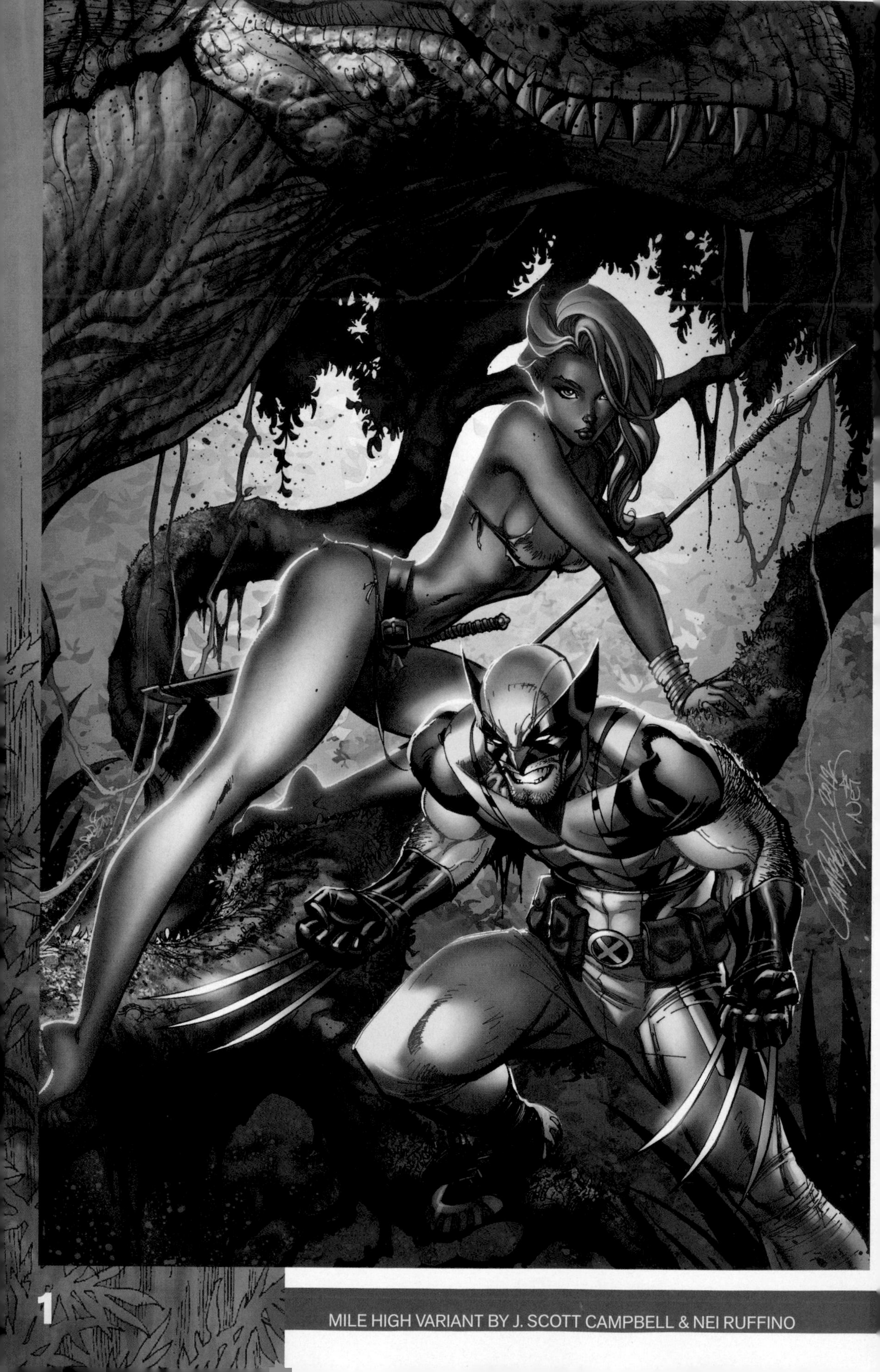

1

MILE HIGH VARIANT BY J. SCOTT CAMPBELL & NEI RUFFINO

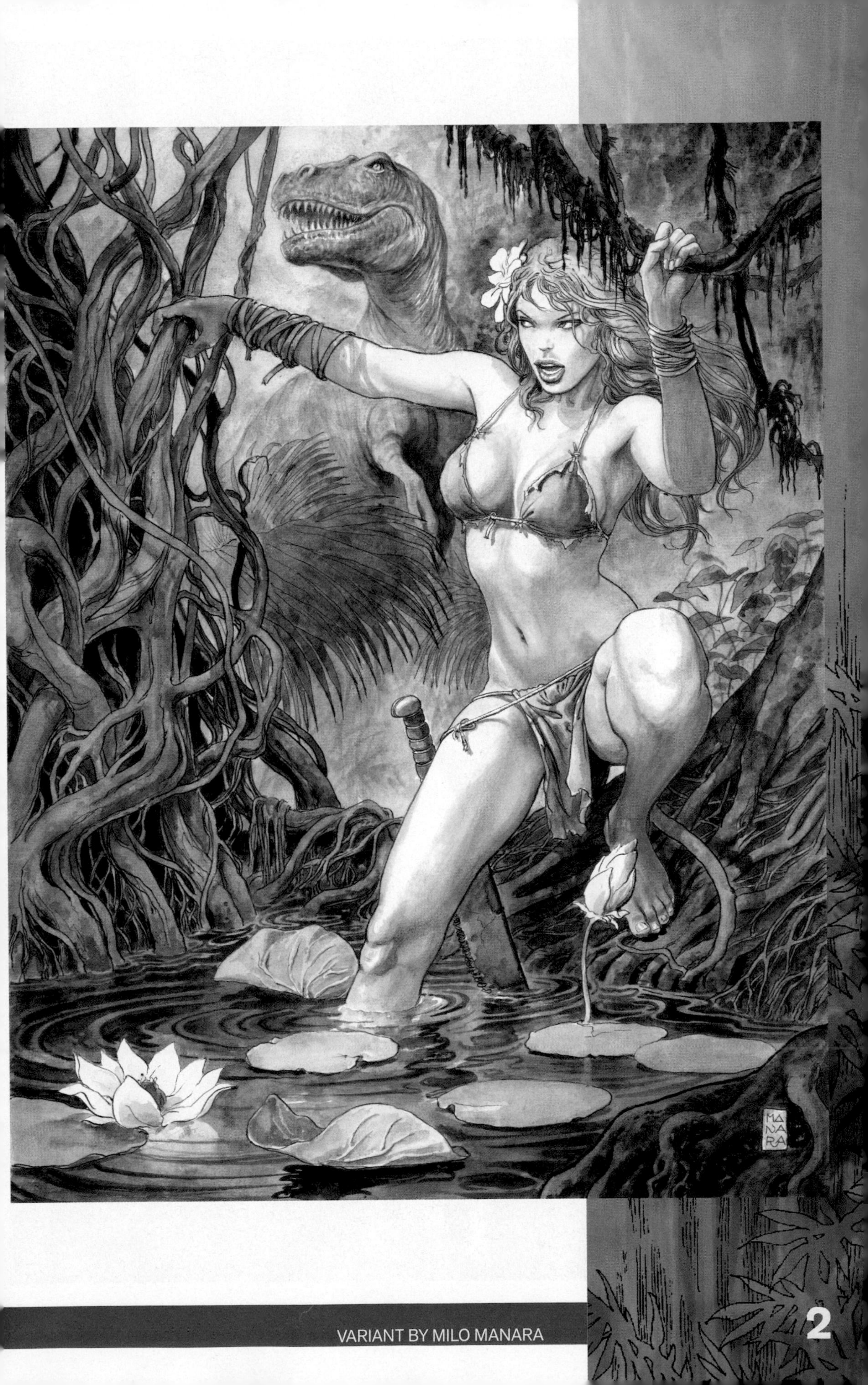
MA
NA
RA

VARIANT BY MILO MANARA

2

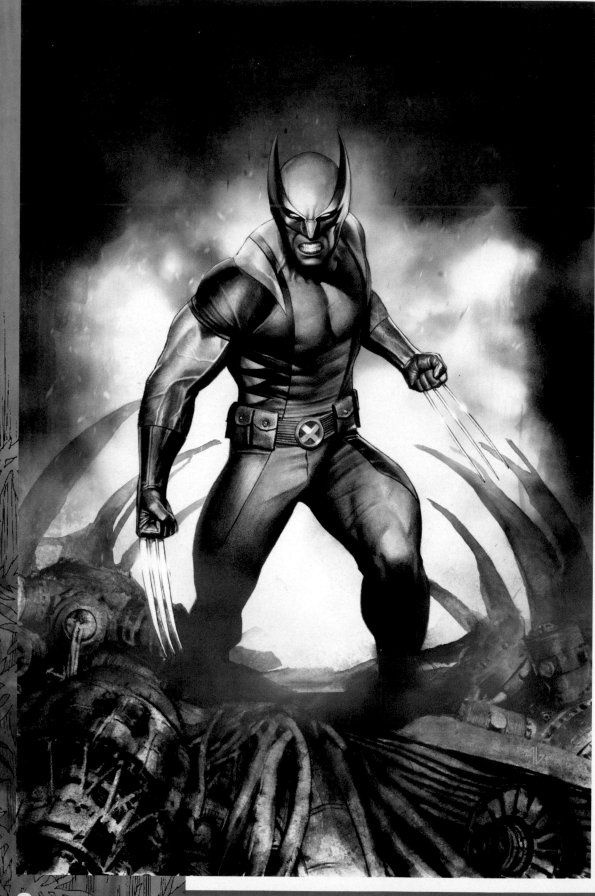

VARIANT BY ADI GRANOV

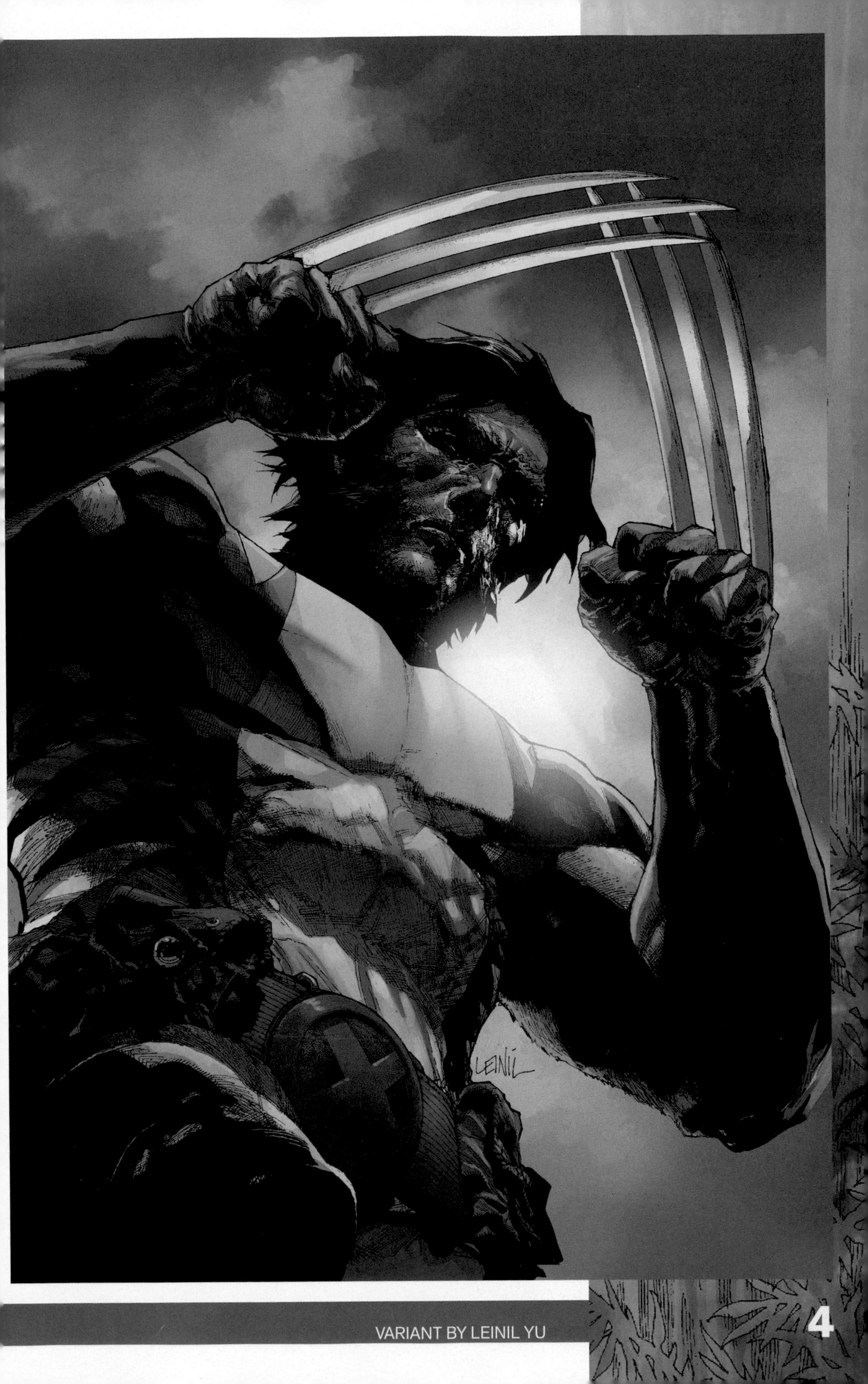
LEINIL

VARIANT BY LEINIL YU

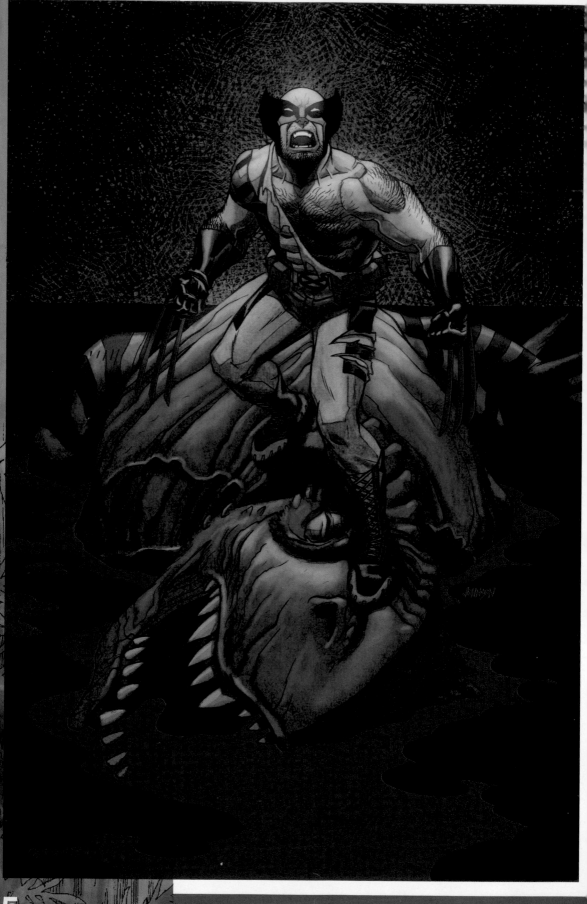

VARIANT BY DAVE JOHNSON

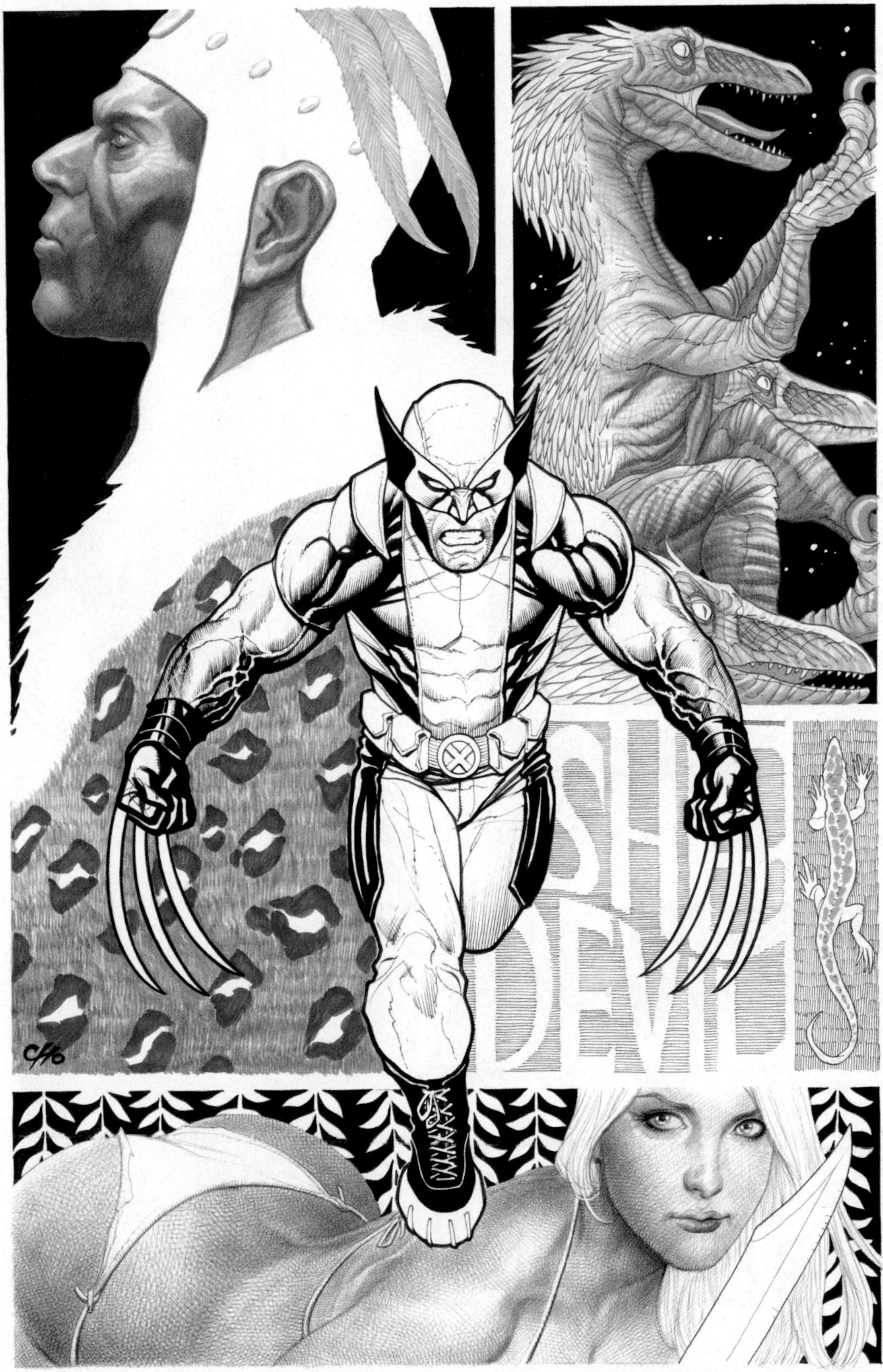

COVER INKS BY FRANK CHO

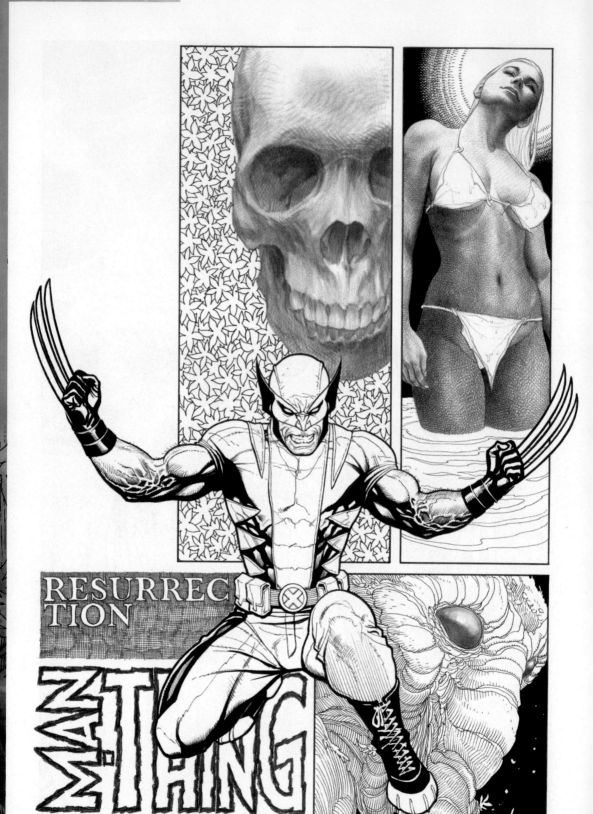

RESURREC
TION

MAN-THING

COVER INKS BY FRANK CHO

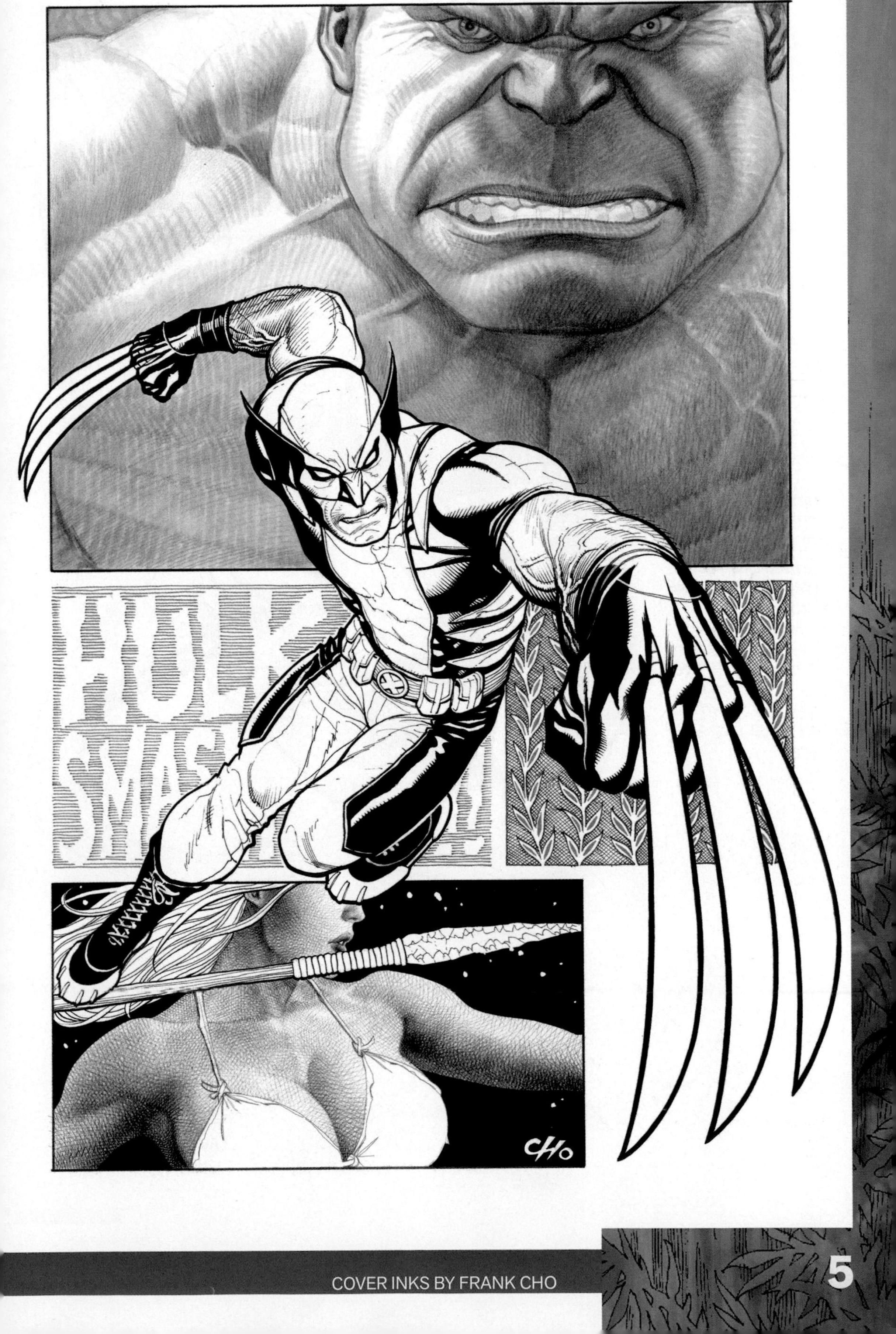
CHO

COVER INKS BY FRANK CHO

MORRIGON

THE HERALD OF VISHER-RAKK

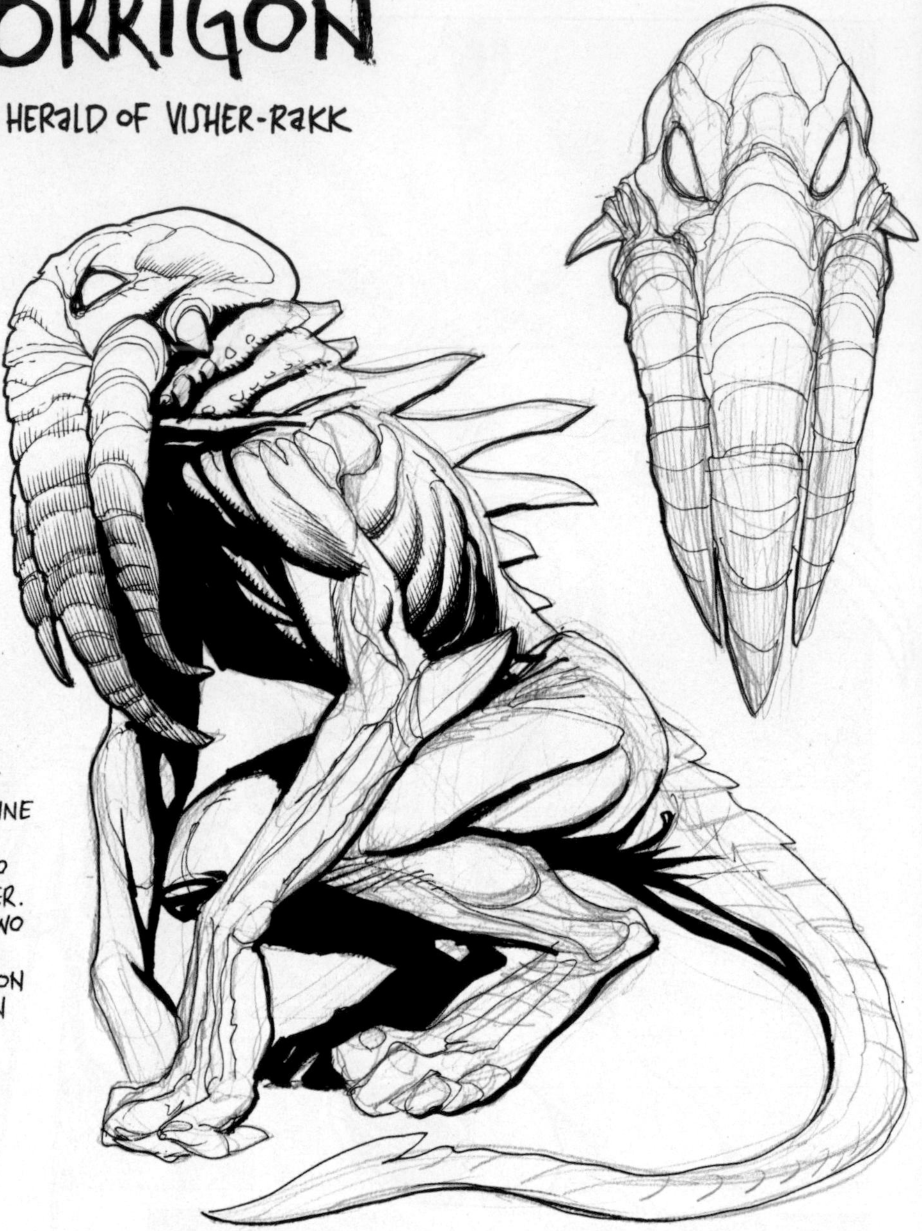

- 150 FEET TALL, STANDING.
- TRAPPED IN THE SAVAGE LAND BUT FREED BY WOLVERINE AND HULK.
- POWER SIMILAR TO THE SILVER SURFER.
- CAN WALK ON TWO LEGS BUT OFTEN CANTERS ABOUT ON ALL FOUR LIKE AN APE.

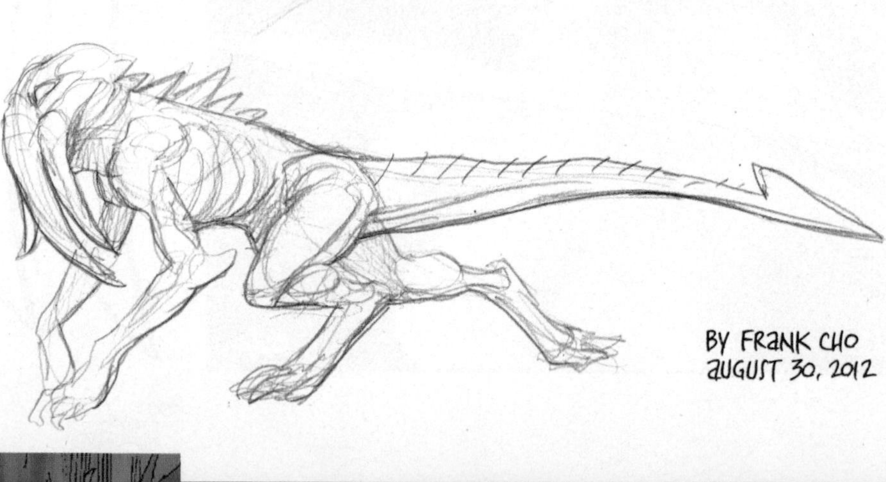

BY FRANK CHO
AUGUST 30, 2012

CHARACTER MODEL SHEET BY FRANK CHO

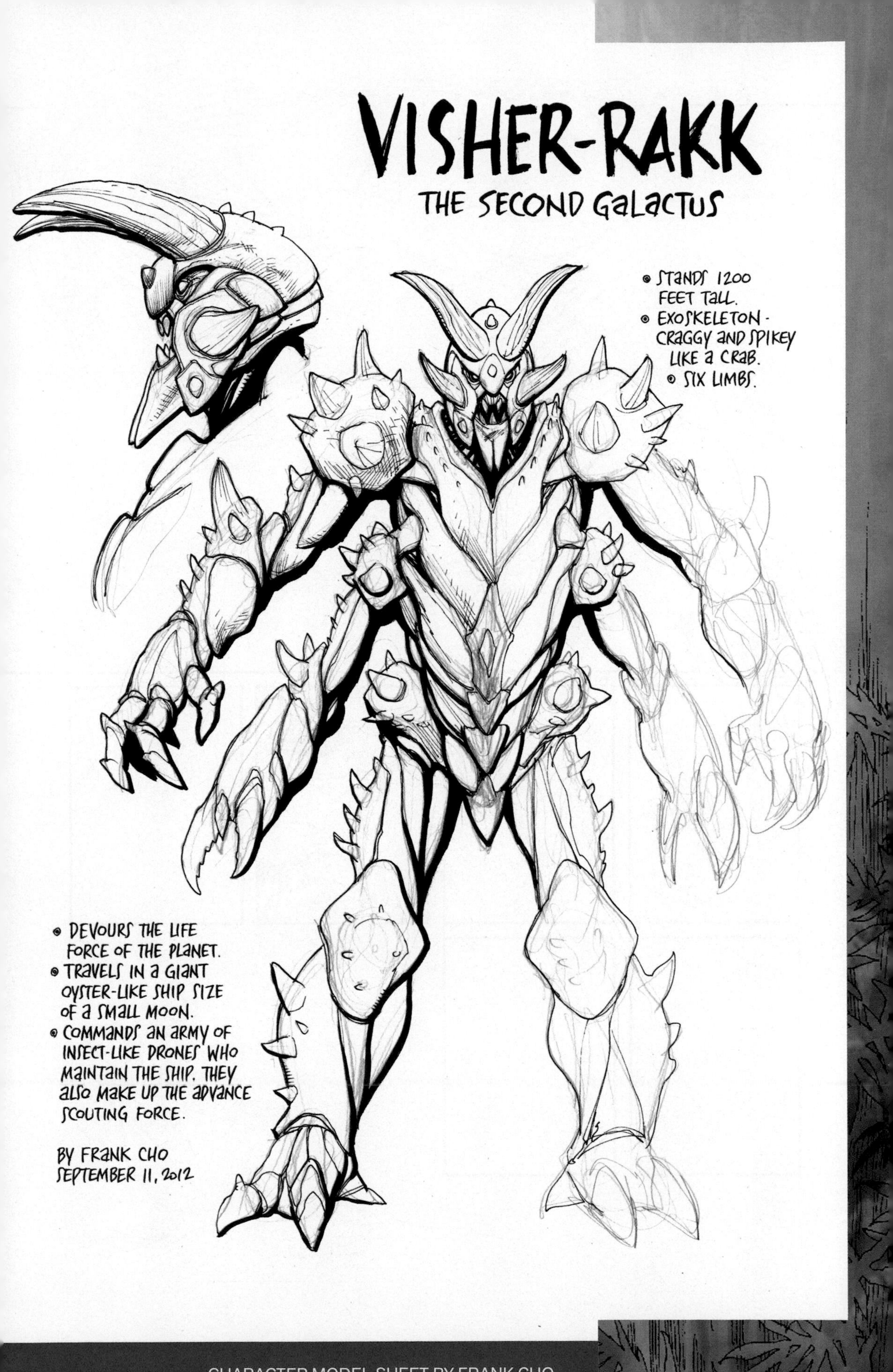
VISHER-RAKK
THE SECOND GALACTUS
• STANDS 1200 FEET TALL.
• EXOSKELETON - CRAGGY AND SPIKEY LIKE A CRAB.
• SIX LIMBS.
• DEVOURS THE LIFE FORCE OF THE PLANET.
• TRAVELS IN A GIANT OYSTER-LIKE SHIP SIZE OF A SMALL MOON.
• COMMANDS AN ARMY OF INSECT-LIKE DRONES WHO MAINTAIN THE SHIP. THEY ALSO MAKE UP THE ADVANCE SCOUTING FORCE.
BY FRANK CHO
SEPTEMBER 11, 2012

CHARACTER MODEL SHEET BY FRANK CHO

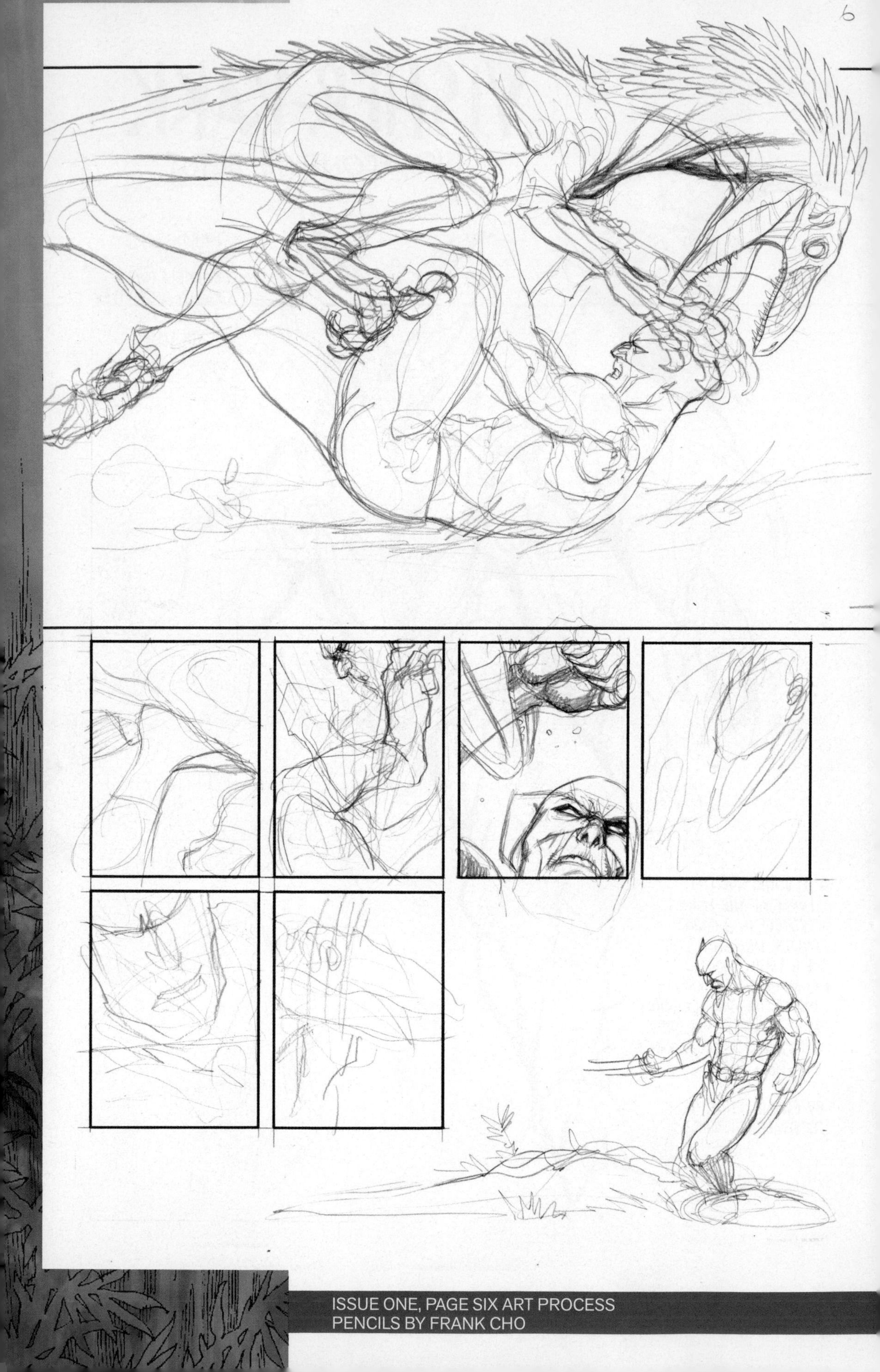
6

ISSUE ONE, PAGE SIX ART PROCESS
PENCILS BY FRANK CHO

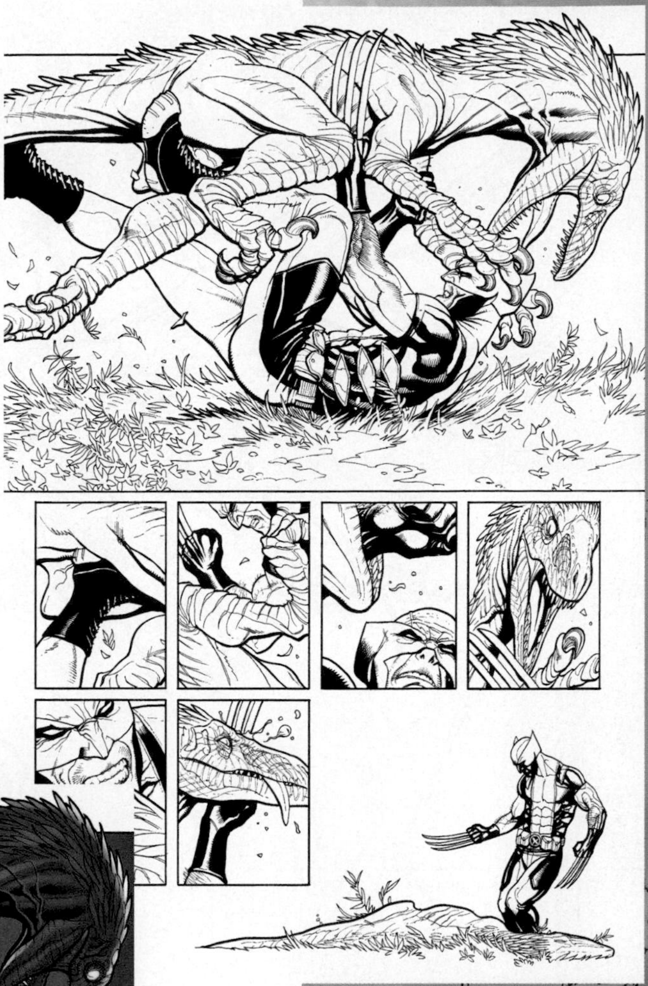

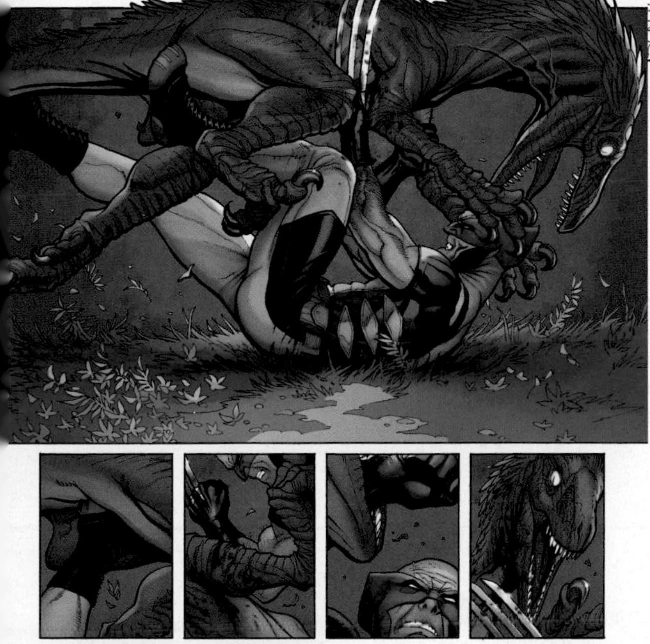

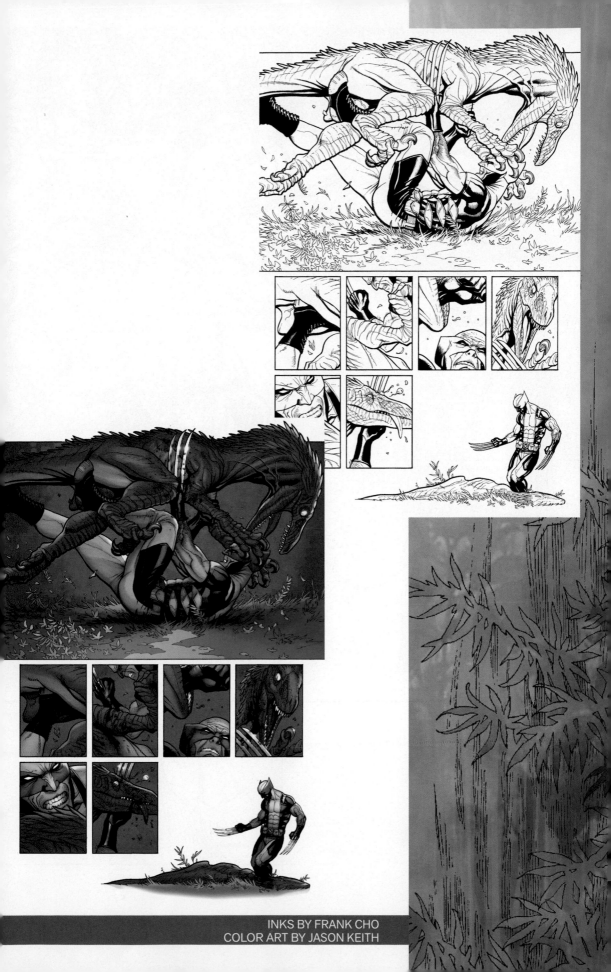

INKS BY FRANK CHO
COLOR ART BY JASON KEITH

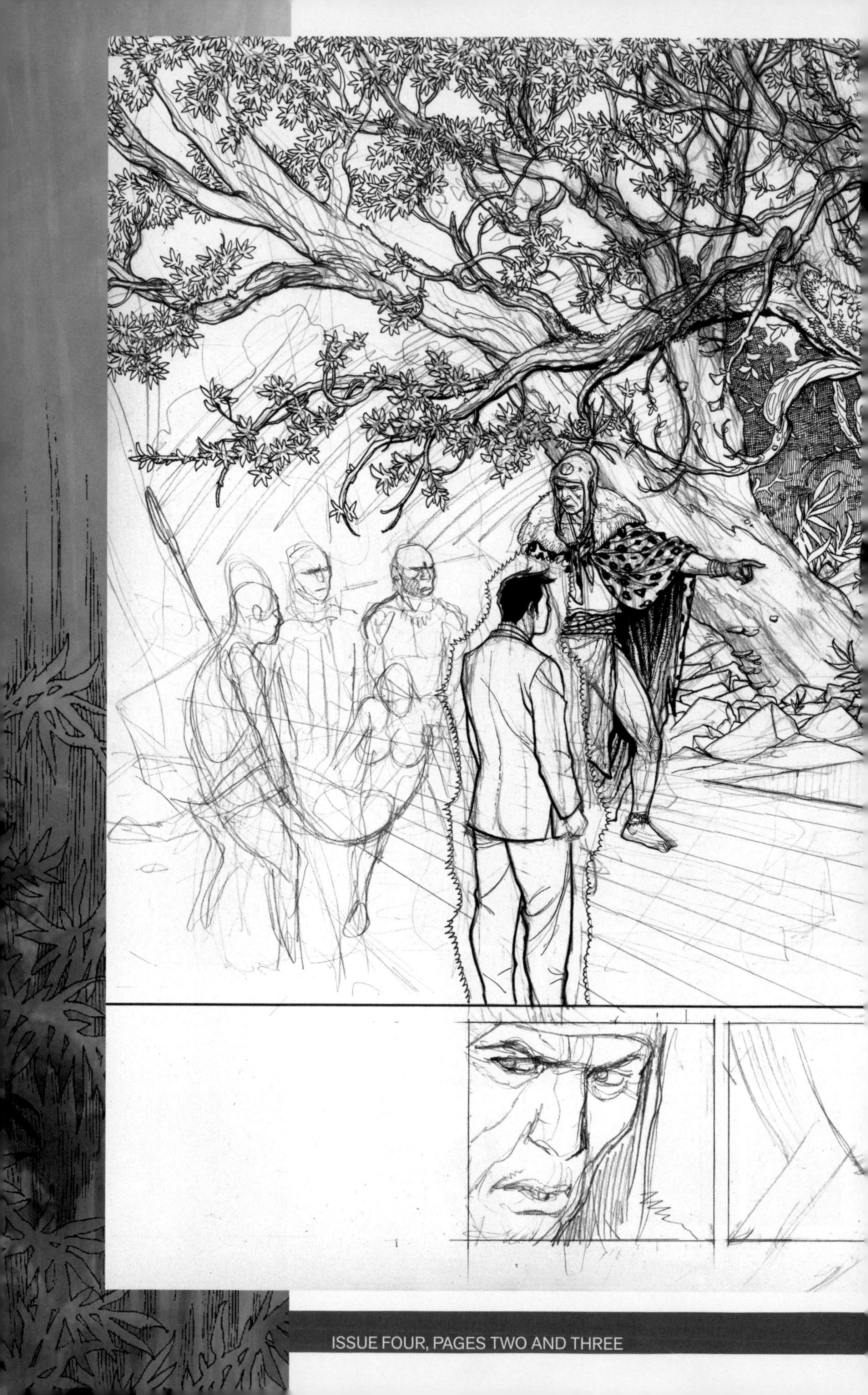

ISSUE FOUR, PAGES TWO AND THREE

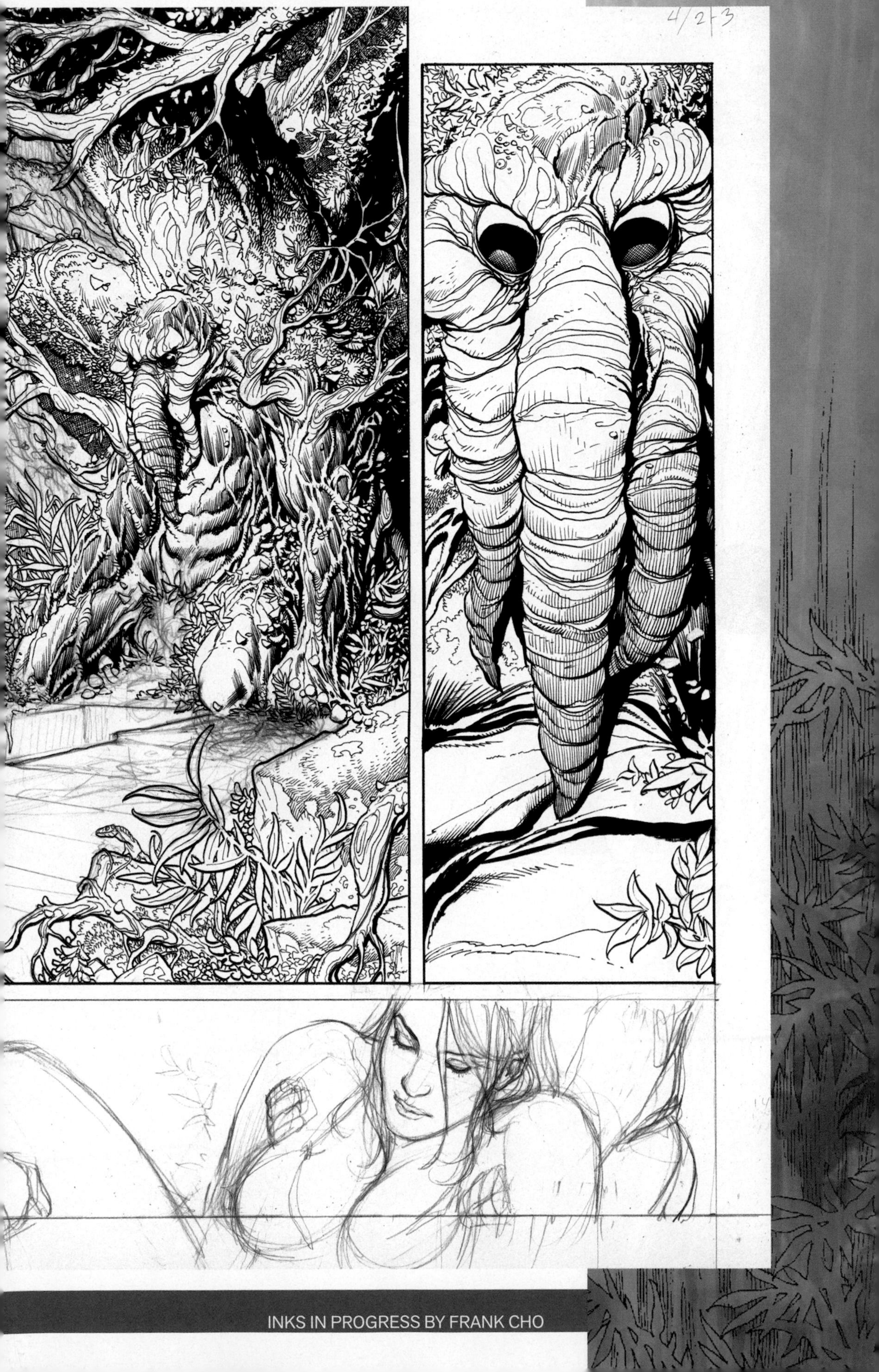
4/2-3

INKS IN PROGRESS BY FRANK CHO

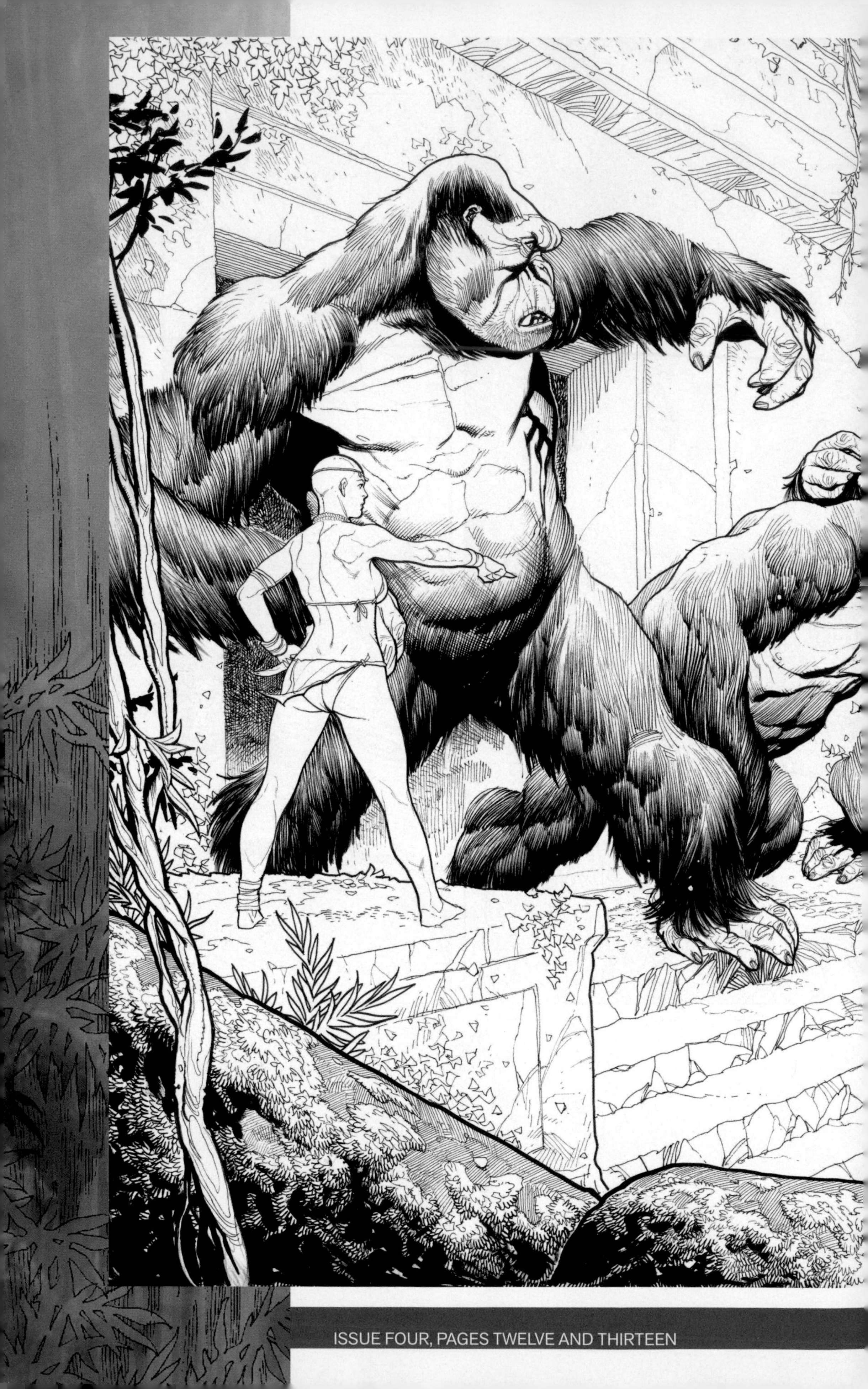

ISSUE FOUR, PAGES TWELVE AND THIRTEEN

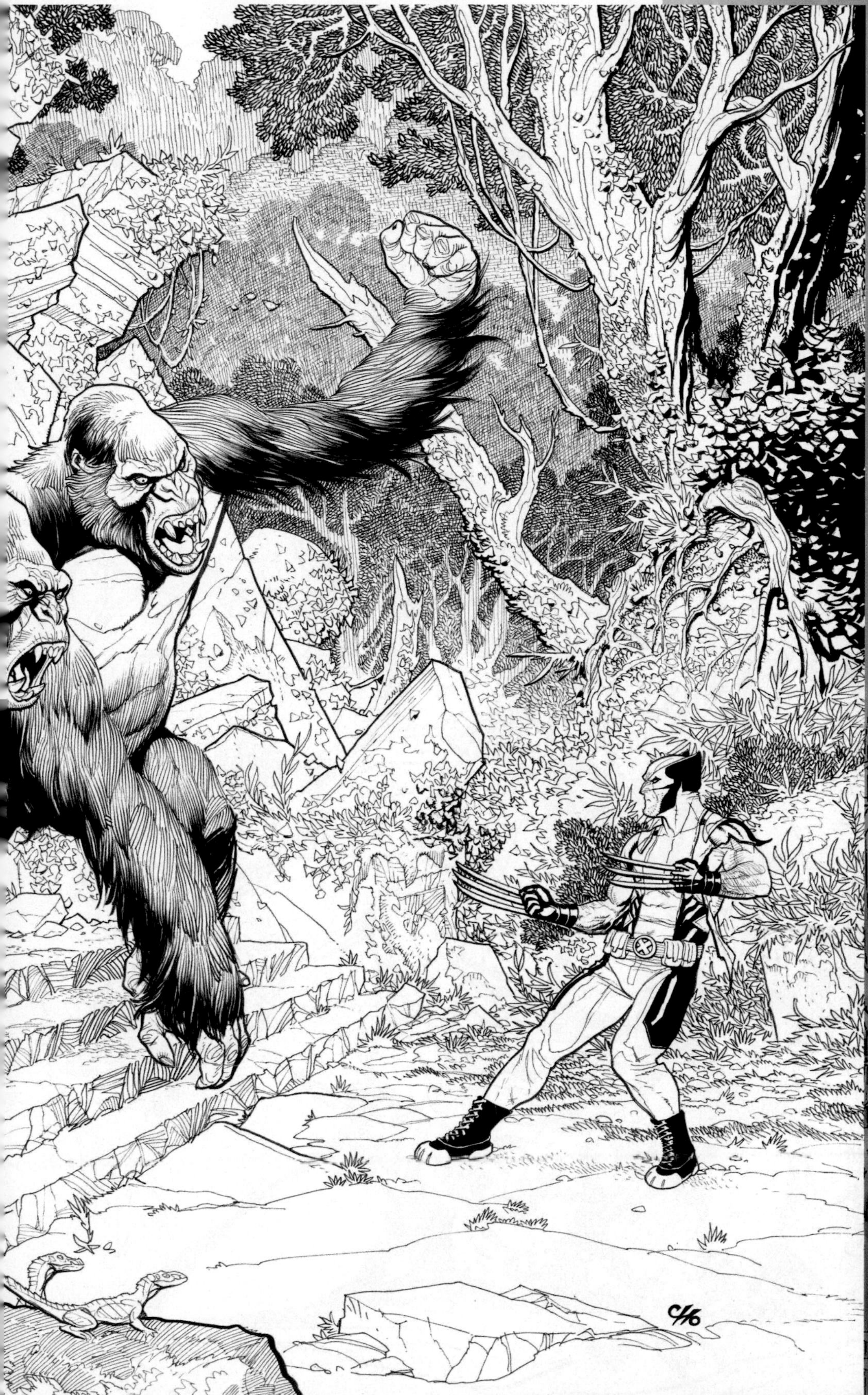

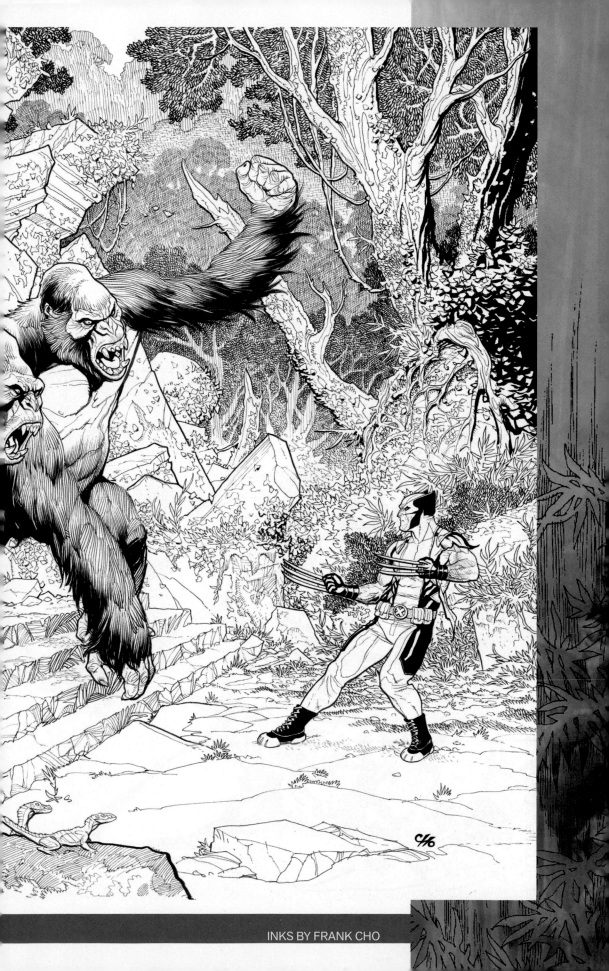

INKS BY FRANK CHO

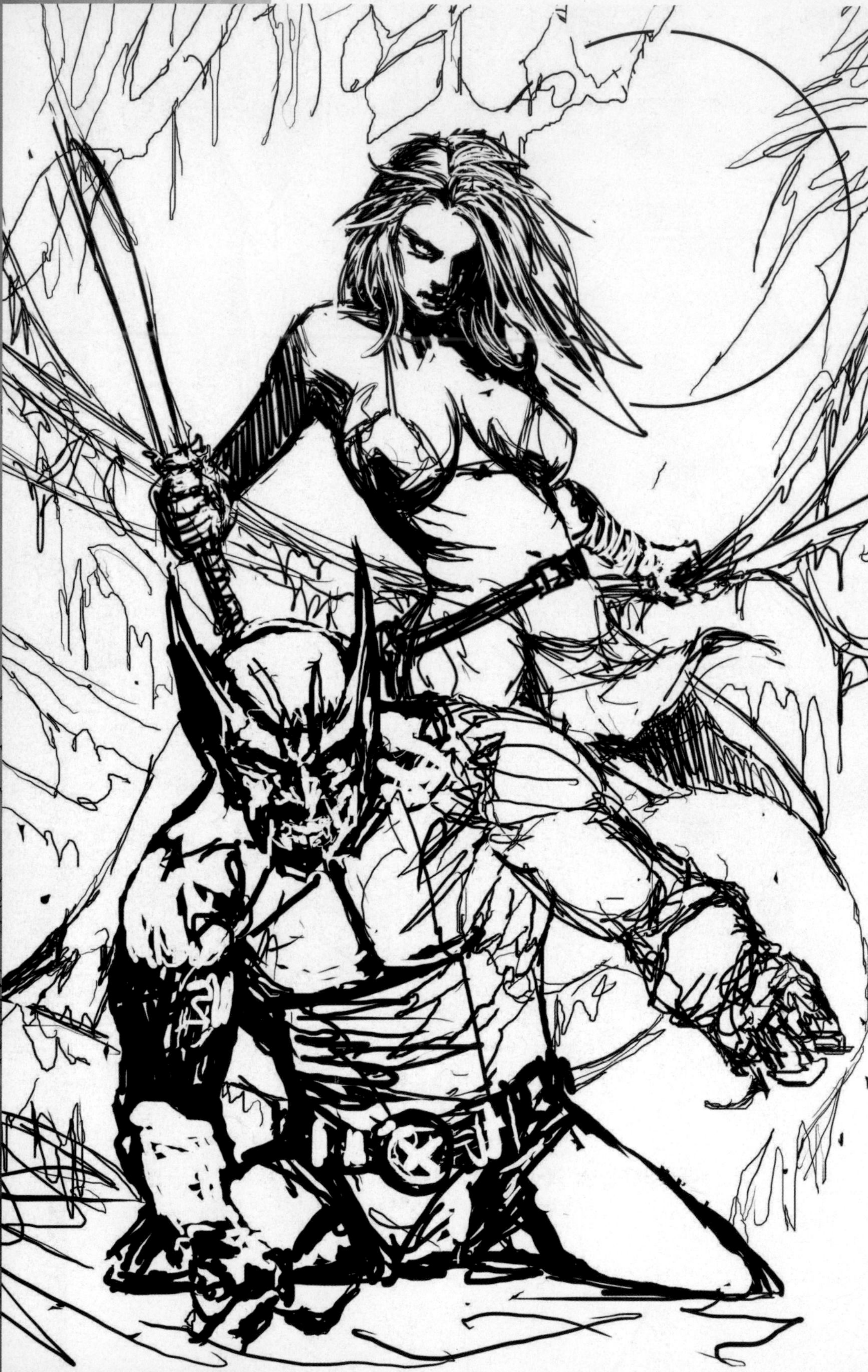

HASTINGS VARIANT COVER SKETCH BY GABRIELE DELL'OTTO

"Hold on to your hat because this is one heck of an X-Men book."
–IGN.com

"Bendis is off to a great start."
— ComicList.com
UNCANNY X-MEN
REVOLUTION
BENDIS
MARVEL NOW!
BACHALO
IRVING
BONUS DIGITAL EDITION Included

UNCANNY X-MEN VOL. 1: REVOLUTION
978-0-7851-6702-0 • DEC130777

"The setup and payoff will rock your socks, so hold on to those, too."
– IGN.com

MARVEL NOW!

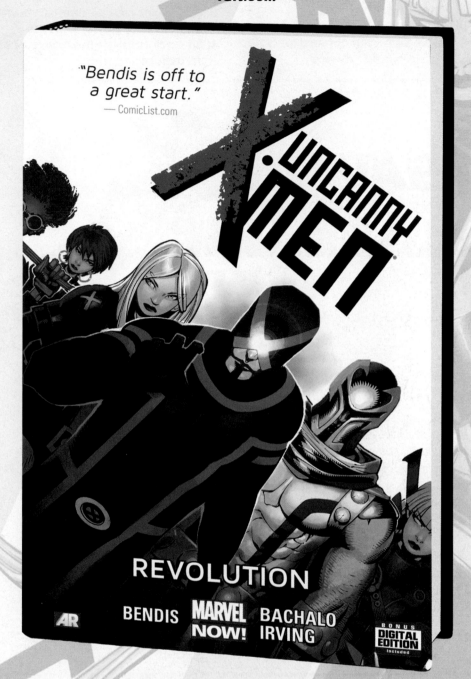

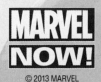

TO ACCESS THE FREE *MARVEL AUGMENTED REALITY APP* THAT ENHANCES AND CHANGES THE WAY YOU EXPERIENCE COMICS

1. Download the app for free via marvel.com/ARapp
2. Launch the app on your camera-enabled Apple iOS® or Android™ device*
3. Hold your mobile device's camera ove any cover or panel with the AR graph
4. Sit back and see the future of comics in action!

*Available on most camera-enabled Apple iOS® and Android™ devices. Content subject to change and availability.

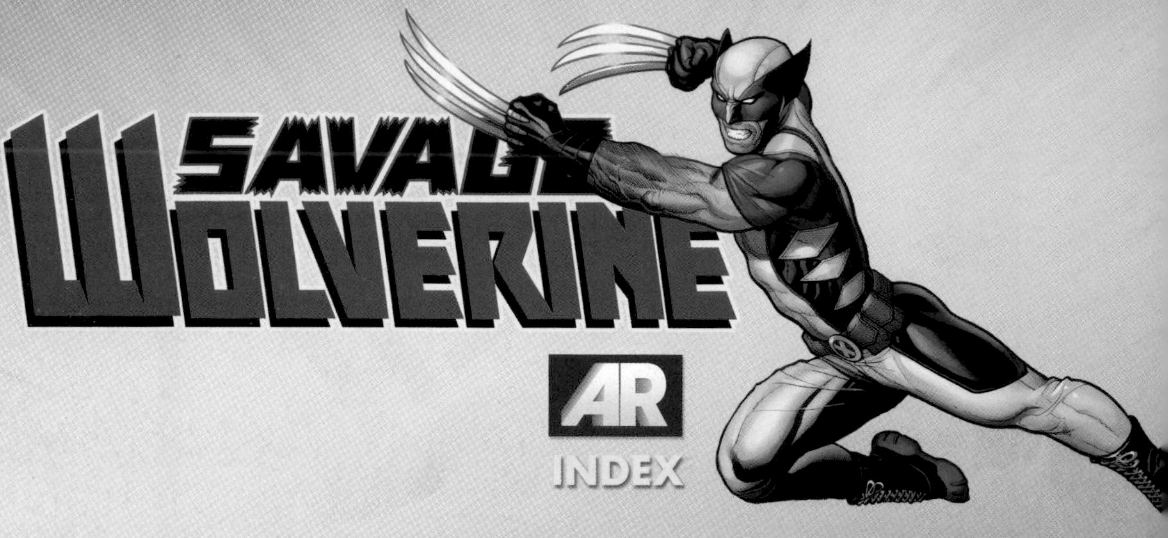
SAVAGE WOLVERINE

AR
INDEX